FREE TO TEACH

Achieving Equity and Excellence in Schools

JOE NATHAN

Winston Press

The poem on page 72 is from *A Coney Island of the Mind*, by
Lawrence Ferlinghetti. Reprinted by permission of the New
Directions Publishing Company.

Library of Congress Catalog Card Number: 84-51117
ISBN: 0-86683-859-7
Printed in the United States of America
5 4 3 2 1

Winston Press, Inc.
430 Oak Grove
Minneapolis, Minnesota 55403

CONTENTS

ACKNOWLEDGMENTS   v

FOREWORD BY HERB KOHL   vii

INTRODUCTION   xi

DAY IN THE LIFE OF AN ASSISTANT PRINCIPAL   3

EFFECTIVE LEARNING   20

REQUIRING COMPETENCE FOR GRADUATION   39

COMPUTERS   56

PARENTS   65

DISCIPLINE   75

TWO GOOD PUBLIC SCHOOLS   93

VALUABLE STRUCTURAL CHANGES   121

RESPECTING FAMILY CHOICE   141

REMINDERS FOR REFORMERS   186

CONCLUSION   199

UPDATE FOR THE PAPERBACK EDITION   206

BIBLIOGRAPHY   219

ACKNOWLEDGMENTS

Unfortunately, only people who have written a book know how much help others can give to an author. "Thanks" is not nearly enough to the following people who questioned, debated with, and encouraged me: Harry Boyte, Dick Broeker, Ronnie Brooks, Bill Dirks, Bruce Dollard, Tom Dewar, David Evertz, Colin Greer, Phelps Hawkins, Diane Hedin, Arthur Himmelman, David Hunt, Wayne Jennings, Curt Johnson, Peter Kleinbard, Herb Kohl, Mary Conway Kohler, Ted Kolderie, Jonathan Kozol, Tony Morley, Dave Nasby, Jonathan Sher, Joan Sorenson, Margo Stark, Ann Wynia, and Betty Jo Zander.

None of the people who helped agree with everything in this book. They all helped me clarify exactly what I meant.

Terry Lydell and Corky Wicker were extremely generous with their time, helping me learn to use our computer.

Pilgrim Press editors Pamela Nelson and Esther Cohen provided thoughtful, sensitive assistance in refining this work. Wayne Paulson, Hermann Weinlick, and Winston Press encouraged me to update my thoughts for this paperback edition.

Russell Ewald, Arthur Himmelman, and the trustees of the McKnight Foundation decided that research on expanding educational choices, particularly for low income and minority students, was worth supporting. Major revisions and expansion in the "Other Structural Alternatives" and

"Respecting Family Choice" chapters were possible because of their assistance. I deeply appreciate their generosity and faith.

Another organization, the Northwest Area Foundation, made it possible for Senator David Durenberger to distribute this book to his colleagues in the U.S. Senate. I am indebted to Senator Durenberger for the high honor he paid me, to George Thiss of his staff, and to John Taylor and Judy Healey of the Foundation for their courtesy and generosity.

Another person stood out in the last year for his courage and openness. Minnesota State Representative John Brandl has been willing to consider and challenge the conventional wisdom about education and to propose fundamental reforms.

The Sequoia Institute graciously supported my research on new roles for teachers which is included in the update. Thanks to Bob Hawkins and Deanna Marquart.

Everyone in my generation knew people who died, left the country, or were placed in prison because of the war in Vietnam. I feel a deep personal duty to those brave people to help build a better world.

Dr. George Young, Dr. Erma McGuire, and Dr. Jim Phillips provided opportunities to test some of the concepts in this book. There are thousands of excellent teachers and administrators in our schools. I've been fortunate to work with and learn from some and know there are many more.

My parents, Ruth and C. Henry Nathan, provided lifelong models of commitment to a better world and the pursuit of excellence.

Joe and Esther Lukesh have been of incomparable assistance. They provided quiet, thoughtful advice and encouragement—and gave us much needed relief from the demands of two young children.

Our children: David and Elizabeth Nathan. I hope these words will open up greater opportunities for them—and millions of other children in this country.

The most important person in the world for me is JoAnn Nathan. I hope we find in years to come that this book was worth the extra burdens JoAnn graciously accepted.

FOREWORD

by Herbert Kohl

I was born, raised and indoctrinated into the New York City left. Anywhere west of New York seemed to be a vacuum that needed to be educated about issues such as cooperation, collective action, caring education, and justice. In other words, I was another parochial New Yorker when I made my first trip to Minneapolis/St. Paul in 1968. I was invited to talk to the University High School in Minneapolis, and I brought a number of my high school students with me. To our surprise there were about 800 people who showed up on the coldest day we'd ever experienced. As is my usual custom I wandered around for about half an hour before the event was to begin, to listen to the people who were waiting to hear what we had to say.

The common theme of their conversation was that schools needed to be changed. They felt isolated. Over and over I heard that no one in the Twin Cities was willing to take initiatives. I decided my talk should be brief and addressed to one point alone: act on problems when you see them. My talk lasted about fifteen minutes and ended with a suggestion that the audience meet together in the basement to form organizations that would work to change the schools. To my surprise, that's just what happened.

People in the group knew how to organize themselves. Not only that, they knew how to choose natural leaders and to get things done. Over the last fourteen years I have returned to the Twin Cities many times and found a nurturing of change and progress that we in New York only discussed.

It's important to understand the central role that Minnesota and other midwestern states have had in the history of progressive educational movements in the United States. It is easy to forget that John Dewey was a midwesterner and that most of his early work was done in Kansas and Iowa and not at Columbia University. It's also easy to forget that much of progressive education was accompanied by the populist philosophy of the Progressive Party of Bob LaFolette and his followers as well as Eugene Debs, another midwesterner. As a New Yorker, it has been a privilege for me to learn of the roots of progressive thinking and education from people who know more than to be taken in by the self-celebration that seems to be characteristic of many on the East and West Coasts.

Joe Nathan, my host in the Twin Cities, became a friend. Joe is the kind of person you want to run a school. He works twelve hours a day, can work with paper as well as people, talks respectfully and truthfully to everyone, and doesn't forget that his main responsibility is not to his staff or the system but to students.

My last trip to St. Paul was several months ago. I visited the junior high where Joe was assistant principal. We walked down the hall together talking about education and planning our time together. It must have taken us half an hour to walk down the hall. Joe stopped to talk to every student we passed. Good schools develop from caring.

This book comes out of Joe's experiences in trying to change public education, first at the St. Paul Open School, then at Murray Junior High. It also comes out of another side of Joe's life, the scholarly and informed side that has led him to contribute dozens of articles to educational journals and papers.

What makes this book important is the way Joe Nathan uses an academic view of the history of public education to deepen his understanding of being a working administrator. Joe's disillusion with the possibility for changing public education given the structures currently available comes out of a measured, experienced and fundamental condemnation of

what our public schools have become. I am inclined to agree
with the ideas in this book, yet I still resist some of them. I
want to see public schools work as they are yet the sensible
part of me says they can't. People like Joe who have
experienced the pain in our school system and who never quit
the kids are convincing when they plead that for the sake of
our children and therefore our future, we have to rethink and
recreate public education.

This book does not confuse the public schools with public
education and that is its particular strength. It is an affirmation
of our need to have free quality education for all people in our
society. At the same time, it makes clear that what we have
done so far has just not worked. It's time we listen to people
like Joe Nathan, and rethink the very nature of our schools.

Herbert Kohl is the author of many books about education, including
36 Children, On Teaching, and, with Judith Kohl, the National Book
Award winning *View from the Oak.*

INTRODUCTION

Because Americans believe in the value of education, our public schools are the focus of considerable debate. What are the most important goals? What is the most appropriate curriculum? Which are the most effective teaching techniques? What courses should be offered? Which ones should be required? How should schools be organized? What rights should teachers have to organize and bargain collectively? How large should schools be? Are schools doing an adequate job of preparing technologically knowledgeable graduates?

This book will describe solutions to these problems. The answers do not lie in spending more money, but in spending the money presently allocated in a more efficient manner. If our children are more successful, educators will be justified in asking for more money to do an even better job. This book is for people concerned about how to attract and retain our most talented teachers, and how to create the most powerful and effective learning opportunities. It is for those who believe in democratic ideals and don't want to sacrifice or deny those values in selecting a school for their children.

Within the last few years, research has caught up with what the finest teachers knew all along: Certain schools and particular teachers have a greater positive impact on students than others. Schools *can* make a difference in the lives of young people. Disturbing research shows that many schools reinforce our poorest childrens' problems.

Just as disturbing is the lack of interest in a teaching career among many of the nation's brightest, most technically minded youth. Colleges and universities are not training enough science and math teachers to meet our needs at a time when the economy demands greater sophistication and knowledge in these fields. Young people with technical skills look at the teaching profession's combination of minimal security, low starting pay, and poor reputation. Most of them decide to look elsewhere for work. College students may be reflecting the public's attitude toward teaching. In several national polls, George Gallup asked adults whether they would like to have a child of theirs choose public school teaching as a career. In 1969, 75 percent answered yes. This figure dropped to 67 percent in 1972, and fell to 48 percent in the 1980 survey.

Many outstanding senior teachers are disgusted by the restrictions placed upon them, and by administrators' tolerance of inadequate performance. A disturbing number of teachers report they would not enter the profession if they were young. "While in 1961 and 1966, about half of public school teachers indicated they certainly would go into teaching if they could start over again, by 1981, only 22 percent expressed this positive attitude" (Dearman and Plisko, p. i).

There is no lack of proposed solutions to public education's doldrums. Many professional educators respond with a simple statement. "Give us more money." Dissatisfied with their pay, many teachers go on strike or reduce the time they spend with students. Many educators insist that additional funds are needed to reduce student-teacher ratios and pay teachers higher salaries.

More funds won't solve the fundamental problems of American public schools. Scholars, teachers, administrators, and foundation officials spent billions of dollars trying to improve our public schools over the last 20 years. The Ford Foundation's fascinating report, *A Foundation Goes to School,* describes its efforts to produce more effective schools by spending $34 million over a decade. The Foundation's experiences are depressing and typical. Most of their projects ended after the Ford money was spent. Most of the remaining programs depended on charismatic leaders. When the leaders left, the innovation died.

Although some schools are more effective than others, it's difficult to sustain such "lighthouse" schools. Ten years after their founding, many are either struggling, closed, or virtually identical to surrounding schools. (A respected public school superintendent, Richard Doremus, recently described his visits to programs which have received national acclaim over the past 15 years. He found little left of the former innovations, and few people who even knew that their school had received acclaim for its improvements!)

A few extraordinary public schools have survived. During the last several years, an education writer from the Cincinnati *Post* traveled throughout the country on a Ford Foundation fellowship, looking for schools which were unusually effective with low income, urban students. He found a few, "minute points of brilliance in a vast, intolerably bleak field" (Benjamin, p. 200). Why don't we have *more* effective programs? Why must excellence be the exception, rather than the rule in public education? This book describes obstacles and barriers frustrating school improvement efforts. There is little theory here—just the day-to-day struggle to serve students and their parents. Equally important, this book illustrates extraordinary learning programs that can be available to all students *without* spending more money.

Of course, some schools would spend additional money wisely given the opportunity. In too many cases, however, a substantial portion of the money intended to serve young people goes instead to the "care and feeding" of school district bureaucracies.

I'm not suggesting that all private schools are better than all public schools. It's impossible to generalize. There is even more diversity among private than among public schools: Some operate for a few students in their parents' basement; others maintain a 150-year-old campus and grounds, with extraordinary facilities and a huge endowment.

However, the most effective private schools have much to teach us. They work closely with parents. They have high expectations of students. They provide a variety of ways for students to demonstrate talents and skills. They demand not just accumulation of credits, but demonstration of competence. They encourage service to others. They've resisted creation of large bureaucracies. Many private schools, particularly in urban areas, are more racially integrated than the public schools in exclusive suburbs.

The fundamental dilemmas in our schools are not whether to teach about sex or evolution. Instead, we must decide: Do we have the courage to reexamine cherished beliefs about public schools? Do we have the confidence to use proven learning principles? Do we have the commitment to establish effective schools for all children?

Americans justifiably are skeptical of "quick fixes." However, more effective schools will not cost more money—there is compelling, conclusive evidence of that.

The first half of this book describes effective, efficient programs which every school in this country can use without spending more money. The second half illustrates barriers to widespread excellence in public education and proposes a fundamental shift in the way we allocate money for our childrens' education. A new method of organization will encourage our best teachers, remove barriers inhibiting adoption of proven practices, and provide opportunities for all parents to select the most appropriate programs for their children.

Fundamentally, my criticisms are of the public education system, not those who occupy positions of influence and authority. There are no heroes and villains in this book, only people struggling to do the best they can for youngsters. Talented teachers and administrators in public education face enormous barriers in providing responsive, effective education. We must reverse the incentives, so that there will be rewards for competence, not compliance; innovation, not inaction; creativity, not conformity; and results, not rationalizations.

DAY IN THE LIFE OF AN ASSISTANT PRINCIPAL

"What does an Assistant Principal do, besides yell at kids?" This chapter describes a typical day—neither particularly easy nor unusually active. Countless other A.P.'s have similar daily experiences. We begin with a typical A.P. day because this has been my vantage point for the last four years. Understanding this viewpoint will provide a context for everything that follows. Exploring the variety of problems an urban school must respond to will help readers evaluate my proposals.

However, before recounting the events of May 21, 1981, it's probably helpful to know a little about St. Paul, Minnesota, where our school is located. For many, St. Paul is best known as the place across the river from Minneapolis, where Mary Tyler Moore pranced down streets throwing her cap in the air. Minneapolis and St. Paul are known as the Twin Cities. In fact they are no more alike than David and Elizabeth Nathan, our four-year-old twins. Our kids have some superficial similarities but different personalities.

Just so with Minneapolis and St. Paul. St. Paul has almost 300,000 residents, Minneapolis about 400,000. St. Paul is considerably older than Minneapolis and is the state capitol. Many Minneapolis residents view St. Paul as their "country cousin"—dull and stodgy compared to Minneapolis. Many St. Paul residents like it that way.

Each city's most prominent building says a good deal about

3

its character. In Minneapolis, that structure is the strikingly modern 52-story I.D.S. Center, the tallest building between Chicago and San Francisco. St. Paul is proudest of its Landmark Center, a completely restored former Federal Court Building erected in the 1880s and now used as headquarters and performing arts center for a variety of artistic and civic groups.

Though more than 80 percent of each city's population is white, there is considerable ethnic and racial diversity within and between the "Twins." St. Paul is heavily Catholic while Minneapolis is predominantly Lutheran. St. Paul has several thousand more Hispanics than Minneapolis, which has more Native Americans than any other American city except Chicago. Blacks make up about 8 percent of each city's population and a number of Southeast Asians have moved into the area within the last five years. Minorities comprise 25 to 30 percent of the public school population in each city.

The politics of the two cities are similar. Both are represented in Congress by liberal Democrats and have mayors who are progressive Democrats. Both City Councils include Republicans and Democrats, with the Democrats having a slight majority. As in most places, residents are concerned about education. The cities have separate school districts which sometimes cooperate with each other.

I've lived in Minneapolis or St. Paul since 1970, and presently own a home in St. Paul. On May 21, 1981, I'd worked in the St. Paul Public Schools for almost ten years, the last four as Assistant Principal at Murray Junior High School.

Here's what happened that day:

7:15–7:30 Arrived at school, answered two phone calls from parents asking why a certain bus had not picked up their children. (Turned out the bus was ten minutes early and left without them, something this particular bus driver does an average of twice a week.) I promised to check with our district's transportation department and get back to the parents. Then I reviewed some of the problems teachers had referred to me from the previous day: Students not in class and not listed as absent, students who left class early, a student who refused to discuss problems with his teacher, and a student who had been sleeping through a certain teacher's class.

7:30–7:45 Conference with two parents and their daughters. The two 13-year-olds had a nasty fight the previous day, which was the product of an ongoing "he said, she said, you said, they said" game they were playing. (The game involves people telling each other about comments other people allege they made or were made about them.) The girls had torn hair, scratched, and called each other names ranging from "whore" to "shit-eating nigger." The grandmother of one of the girls was angrier with me than she appeared to be with her grand-daughter. She disagreed vehemently with my sending both girls home for the rest of the day and insisting they return the following day with a parent or guardian (standard procedure if there's a fight which appears to have the potential for breaking out again).

I asked the young women to explain why fights aren't a good idea: People can get hurt, people can spend more time thinking about fights than their assignments, and they can lead to others coming into school to settle scores, which creates a dangerous situation. The grandmother had heard all this before, since her granddaughter had been in several previous fights, but wanted to know why we didn't have a room to isolate and punish students who fight. I invited her to a previously scheduled discussion about assigning a staff member to an "in-school suspension room." (More on this topic later.)

The girls agreed that there were better ways to settle disagreements. Both admitted shyly that they really had no argument with each other, but had been set up by other students' going back and forth between them telling various stories. Convinced the girls were ready to return peacefully to class, I readmitted them. As the grandmother left the office, she muttered that I was a "honky bastard" just loudly enough for several nearby students to hear. I couldn't think of a witty response so made no reply and continued walking down the hall.

7:45 Met briefly with a substitute teacher to review procedures. The regular teacher, despite our requests, had not left assignments for the substitute. The office staff tried to reach the teacher but his phone was busy. An hour later a clerk was able to make contact with the teacher, who said he'd given his assignments to another teacher. Turned out that teacher was

out sick. In any case, the clerk got the assignments which
were subsequently given to the substitute.

7:50   Took a phone call from a parent complaining that I had
forced her son to pay $5.00 for a window broken as a result of
a scuffle involving him and several other students. Her son
clearly had not delivered the letter I'd given him to take home
explaining the situation. (My mistake—I should have mailed
it.) The incident involved 14 students, each of whom was
being asked to pay $5.00 as their part of the $70.00 replace-
ment cost of the window. Her son had agreed to pay his share
the previous day, asking whether I would contact his parents
if he paid the money right then. I answered "Yes." The parent
didn't believe me. "Would you like to talk with your son and
the other participants?" He definitely would talk that evening
with his son when he returned from school. The parent promised to call the following morning.

7:55   Took a phone call from a poet we'd arranged to bring
into several classes. The artist cooperative she worked for
hadn't told her when these classes met (as they had promised
to do). I gave her this information and asked her to come in 10
minutes early to meet with the teacher. Then I listened to
several students' frustrations with my inability to get their bus
driver to stop at the places his printed schedule listed. (It
turned out that the driver was a substitute who insisted the
bus company had not given him an up-to-date route map.)

8:00–9:30   Our Pupil Problems Committee, which all St. Paul
Public Schools have, met with a student, who had called in a
false bomb scare, and his father. We discussed what further
disciplinary action should be taken. The student had already
been suspended for five days and we had filed charges with
the police. As chair of the committee, I made sure everyone
present (nurse, social worker, two teachers, counselor) introduced themselves to the father (who already knew most of
us well). Then I reviewed five options:

1. Recommendation that the student be expelled from all St. Paul
   Public schools for the remainder of the school year (eleven
   school days remained). This recommendation would have to
   be approved by the School Board. No one had been expelled
   for several years.
2. Recommendation that the student not be allowed to attend our
   school and be transferred elsewhere for the remainder of the

school year. This recommendation required Central Office approval.

3. Recommendation that the student be allowed to complete his assignments at home for the rest of the year. This recommendation required Central Office approval.
4. Readmission of the student while denying him certain privileges, such as eating with his friends and going on the final field trip. This recommendation required the Principal's approval.
5. Readmission of the student, returning all his privileges. This also required the Principal's approval.

The father's response to these options was that he had three older children in various penal institutions, he was fed up with his son, had beaten him and taken away all privileges at home for the next month, and that we could do whatever we wanted to do.

Several attending staff members discussed the possible effects on other students of readmitting this youngster. Some of the staff wanted to see the student transferred to another school, an indication to other students that his behavior was unacceptable. Other staff members pointed out that he had made real progress over the last two years; they asked his father about a program where the young man would come to school three hours a day, and be isolated from the other students. The father said that he didn't want his son at home; he felt the best action would be to send the student to his grandparents' home in Iowa. This surprised most of the committee members, but after some discussion, they agreed to the father's suggestion. An important part of the committee's agreement was the knowledge that when the student had previously spent time with his grandparents over Thanksgiving, he came back very happy and well-behaved for several weeks. It appeared that the father's solution was in the best interests of both his son and the other students at our school.

The meeting, which I feared would be both bitter and nasty, ended amiably, with the student thanking various staff members for helping him through the two years he'd been at our school. He told us that this was the best school among the nine he had attended. (He was 13 years old.) As the meeting ended, the father, student, and I walked to the office, where secretaries gave us the forms necessary to check out of school.

9:30–10:30 Another conference, this one with two students and two guardians. This involved a fascinating and disruptive situation which had nothing to do with school work. The two students were half brother and sister. Until the previous week we thought they both had the same parents. We learned that the young woman had run away from home and gone to live with her sister. Her uncle (who we mistakenly thought was her father) came into the school to bring her home.

The young woman begged us not to let her uncle take her away from the school. She explained for the first time that the information her family had given us in the fall was incorrect, that her real father was in a nursing home and her mother was dead. She claimed that her uncle abused her, and she wanted to leave his home. Under state law, school officials are required to report child abuse to the welfare department and police if it appears the claim is justified. Obviously, this does not help to create positive relationships between school officials and parents. But, we had made a report because the young woman had several bruises on her arms. The police had been at our school the previous day to investigate and said they would be in touch.

The girl's half brother learned somehow that she had filed a complaint. He began swearing and screaming at her, and she returned his comments in full. I'd stepped between them to prevent the boy from striking his sister and told him to go home for the rest of the day. He and I walked to the door together and I urged him to go directly home to cool off. Fifteen minutes later he was back in school with a two by four board several feet long! This time I warned him that he was to leave immediately and that if he came back into the building today, I would call the police and ask them to arrest him on trespassing charges.

The counselor brought the sister into her office to wait for the bus at the end of the day. Our plan was to escort her to the bus, just in case someone else was planning something. Several hours later, when the final bell rang, the counselor and I went with her to the bus. The half brother was there. I had to step between them again and then hold him so he wouldn't attack her. Finally he left. I went back into the building and called the father. (I'd tried several times without success to reach him earlier in the day. This time I was successful.) He apologized and promised to bring his son in the following day.

A mental review of these events of the previous day reminded me why I was not looking forward to the conference! Despite my expectations, the meeting was not a repeat of the previous conflicts. The girl's elder sister and her uncle already had decided to keep the young man home for the last 11 days of school. They felt other students would harass him, and that the boy and girl would be unable to get along. The father asked us if we'd be willing to allow assignments to be completed at home. I readily agreed. We also convinced the family to begin some counseling at one of several available neighborhood centers. The counselor gave them a list she'd prepared, and they used the phone in my office to make their first appointment.

As they left, I thought about the previous two conferences. Over the year we'd spent an enormous amount of time with these three youngsters. I felt each had made some progress toward acceptable behavior, but still had quite a way to go. Sadly, our ultimate solution to their problems was to agree to their removal from school. Deep down, I felt we had failed these kids. Long ago I accepted my inability to solve all the problems I encountered, but failure still bothers me—a lot.

10:30–10:45   I took several phone calls. One was from a freelance journalist in Virginia who wanted more information about our peer counseling program. I explained that it was really hectic right now and asked if he would call back about 3:00. The evaluator of our Federal crime prevention project also called and agreed to call back at 2:45.

A parent called to challenge a decision we made about students who were on the work program. (They spend three hours in classes at the school, and three hours working at various jobs, mostly fast-food restaurants.) All eighth and ninth grade students were going to spend one of their last school days at an amusement park. The work program coordinator and Principal had decided to allow students who were working to go to the amusement park later in the day. The coordinator would drive them to and from the park. Several of these youngsters wanted to go with the rest of the student body. The work program supervisor's position was that the

employers depended on these kids and would be less interested in hiring students the following year if they asked for a
day off just to go to a party at an amusement park. He also
thought students needed to learn that they had responsibilities
to their employers. I explained all this to the father.

He insisted that he had talked directly with his daughter's
manager who didn't mind if *she* went to the amusement park,
as long as the other two students from our school remained at
the restaurant. Since the Principal had made the decision on
this one, I referred the parent to him (and thought to myself,
"Good luck, Vern"). I also made a note to tell the Principal
that the father would be calling. This appeared to be one of
countless situations where divinely inspired wisdom and
negotiation powers would come in handy.

10:45–11:00   Several students were just arriving for the day.
This late arrival was a pattern for them. We'd talked with their
parents and assigned after-school detention, neither of which
had much impact. I talked with each of them. They all said
they liked their morning classes and did well when they attended them. However, they also liked staying up late and
watching movies on television. Two of the three said their
parents left for work before they left for school. Each understood she would be staying after school and either working for
half an hour or sitting for an hour each time she was tardy for
the rest of the year.

11:00–11:30   A teacher sent in two students who had been
fighting. One was a boy with whom I'd had no previous contact, the other a youngster who constantly had problems. I
talked with each individually to get his version of the fight.
One had called the other a "muscle-bound dummy," and the
other retorted with, "drug-running burnout." Both had challenged each other to "do something about it" which immediately produced flying punches.

After determining that they clearly were ready to go after
each other again, I called both sets of parents. I reached only
one of the four parents, told her that I would be sending both
youngsters home for the rest of the day and that they had a
writing assignment about how they would avoid conflicts with
each other for the rest of the year. I've found that these writing assignments are helpful for teachers, administrators, and

students. Keeping students' written statements helps convince them I respect and believe what they say and will hold them to what they've expressed. It doesn't always work, but it can be helpful.

The parent's response was that the fight must have been all the other student's fault because her son never fought. While agreeing her son had not been involved in fights before, I reminded her of his comment, "What are you going to do about it," which clearly challenged the other student. She said she would call her husband who would be contacting me. Several minutes later he called and asked if I would be willing to meet with him about 3:30, instead of waiting until the following morning. I agreed. (He arrived shortly after 4:00, but that's getting ahead of the day's events.)

11:30–12:00   Six times I tried during this half hour to get out of the office and walk around the school, as I try to do every lunch hour. We have three different groups of students eating between 11:00 and 12:30. Despite trying to leave, I never made it. Students came in asking for bus cards, and when the secretary reminded them the cards were given out only before and after school, the students came to me to complain. They had no particular reason for not wanting to come in before or after school, but didn't like the idea of not getting them now. I explained that we were currently short one secretary and that we had to make some decisions about how to use the limited time of the office staff. Not particularly satisfied, the students left. (I wasn't very satisfied with the explanation either—it seemed a bit rigid. I made a note to discuss this; possibly a student in the office could help do this 30-second task.)

A substitute teacher came in and said the key we had given her was stuck in the door of a classroom near the office. The secretary tried unsuccessfully to find the custodians, who I knew were in the lunchroom, also short-staffed because one person had resigned two weeks before and the position was not yet filled. The teacher and I walked over to the classroom. Neither of us was able to get the key out. By this time, a custodian arrived and I left to check on other things.

Several teachers stopped me at the office door to ask when they would be receiving extra pay for chaperoning a four day out-of-town field trip. I asked them to check with the secretary to see if the time sheet had been sent to the Payroll office, promised to follow up, and wrote myself a reminder on the small index card I always carry headed, "things to do."

Earlier I'd asked several students who were helping out in the office to sort through slips I've received in the past two days from teachers referring non-emergency problems (such as skipping class). I picked out several of these and asked the school service person in the office to find what classes the students were in and bring a hall pass to their rooms so I could see them. While waiting, I took a short walk down the hall to calm down several students who were playing loudly on the way, it turned out, to the restroom. "Relax and cool it," was my initial comment. That was enough to produce smiles, end the shoving, and get them moving directly to their target.

By this time, the two students I'd called for were in my office. The first insisted he had been absent all day yesterday and that a mistake had been made by his homeroom teacher. I asked my secretary to call his house to get confirmation of this, and asked the student to wait. Checking was a clear indication to the student that I wasn't sure he was telling the truth. However, I've found many students don't give me the facts in such matters. We've asked parents to write a note when their children are absent, but unfortunately, everyone doesn't do this. In any case, this parent confirmed that her son had been home all day yesterday and apologized for not writing a note.

This called for a note to the homeroom teacher, whose failure to notice the student's absence had wasted time of his five other teachers who had to send a note to me about his absence. Unfortunately, more than a third of the skipping referrals I get are due to a teacher's error in not marking a student absent in homeroom, or not looking at our daily attendance bulletin to see who is excused.

After writing the note, I apologized to the student. "Sorry to waste your time, and to question your honesty. I don't always know who to believe."

"No problem—glad to see you're going to say something to Mr. Adams. He often forgets to do the attendance first thing in the morning. I'd be glad to help him, if it's ok."

"Thanks, Jack, that's a good idea. I'll include your offer in the note."

Then I called in the second student. He had skipped. We briefly discussed the reasons, which were that it was a beautiful day, he had not been truant at all this year, and he thought it would be fun to walk around the neighborhood. He asked if I would notify his parents, and when I said "of course," he began to cry. He explained that his parents were discussing divorce and had a bitter, screaming argument two nights before. The 13-year-old described how his Dad wanted to "Get it on with as many women as I can before I die!" and his mother's angry response, "You don't have much to get up, so I can see why you need to practice!"

I gave him a Kleenex and closed the door to my office. I asked if he felt bad about these arguments between his parents.

"Shit yes," he replied.

"And do you feel your parents argue about you?"

His weeping started again and he nodded. I moved to sit next to him and put my arm around his shoulder. He moved closer to me, and the tears slowly subsided.

"Would you mind if I asked Ms. Kaiser, our counselor, to come in?"

He muttered that it would be ok. I phoned her on the intercom, but got no answer in her office. I asked our clerk to try to find her. As usual, the secretary came through and in several minutes the counselor joined us. When she arrived, I briefly reviewed the situation and, after the student agreed to talk with her, she led him into her office.

It was now 12:20. I'd been at school since 7:15 and was ready for a break.

On my way through the halls to the faculty room, I stopped to compliment an eighth grader on her new haircut, asserting that it made her look older. She beamed. People like to be noticed!

Several student council members walked with me, asking about their proposal to allow students to go outside into a courtyard at lunch. I reminded them that such recommendations went to the Principal and urged them to make an appointment to see him. My "to do" card got another item as I promised to remind him of their concern.

Finally, the faculty room and a few minutes of potential peace. Several staff members came over and mentioned that they'd heard it was a busy day. I smiled and muttered something innocuous like "Oh yes, busy like most days—full of challenge and opportunity." I couldn't think of anything more intelligent or witty to say, but they laughed. Humor doesn't stop the rain from falling, but it can serve as an umbrella.

12:32 Exactly eight minutes after I arrived in the faculty room the public address speaker summoned me back to the office. "Is Joe there?" "Yes." "Please come to the office immediately."

On my way to the office I encountered a teacher so angry she didn't want to wait until I got back. "Six or seven little monsters just picked up my car and tried to move it. I have no idea how much damage was done. Mr. Jackson saw them too. I just know two of them—Sammy Carlson and Robin Adams." She was shaking with rage and screaming at me. I walked with her to the street where her car had been parked, next to the building and her classroom. We talked briefly with the teacher in the classroom next to her, who confirmed the two names she'd given me and who also wasn't sure of the others.

I immediately called the office and asked them to find those two students and have them there when I got back in several minutes. Turning to the furious teacher, I asked if she would please drive her car around the block to check on any immediate damage while I watched her class. Nodding, she insisted that some damage might not be readily apparent but could show up later. I agreed but explained that it would be helpful to determine whether any readily observable damage had been done.

She drove off, returning several minutes later, somewhat calmed down (which was the other reason I suggested that she take the car around the block—to cool off). She apologized for yelling at me and I assured her no apology was necessary. She reported that there was no apparent damage and reminded me it could show up later in the transmission or parking brake.

When I arrived back in the office several minutes later, the two students who had been identified were waiting for me. I gave the secretary a quick "thumbs up" in thanks for her help. The two students readily admitted their part in the incident. I explained that the punishment would be less severe if they told me who else was involved and said it would take just a bit longer to find out if they wouldn't cooperate. They decided to give me the other names, and within three minutes all six involved students were in my office.

"Jack, did you pick up Ms. Armstrong's car?"

"Yes."

"Sam, did you pick up Ms. Armstrong's car?"

"Yup, just to show that I'm a real man!" (Big smile.)

Each agreed he had been involved. Then I asked what problems they could have created.

"Well, I suppose someone could have been hurt."

"Agreed. In fact the injury could have been extremely serious. Ever see an arm or leg that's been under a 2,000 pound car?"

None of them had, and several began to look a little nervous.

"And how about the car—she says you moved it. That could have torn up the transmission or parking brake. We're talking about a $5,000.00 car. Anyone want to pay for repairs?" No volunteers.

I told them that each would be suspended for two days, and that they would have to come back with their parents before being readmitted. Then I began the 45-minute process of completing the page-long form required by Minnesota's Pupil Fair Dismissal Act whenever a student is suspended. The form asks for the student's name, address, etc., reason for suspension, facts, testimony received, name of administrator who heard the evidence, time and day of the hearing, and plan for readmission. We had to complete one form for each of the six kids. I dictated the original form and then had the secretary fill in the rest. Then I began calling parents and suggesting that the students should have tasks around the house so that they would not regard the suspension as simply vacation. The first phone call set a pattern which was repeated with four of the six parents, all of whom are affluent and live in nice sections of the city.

"Hello, Mrs. Jackson, this is Joe Nathan from Murray Junior High. Your son Jim is being suspended because he was involved in an incident which could have resulted in serious injury or major property damage." I then described the situation, her son's response and the readmission plan.

"Well, Mr. Nathan, don't you think you're being rather harsh? I mean, wouldn't it be sufficient to warn them?"

"On relatively minor matters, such as skipping for the first time, we do warn students. However, your son and his friends could have been very seriously injured. Or they could have wrecked the staff member's car."

"Well, I suppose you're going to do what you want regardless of what I say. Send him on home."

"Would you please consider making his day full of jobs so he won't view this as simply a vacation?"

"It's going to be a real bother to have him home. I'll see what we can do."

This was the response of four parents. The other two parents asked me to apologize for them to the teacher and thanked me for calling. All promised to come in at 7:30 A.M. in two days.

By this time it was 2:15, and time to check with a bus driver who the students claimed was not following his route. School ended in less than 15 minutes and I wanted to make sure he had the correct directions. The substitute wasn't on the bus— a brand new driver was! I asked if she had a copy of the revised route. She did, but had several questions about discipline procedure on busses. We reviewed the rules: Students are to follow drivers' directions; drivers are responsible for students' safety; misbehaving students should be warned, and if they don't stop causing problems, the driver should report them immediately to the school.

More than 60 percent of our school's students arrive by bus, so we try to keep a close working relationship with the drivers. The new driver and I chatted informally for another few minutes, and then watched as the final bell rang.

2:30 Time for the students to go home! Laughing, yelling, the students burst out of school doors toward the busses, their homes, or the athletic field two blocks away. It was time to return phone calls, write letters to several parents, and meet with teachers who'd asked to discuss one situation or another.

2:40–3:00 Talked with the Virginia freelance writer. After a brief discussion, I put the peer counseling teacher on the phone. The writer was impressed and asked us to send him some written information. We did, and never heard from him again. The teacher and I also talked about a conference during the summer for faculty interested in peer counseling. The teacher promised to think about it and give me his ideas the following day. This surprised me; I had expected him to be really enthusiastic.

I learned the next day that he was angry about the district's policies discouraging teachers from attending conferences during the "school day." The Board of Education had received complaints from several parents about their children having a number of substitutes. Apparently, one of the reasons was a conference teachers had attended. As a result, the Superintendent recommended that the district not provide substitutes enabling teachers to attend training workshops. This became district procedure. It was a classic case of bureaucratic response. There was a complaint, and apparently a problem. Every rule, no matter how trivial, has a reason; it is intended to solve some problem or abuse. Unfortunately, making broad policies often creates other difficulties.

The following day the teacher and I talked about all this. He pointed out that administrators were able to miss school days to attend conferences. He felt teachers shouldn't be restricted to attending conferences during the summer. We were able to hold a two-day peer counseling workshop the following fall during "school time" by working closely with principals and not asking for substitutes.

3:05–3:30   Talked with our federal program evaluator in California. She wanted to see me in St. Paul as soon as I could spend two or three days with her. I suggested that the week after school was out would be the soonest possible time. She promised to check on whether she could do this and notify me by the end of the week, either way. (She didn't.)

3:30–4:30   Wrote letters to or phoned several parents about problems or progress. One conversation went something like this:

"Hello, Mr. Taylor? This is Joe Nathan from Murray Junior High. How are you this afternoon?"

"What's that damn son of mine done now. Lord, we just talked a week ago."

"That's why I'm calling—to tell you that whatever you said to him really worked. His conduct in science class has improved dramatically. He's bringing his materials to class, and the teacher reports that he's turned in several back assignments. She also says he is raising his hand when he wants to say something. We're really pleased and wanted to share this progress with you!"

"Say what? Hey, who is this really?" I assured him that he was talking with his son's assistant principal.

"Do you know that this is the first time anyone from a school has ever called to say something good about my son? Thanks, thanks a lot, man."

Hard to think of a better way to use the three minutes between 4:18 and 4:21 than that call. We need to let parents know when things are improving or going well, in addition to contacting them when problems develop. It makes sense to have at least one positive phone conversation or to write a happy letter each day. Good for me, as well as the student.

About 4:25 the Principal and I met to discuss classes for the following school year. We were interrupted by a phone call from the Assistant Superintendent. He wanted a written report about two problems we'd discussed with him. The first involved an assault by two outsiders on several of our students. That happened 10 days ago. We'd called the police, taken the students to the hospital, and contacted the parents. "Well, I want a written report. Several Board members have heard about the incident, and want to know the details." We knew that protocol demanded Board members not call building administrators directly, but rather ask central office administrators for information. So, we promised to write the report immediately.

The second document he wanted involved an assault which had taken place in a park after several students got off their bus. I had met with the involved parents and recommended that they file charges with the police. Instead, they had an older friend go to the park the following evening and knock around the 14-year-old who'd struck their 13-year-old son. They called the Assistant Superintendent when they learned that the 14-year-old's parents were going to file charges if they pressed the issue. The parents of the younger boy wanted us to file charges.

We explained all this to the Assistant Superintendent. He pointed out that we needed to be involved in student problems that had to do with transportation. We recognized it was impossible for him to keep thousands of incidents separate in his mind, and that he would use our report to help him deal with the complaining parents. If he didn't call these parents back, it's likely they would have gone to the Superintendent complaining about him, as well as us. So, we reluctantly added writing two reports to our "to do" lists.

The Principal and I smiled at each other. (The option was to scream.) We decided to leave the reports for the following day, violating the old rule about "Don't leave until tomorrow anything that can be done today." The person who suggested that policy didn't have a band concert coming up in 90 minutes!

We went out for some dinner before the spring band concert, which was scheduled to start in less than two hours, at 7:00 P.M. At 6:45, we opened the doors and asked the band director how we could help. A number of parents stopped to talk before, during, and after the concert. They were concerned about layoffs, next year's class schedule, lost textbooks, and why their son or daughter didn't have a solo in the concert.

The program went well, with most of the parents and students really enjoying themselves. It was a great chance for some of the kids to achieve positive attention. We need to develop opportunities for all kids to get acclaim from their peers and adults. The concert was a nice way to end the day. The Principal and I complimented the students and the band director and agreed with several parents that the kids had done a terrific job. Then we walked to our cars. It was 9:45 P.M.

EFFECTIVE LEARNING

At one school, students decided that their playground needed improvement. Bleak and uninviting, it contained a slide, two trees, and some scruffy grass. Working with a University of Minnesota architecture student who volunteered his service, the students, aged 6 to 13, and I began by gathering books and articles about playgrounds around the country. We talked with local architects and visited several outstanding sites. Gradually, the students developed ideas about the kinds of equipment and materials they wanted.

The next step was to develop a plan for creating the ideal playground. Older students helped younger ones measure the available area, and the architecture student helped them draw a map to scale. Suddenly, the multiplication and division they'd been studying made more sense. With more help from the architect intern, the students built a scale model to help others visualize their ideas and give reactions. Parents, other students, teachers, and school administrators reviewed the model, made suggestions, and gave the project a name: FUFY (Fix Up the Front Yard). After considerable negotiation and revision, approval was given.

The first, most obvious question was: Where would the materials come from? The answer: From both the group's ingenuity and community generosity. After listing the various materials needed, students divided into committees. There were groups assigned to obtain tires, railroad ties, sand, and a concrete tube. Before the committees started their work, we practiced making phone calls. Students wrote down what they intended to say on the phone, shared it with classmates, and got helpful responses.

Then the calling began. The sand committee members made 17 phone calls before ultimately finding a contractor who agreed to donate six dump truck loads of sand. The day those two tons of sand arrived was unforgettable for everyone involved, but especially for the valiant six sand committee members.

Several students found a parent whose company donated the concrete pipe (an imperfect tube, five feet in diameter, which they would have scrapped but which youngsters found irresistible). However, it took two months from the time the company agreed to donate it until the pipe finally arrived. Transportation had to be arranged, and a fence surrounding the playground had to be taken down so that the delivery truck could place the pipe. Committee members had hoped that the pipe would be in place before the sand was delivered, but this just was not to be.

Railroad tie committee members faced different problems. The students encountered what they came to call the "circle game." Person A referred them to Person B who told them about C who suggested calling D. That person thought the idea was terrific and was sure that A could help! Finally, a supply of ties was located, provided the students pick them up. The kids arranged for a van and driver, only to discover that the van could carry only five at a time. They figured this would require six round trips. The group switched goals and was able to borrow a dump truck and driver the following day. The 30 ties were delivered in a single load.

Building the new playground took four months. It was slowed by a typically severe Minnesota winter and a major miscalculation on my part. The railroad ties were stacked in the yard when unloaded. I did not foresee that the ties would freeze to the ground when the snow began in mid-November. I also forgot that frozen ground is similar to steel when one is trying to help an eight-year-old pound a spike into it! We decided to thaw the ties by bringing them into the school's front hall. This solved one problem, but created others. Few interior designers would recommend placing defrosting railroad ties in a building's foyer to enhance its attractiveness. The custodians weren't overjoyed by the melting snow, so we placed paper under the ties. That quickly became saturated, and soon began to smell.

The attachment of railroad ties to the ground went on (somewhat inhibited by minus 20 and 30-degree temperatures, and very resistant frozen ground). The students persisted and finally were ready to pound in the last spike connecting the railroad ties. Several of the students, in their U.S. history class, had read about how the transcontinental railroad's final ties were joined with gold spikes. They suggested we paint the final spike gold. This triumph was toasted with grape juice donated by parents.

What did the students learn from this project? They saw the value of basic computation and communications skills. They used and strengthened those skills. Equally important, they gained confidence that they could complete complicated, difficult tasks. They learned how to work with others in a cooperative, task-oriented manner. When faced with obstacles, they shared creative solutions. How often do we find these skills lacking in our high school graduates?

Comments by educators that our schools are doing the best they can with the available money are shameful. Americans have committed extraordinary resources to their schools. In the last 20 years, more money has been spent on education than for any other single purpose in most states. Student-teacher ratios have reduced and teachers' salaries have increased (although in many places, teachers' salaries have not matched inflation). Citizens have raised taxes to build and equip shiny temples for education.

Despite these expenditures, our functional illiteracy rate is high, scandalously high. An important national study of more than 20,000 adults showed that over 20 percent did not have the reading or computation skills they needed daily (Fogg, p. 1A). Many adults could not determine which is a better bargain, a gallon of milk costing $1.75 or two half-gallons at $.90 each. Too many cannot write a clear paragraph, and struggle to fill out job applications.

Attitudes toward school, self, and learning are as disturbing as skill levels. Two recent reports (Proctor, p. 4; Hedin, 1982, in Thomma, p. 1C) show that a majority of students value education but don't feel sufficiently challenged. Important research by Alabama professor Dr. Robert Bills shows that as students move through schools, they feel less able to have much impact on their own lives. There is mounting evidence that "the longer students remain in school, the more they reject values such as honesty, trustworthiness, truthfulness, sincerity, cooperation and others vital to the survival of our society" (Bills, 1982).

These research projects don't convey the enormous individual and collective tragedy our schools help produce. Few people achieve their potential. Every youngster comes to kindergarten eager to learn. Every teenager, no matter how alienated, hopes in September that the new school year will be better than the last one. Usually they are disappointed.

Meanwhile, teachers report mounting frustration. Less than 25 percent feel they made the right professional choice. They are being blamed for widespread incompetence, poor discipline, and an unprofessional attitude toward money. Teachers often point to poor teaching conditions, inadequate support from administrators, too much time spent on forms and not enough on teaching, and lack of respect from youngsters and their parents.

We need to rethink learning and schooling. Let's start with walking and talking, two of the most difficult skills we ever learn, according to many physicians and psychologists. More than 95 percent of our citizens achieve enough proficiency to get around and communicate clearly. The few who do not gain these skills have clear physical or psychological impediments. It is nowhere near the 20 to 30 percent of our population who lack necessary reading, computation, and writing skills.

Why can people learn to walk and talk, but fail to gain writing, computing, thinking, and reading skills? Analyzing the environment in which people learn to walk helps answer this question. First, there is a strong, clear expectation that each child will succeed. Next, the skill to be learned is an important one, something that the child knows is useful. This learning takes place in an extremely supportive environment. The child is allowed to make progress at her or his own rate. There is no standardized, coordinated curriculum. The parent emphasizes achievement. When the child makes progress, she or he is praised. When progress is slow, the correct way is modeled. The child rarely is criticized or ridiculed. Little children are not isolated into groups of two-, three-, or four-year-olds (until they go to school). At home the young child has opportunities to watch and learn from a variety of models who make learning enjoyable. Success brings a hug, or sometimes a snack. Finally, the student-teacher ratio is low.

In such an environment, virtually everyone learns to walk. This is not the permissive "do your own thing" situation which some suggested in the late 1960s; expectations are clear and high—the child *will* learn specific skills. But neither is the atmosphere a harsh, rigid one.

I'm not suggesting all schools should be the same, any more than all families are identical. Parents and youngsters have different values and learning styles. Families should have a far greater role in determining the kinds of schools young people will attend. All schools should consider the child's earliest (and more successful) learning environment when planning their own organization and program.

If I had a chance to create it, my children's school would include a variety of learning experiences patterned after the environment in which they learned to walk and talk. I'd insist on "youth participation projects." These programs have been developed and promoted by a group called the National Commission on Resources for Youth. NCRY was founded by a remarkable juvenile court judge, Mary Conway Kohler. Kohler believes that there are better ways to assist learning and development of responsibility. Her group described four important characteristics of youth participation projects:

1. Young people help to solve a real need.
2. Young people work cooperatively with an adult, and help make decisions about their project.
3. There is an opportunity for reflection and consideration of the project's success.
4. Youths gain skills as they work on their project.

To this list, I'd add that the group's work includes a specific product. Youth participation projects have been used with children as young as six. The playground class described earlier is an excellent example.

Another youth participation project in our school required

even more sophisticated skills. It was part of a class I taught on juvenile and consumer rights and responsibilities. The students read a variety of material, wrote reviews of articles and books, visited courts, and interviewed employees of the Better Business Bureau, Minnesota Consumer Protection Agency, Minnesota Public Interest Research Group, and Mayor's Information and Complaint Office. They also helped solve actual consumer problems. Two cases are typical of the more than 250 which the students handled, successfully resolving about 70 percent.

In the first case, an area woman wrote to ask the students' help in obtaining a radio she claimed was owed to her by a car dealership. The class began by listing possible first steps. These included writing to the woman for proof of her allegations, calling the Better Business Bureau, calling the dealership, or picketing the dealership. After some discussion of each alternative's strengths and weaknesses, the students voted to write the woman. They knew how easy it is to complain; responsible action requires proof. (A note: I retained the right to veto any action students selected, but never had to use the power during the three years the class functioned. The students and I didn't always agree, but their rationale always was logical. Often I was unsure about which of several steps was most appropriate. My veto was only for potentially illegal, unethical, or dangerous actions. They never picked a strategy which worried me.)

Several students in the class of 38 volunteered to "take the case." That meant they would be responsible for carrying out steps the class agreed upon and keeping the group informed of their progress. The students wrote a letter to the woman:

Your case was brought up in our class and we have agreed to work on it. We have discussed it and we would like a copy of your contract. From there we will write to you and tell you our next step.

Sincerely yours,

Consumer Action Service Students

The woman wrote back and enclosed her copy of the contract, which indeed stated that the dealership owed her a radio. The students made several copies of the contract and sent the original back to her. Then they went through another brainstorming discussion and selection process to pick a strategy. After considering several possibilities, they chose to call the dealership's owner. They had learned that starting at the top can be useful.

Before making any phone calls, the students rehearsed. One student played herself, another the dealer's secretary, and a third the dealer. Through this role playing, the students quickly learned to accept being put on "hold" and to handle attempts to divert them from the person they wished to speak to.

Finally, one student talked with the dealer.

"Hello, Mr. Jackson, this is Kurt Johnson from the Consumer Action Service. We received a letter from Mrs. Zumalt regarding a radio which was to have been put in a car she purchased on October 15. Apparently the radio wasn't available that day, so a notation was made on the contract that it would be put in. Mrs. Zumalt says she has been trying to get the radio for the last four months, but has not made any progress. Can you help her out?"

"Hmmm, I'll need to know more about the situation, Kurt. Can you give me her name and the date of the sale again? I'll be glad to look into it." Kurt did this. "Now, I'll need a few days to take care of it, ok?"

"That's fine, Mr. Jackson. May I call you early next week?"

"Won't be necessary, Kurt. But I appreciate your interest."

"We appreciate your help, Mr. Jackson, but our procedure is to check back. When would you like me to call?"

"Well, how about four days? That should give us time to thoroughly review the problem and take appropriate action."

The student reported back to the class. While pleased, the group had learned to be wary of promises. They elected to write to the woman to tell her what had happened.

A week later, a letter arrived for the students.

Mr. Jackson, the owner, called us Friday night about the radio and, because of the holiday, I was able to go and have them install it on Monday. They were very pleasant and even gave us a much better unit than they had planned to because the other one wouldn't fit. Thank you all so much for your help.

Though often successful, students learned that they couldn't help everyone. In one case, a young woman wrote to complain that her landlord had demanded she leave her apartment in 30 days and forfeit the security deposit of $100.00. She insisted the landlord did not like her dog, who was very quiet and did no damage. She also said the landlord made advances when she'd answered the door in a nightgown.

The students wrote back to ask for a copy of her lease. She had lost it. Next the students contacted the landlord and asked him for the lease. When it arrived, the students read it carefully (something the young woman apparently had not done). The lease included two key provisions: 1) No pets whatever were allowed in the building; and 2) Any person violating any provision of the lease could be given 30 days notice by the landlord and would lose their security deposit. The students asked the landlord about his comments when the tenant had answered the door in her nightgown. He said the nightgown was revealing, but denied making any comments beyond noting that she was more attractive than he had realized.

Students reviewed what they learned with an attorney who volunteered to advise them occasionally. Reluctantly they concluded that there was little they could do to help the woman, other than strongly suggest she read and understand whatever she signed. They also urged her not to answer the door with nothing on but a nightgown.

Many adults have asked me whether other adults treated the students seriously in these cases. The answer is almost invariably, yes. We used letters as often as possible. Sometimes the students made phone calls, but only after careful preparation and practice. In a few cases, though, the youngsters' age and status clearly was an issue. One taxidermist refused to respond to the class's letters. When contacted by phone, he laughed at the students and dared them to do anything about his lengthy delays in returning animals to their owners. The students finally turned this case over to the State Consumer Protection Agency.

One case almost got me arrested. The students were working with a parent who lived in a Housing Authority apartment. Considerable damage had been done to clothing in her basement due to a backed up water pipe. It appeared to the students that the Housing Authority was at least partially responsible for the damage, because one of their workers had inadvertently neglected to turn off all the pipes while doing some repair work.

After getting nowhere by negotiating with various officials within the agency, the students made an appointment to be on the agenda of the Housing Authority Board. They arranged for an attorney to represent the woman at the meeting. However, the chair of the housing authority board refused to let the attorney speak, because he had not asked for time. He refused to let the students speak, because, although they had placed the time on the agenda, they had no legal standing with respect to the woman. It was a classic "Catch 22" situation and I began pointing this out to the Board. A police officer was directed to get me to sit down. We had a brief, heated discussion in which my alternatives were laid out: "Sit down and shut up, or be arrested for disorderly conduct!" Fortunately, the students were a good deal more relaxed about the situation than I. They convinced me to go outside to cool down.

Although this case took more than seven months, we were able to help the parent—the Housing Authority ultimately paid her more than $700.00.

Students learned important lessons from these and more than 200 other cases. First, they applied and strengthened academic reading and writing skills. They used those skills constantly and came to understand the necessity of accurate, clear writing and careful, thoughtful reading. Their consumer action activities were probably more valuable than reading a chapter about consumer problems and answering questions at the end. Also, they learned they could be helpful to others. The students wrote a booklet about the class. When the national Sunday newspaper supplement *Parade Magazine* ran an article about the class, more than 5,000 subscribers sent in a dollar to get a copy. (The booklet is still available by writing to the Principal, St. Paul Open School, 1023 Osceola, St. Paul, Mn. 55102. It's still $1.00.)

Learning that they could help others changed the students' views of themselves; they saw themselves as capable, productive people. The class demonstrates that improving students' self perceptions can coincide with their acquiring basic and applied skills. Students who don't have those skills won't "feel good" about themselves regardless of how many sensitivity groups and trust building exercises they participate in. Too much "touchy-feely" work has been done in schools which ignores this basic principle.

The students learned how they can use law. Without these activities, many youngsters have the attitude expressed by one of the consumer action students on the first day of class: "Law is just a way rich people keep us in our place." In fact, students learned that laws can help protect them from people with more power and wealth than they have—and that this is an appropriate use of courts.

Our kids took a number of cases to small claims court. In one, students pointed out to an incredulous judge that the law on which he was basing his decision had just changed. The students were working on a case involving about $820.00 worth of damage to a friend's car. The judge explained that small claims court had authority to award up to $750.00. The student told the judge that the legislature had just given these courts authority to award up to $1,000.00. The student won not only the case, but a congratulatory phone call from the judge.

The playground design and consumer action classes are only two examples of youth participation projects. Hundreds of schools throughout the country have one or two such projects. In virtually every case, they are not more expensive and do not require special equipment beyond what already is available in schools. Youth participation projects do require several things from teachers:

1. Willingness to work cooperatively with students, rather than be completely in charge and totally directive;
2. Willingness to be creative, thoughtful, and hardworking, rather than reuse the same lecture and class materials hour after hour, year after year;
3. Willingness to accept questions and criticisms from colleagues who continue to use the same lectures and regurgitation-of-answers test methods so popular with many secondary school teachers.

Other examples of youth participation demonstrate its range and variety.

Many of the most interesting youth participation projects have been conducted in inner city schools. Students and staff at Philadelphia's Simon Gratz High School created a new approach to biology and health education by working with local Tuberculosis and Health Associations. They used puppet shows, comic books, posters, and cartoon strips to teach good health practices to elementary school students. Their presentations covered drug abuse, alcoholism, venereal disease, and tuberculosis, among other topics, and received positive response (National Commission on Resources for Youth, 1974, p. 25).

In New York City's South Bronx, at Intermediate School 139, students and staff created GUTS (Government Understanding for Today's Students). Students conducted a survey to identify the most prevalent problems in their area. They discovered a need for accurate information on health care, and organized a community health fair, giving free information, testing, and referrals. In another project, the students improved their community's appearance, replacing abandoned lots with a large garden. The garden was also an educational source for English, Art, Home Economics, and Science classes. GUTS and similar programs can bring hope, learning, and excitement to depressed communities (National Commission on Resources for Youth, 1981, pp. 16–17).

One talented math teacher named Jon Scholten decided to help students see immediate value in algebra. As part of their course work, students identified and studied the relative cost of different insulation materials. The class was able to acquire several kinds of insulation for their classroom's windows. Results were shared with other students and parents.

Pennsylvania high school students in advanced physics classes started a service for their families using many of the principles learned in class. They conducted home energy audits and gave families information about low-cost steps to take to conserve energy.

In one school, Dick Larson, a creative art teacher, talked with the Principal about the possibility of extending the work of some of his talented students. The school was having difficulty with vandalism in an unsupervised area near the locker rooms. The teacher suggested the students draw murals depicting various athletes on the walls. The Principal agreed, and within several months the walls were illustrated with a hockey player, skier, swimmer, golfer, quarterback, and basketball player. The swimmer was placed just over the drinking fountain, a cute touch. More important, the vandalism ended.

Another exciting project was the result of cooperation between several schools, a local insurance company, and the police and fire departments. The teacher, Lana Mahoney, had seen teenage vandalism in her school's neighborhood. She discussed vandalism, arson, and assault with her class. They visited some of the places those crimes had been committed and talked with the victims. Then they worked with artists to create puppet shows and a formal presentation about crime. The ninth graders took these products to elementary schools, and worked with the elementary teachers and students. Both teenagers and younger students were affected by this project. The local electrical utility reported that vandalism in the neighborhood went down sharply after this project had been in operation for a year.

Another project began with youngsters surveying their school's student body about which of several projects would be of greatest immediate benefit. The greatest number of votes went to getting in more community volunteers to work directly with students. The class then worked with their teacher, Mike LaBerge, and an expert on media, Jim Gambone, to produce a 10-minute filmstrip on the value of volunteers. A local television newscaster donated his time to help narrate the filmstrip. It was shown to a number of community groups and helped encourage many new volunteers.

Rural areas have produced some of the most interesting projects. A group of students in Watertown, Minnesota, produced a marvelous "living museum." They restored several buildings, including a log cabin. Students, parents, and community members came to understand what rural life was like 100 years ago.

One of the most nationally famous youth participation projects began in a school in Rabun Gap, Georgia. A teacher named Eliot Wigginton found that he was not very successful teaching the rural students to write by drilling them on the parts of speech and other grammar rules. They didn't seem interested. He decided that he would have to leave or change his methods. Fortunately, he started a magazine about the area. Students interviewed long-time residents, took pictures,

and gradually assumed a major share of the magazine's production activities. Their magazine, *Foxfire,* has been sold
throughout the world. Many of the articles from *Foxfire* were
put in books which also are well known.

One of the most powerful articles in the *Foxfire* magazine
described the area residents' reaction to a movie filmed in
their county. They were told that the movie would be sym-
pathetic to their area. It appears that the producers of *Deliver-
ance* deceived these people. Their talent and goodwill were
abused—and the *Foxfire* article explains how it happened.

Foxfire has inspired teachers throughout the country.
Groups of students and teachers in New York City's Lower
East Side *(Fourth Street i),* Maryland's Chesapeake Bay area
(Skipjack), South Dakota's Pine Ridge Sioux reservation
(Hoyekiya), and dozens of other communities, urban and
rural, have started their own magazines. These magazines
give meaning to student assignments and meet important community needs for historic preservation. Too often, youngsters
are given writing assignments with little import or impact—
they are simply exercises to strengthen skills. Far too much of
school activity follows this pattern: empty exercises from dull
textbooks. Many parents can not understand why youngsters
don't learn to write or compute. "What are those teachers
doing with our children?" they wonder. Day after day kids go
to school, bring work home, get decent grades, but in the end,
have minimal skills. What's gone wrong?

People don't do their best work when they're bored. People
don't put much effort into work that appears to be assigned
primarily to fill time. This is how most schoolwork appears to
young people.

Some people demand that schools assign more homework
to students, hoping that this will improve their skills. The
important question is: "What sort of homework?" When work
is meaningful, young people will extend themselves. A number of parents reported their amazement that their teenagers
spent much of a Christmas vacation in a law library preparing
for a mock trial. Some of the students would be portraying
attorneys; others were key witnesses. These youngsters
found the assignments challenging and meaningful. They were
being asked to do more than answer questions at the end of a

chapter about court systems. They had to do more than define various legal terms.

Many community agencies report that teenagers who spend part of their school day volunteering are conscientious about reporting during school vacations. A day care center director called me after Easter vacation to report our school's volunteers had been there each day during vacation, despite being offered the opportunity to take a few days off!

Anyone who's watched a school's doors at the end of the day knows how much human energy bursts out at the final bell. The potential is there, waiting to be stimulated, challenged, and encouraged.

Most youth participation projects make good use of that energy and potential. For more than 20 years, Wayne Jennings has helped create such projects in St. Paul, first as a teacher and later as a principal. One year he decided that his school ought to systematically organize and employ the vast talent and creativity of its junior high youngsters. They surveyed the staff, and identified dozens of tasks to make classes more interesting which the staff did not have time to complete. Then the students worked on these tasks for the staff. Jennings expanded his project when he moved to another local high school. The school developed a Volunteer Bureau which provided services to several dozen community agencies. The program was coordinated by Steve Vanderschaff, Mike Lugar and Jerry Cromer. Students helped distribute literature about recycling, wrote stories and took pictures for the neighborhood newspaper, helped at a nearby day care center, and contributed time to other community groups.

Some of the most fascinating student participation projects combine outside volunteer work with classroom investigations. Our school was able to arrange for several students to spend two hours a day, twice a week, working with a neighborhood day care center. Students combined these experiences with reading about child development and preparing lessons to use with the young children.

In a few schools, students are able to get credit in their government courses by working on political campaigns. Their experiences extend and enrich classroom discussions and reading. Several former students told me they'll never forget their adventures working for one local mayoral candidate as part of their class assignments. We had an agreement that students would discuss what they learned about campaign strategy in class, but not outside of the classroom. Both campaign staffs pressured the kids to divulge what they'd learned about their opponent's financial condition! We finally agreed with the campaign managers that the students' valuable contributions would not include "inside information" about the opposing candidate.

These samples illustrate the kind of cooperation we could and should have between community agencies and schools. Another case shows the possibilities. In St. Paul, the schools have negotiated an agreement with several local hospitals. For many years, the hospitals hosted "candy-striper" programs in which young people helped out during the summer. The hospitals agreed to enrich the program by offering weekly seminars about careers in medicine, patients' rights, cardio-pulmonary resuscitation, and other topics. The school district awards successful participants one credit toward graduation. This program operates under the supervision of a community coordinator. The coordinator checks periodically to make sure that agreements are being maintained and that both the students and hospitals feel good about the program. In each case, the hospitals agreed to cover costs of the program (and one of the hospitals agreed to give students who stayed in the hospital at least three hours a day a free lunch).

As this chapter is being written, we are negotiating with another large company for a new summer program. The large corporation has many employees who are searching for high quality day care for their children during the summer. We're exploring the possibilities of employing youngsters to help staff a day care center. The youngsters would be supervised by a trained early childhood specialist, and would spend part of their time reading and thinking about the needs of very young children. Such a cooperative project serves a variety of purposes: quality day care, productive teenage employment, and education about little children.

These projects are excellent illustrations of how we can improve learning opportunities without spending additional "public money" on education. Day care centers, nursery schools, senior citizen homes, elementary schools, city governments, parks, and service agencies are natural sites for such projects. It makes sense to have a school be a true community resource center, with offices for many of these groups readily accessible to youngsters. As these examples illustrate, youth participation projects can be designed to reflect an individual teacher's expertise and interests. Many teachers find the projects add immeasurable enjoyment to their own jobs: Students are more interested and alert. Rather than viewing the teacher as a person to be worked around, this approach to school reform views the faculty as an enormously valuable resource.

Sher offers an example of a rural high school which discovered that there was no daycare program available anywhere in its county. One of the teachers and the students opened a daycare facility in which the students were trained "on the job." The program was so successful that the high school became a state licensed training program, and one of the school's graduates soon opened another daycare center to meet the enormous demand. Ortonville, Minnesota, students use their school's computers to help make local farms more efficient. Using "what if" electronics modeling, students investigate whether farmers will get a better return from spending additional money on extra feed or fertilizer.

There are many ways to evaluate the effects of youth participation projects. Once I asked a 14-year-old student to help a much younger girl who was having a difficult time—it was the first day of school and the younger child was frightened. The two students became good friends (despite being eight years apart in age). Several months later, the older student told me, "You know, Joe, I was worried when you asked me to help Beth. Didn't know if I could. But it worked out. That was the first time I've ever been in a school and felt I mattered to anyone else!"

More formal evaluation of youth participation programs give equally strong recommendations. Dan Conrad and Diane Hedin asked more than 4,000 young people from all types of schools about their experiences in youth participation programs. Seventy-seven percent said they learned much more and only 14 percent said they learned less than in other classes (Hedin and Conrad, p. 9). A Federal Delinquency Prevention publication describes these programs as "promising broad and

lasting benefits at moderate cost" (Johnson et. al., p. 82).
These programs are appropriate for a wide range of talents
and interests. A number of foundation and government study
commissions have recommended these activities:

> A practicum in civic education should be required for gradu-
> ation from high school. This could be supervised volunteer
> service projects . . . which should be related to work in the
> classroom and monitored by teaching personnel.
> (National Taskforce on Citizenship Education, 1977, p. 11.)

> Educational programs should be inaugurated for the joint
> participation of adolescents and other interested and qualified
> adults in the programs which may be designated "participatory
> education." (Learning by doing what is socially useful, person-
> ally satisfying and health supporting for the individual and the
> community.)
> (Major recommendation #2, National Panel on High School
> and Adolescent Education, 1976, p. 10.)

Adults throughout the country endorse credit for community service. The 1978 Gallup poll shows that more than 86
percent agreed that juniors and seniors should receive course
credit for community service. Despite these recommendations, only about 16 percent of our secondary schools allow
students to "become involved in community service as a com-
ponent of their academic program" (National Center for Service Learning, p. 2).

These projects are not more expensive than traditional lectures, or "read the textbook and answer questions at the end"
techniques. They do require more effort on the part of
teachers and administrators. Most universities don't train
teachers in these methods, in part because most university
instructors have little or no experience with them. A few
teachers say they don't want to use these kinds of projects
because parents will object that the basics are not being
taught. Of course, I don't think students should be required to
participate in these projects if their parents object. However,
in the decade I've worked on such projects, only one parent
refused to allow her daughter in a youth participation project
after we'd discussed it. This was a group which was learning
to provide counseling to other students. The parent wanted

her daughter to get advice only from her parents—no one else.

Some teachers say they don't see much value in these projects. They insist that their traditional lecture methods and textbook assignments provide more direct information to students. They say schools have taken on too many tasks already, and that it should stick to providing students with factual information. "Let their parents help them develop into responsible adults," suggest these teachers, who say they are "going back to basics." It's hard to think of something more basic for this country's survival than responsible actions by our citizens. Equally important, youth participation projects do help students strengthen their academic skills; it's not an either-or issue.

Think of the impact on this country if even 50 percent of the people between ages 9 and 18 spend some time each week on a well-developed youth participation project. There is so much work left undone in this country which youngsters could help complete! There àre lonely, bitter senior citizens who would welcome the chance to talk with young people, listen to their music, and work with them on a building project. There are hospitals with sick people eager to talk with someone. There are thousands of stories young people could tell through a filmstrip, puppet show, or videotape production for cable television companies to show. Legislators and city governments might make better decisions if they had more accurate information, data that young people could help to gather as part of their classwork.

None of this suggests that young people should take jobs away from people already employed. These are tasks presently left undone because there just isn't the staff to do it. The possibilities are staggering. Regardless of how we decide to fund and control our schools, what happens within them is extremely important. People concerned about our youth (and our country's future) should consider the comments of one Consumer Action Service participant.

Wayne was 6'3", 205 pounds. He'd been in trouble several times with the police. Just before being transferred by the central office into the Open School, he'd had a major confrontation with a teacher. Wayne was walking down the school hall one day with a hat on. A teacher saw Wayne and demanded that he remove the hat. Wayne replied that he wasn't bothering anyone and meant no disrespect. The teacher said that the hat bothered him and that Wayne should take it off immediately. Wayne began to walk away. Furious, the teacher knocked the hat off Wayne's head. Wayne then knocked the teacher on the floor. He was placed on probation by juvenile court and transferred into our school. He became involved in the Consumer Action Service (learning other ways to change peoples' minds than knocking them on the floor). Several months later, a newspaper story appeared about the class, and the students chose Wayne as one of the participants who would be in a picture accompanying the story. Several days later Wayne came over to my desk. "You know, Joe," he began. "I often thought my name would be in the newspaper. And I thought my picture might be in there too. But I never thought I'd be in the paper for doing something good." Wayne graduated and has done well in college. He could have spent many years in prisons (which presently cost more per person than tuition at Harvard). Instead, he is a productive, contributing member of our community.

Taxpayers have the right to expect that schools can do the same for more young people. There is no single answer for how to improve our schools. But we know what has failed in the past. The answer is not brand new buildings with marvelous facilities. The answer is *not* more "drill and practice" exercises in our classrooms. It's not in devising new, elaborate curriculums.

Part of any plan for more effective schools must be establishment and extension of youth participation projects. These projects challenge, stimulate, and encourage the best instincts of young people. These programs extend and enrich skills of the most creative teachers.

This country needs competent, caring people. This country has enormous unmet needs which youngsters could help fulfill. Young people need to feel that their ideas and skills are valued. Youth participation projects have a strong, well documented record for enormous impact at minimal cost. They ought to be a part of each young person's education.

REQUIRING COMPETENCE FOR GRADUATION

Dear Friend,

We are writing to you because of your strong interest in effective schools. Our school is considering new graduation requirements in which students would have to demonstrate competence prior to graduation.

What are the most important skills for high school graduates to possess? We would deeply appreciate your opinion.

We'll be glad to share the results of our survey and the graduation requirements we develop. Just note in your reply that you'd like to get a copy of our results when you answer this letter.

Thank you very much.

> *Graduation Requirements Committee*
> *St. Paul Open School*

This letter was sent in October, 1972, to more than 500 businesses and community agencies. Our school was considering adoption of a graduation system different from the traditional credit system. Why were we questioning the plan used in most schools in which students acquire certain credits for passing courses? We were trying to develop the most effective school possible. We were trying to adopt the most reasonable procedures. This meant examining school practices to determine which made sense and which had outlived their purposes.

39

We studied the background of high school graduation requirements. The basic credit system was developed in 1910 by the Carnegie Endowment for the Advancement of Teaching. Hoping to improve the status of college teachers, Andrew Carnegie had donated $10 million to this study. The endowment spent a year trying to decide how best to make college teaching a more attractive profession. Ultimately, the group decided to offer grants which colleges could use to establish pensions.

The Endowment learned that there was no clear distinction between secondary schools and colleges. They found that secondary schools were teaching classes lasting an average of 120 60-minute hours. Breaking that down, they learned that a semester usually lasted 12 weeks, with classes meeting daily. (12 weeks × 5 days/week = 60 class sessions per semester. 60 meetings per semester × 2 semesters = 120.) They decided that a student attending and passing a class which lasted at least 120 60-minute hours should receive one "standard unit." The Endowment said that any college applying for its funds must require for admission successful completion of at least 14 standard units. These units quickly became known as "Carnegie Units."

About eight years later, a National Education Association committee met and, using the Carnegie framework, recommended the areas in which those 14 units should be distributed (i.e., Math, Science, History, English, etc.). Within 10 years, this graduation system had been adopted throughout the country. It still forms the basic graduation requirement system in all 50 states. Like so many of our well thought-out education ideas, this one has been exported throughout the world.

What can be said for the credit system? Clearly it makes counting easier. It's relatively simple to administer—a student either has the required credits, or doesn't. Of course, it's very convenient for colleges. But does it measure what most of us expect from high school graduates? We hope that high school graduates will have a variety of skills including reading, writing, computation, and information finding. We think that high school graduates should know some basic scientific principles, and our country's culture background and heritage.

These are realistic expectations. Do credits measure competence, or only exposure?

Our newspapers and magazines have described young people who've graduated from schools and can barely write or compute. Several years ago the story of a Washington, D.C., valedictorian made national news. The student graduated first in his class and received a number of college scholarship offers. Unfortunately, he quickly learned that he could not write a research paper, and could barely keep up with the college's remedial math class.

A recent survey of colleges showed that enrollments in remedial (high school level) math classes were up 72 percent between 1975 and 1980. Twenty-five percent of four-year public college math class enrollments and 42 percent of two-year college math enrollments are in remedial classes. The study concluded: "The large increases in remedial mathematics confirm evidence from various other sources that a disappointingly large proportion of students in the United States have come to college quite poorly prepared in mathematics" (*Focus,* pp. 1–6).

A local television producer recently told me of his shock when he reviewed a two-page essay written by a senior at one of the most prestigious public suburban high schools in the state. This school was mentioned recently in *Money* magazine as one of the finest in the country. The reporter explained that the student did not know how to compose a paragraph and that her spelling was awful. Yet she had a B plus average at school. Most readers could tell similar stories about recent public school graduates. What is the solution?

Our graduation requirements committee decided to require a demonstration of skills prior to graduation. This meant that students could not graduate simply by "putting in time." They had to prove that they possessed certain talents. The competence system recognized a number of fundamental learning principles. First, we know that people learn at different rates, in different subjects. Personally, I gained writing skills more quickly than most of my classmates. However, I was so bad in the woodshop that my eighth grade teacher just shook his head and said gently, "Joe, if I didn't know your record in other classes, I'd think you were retarded!"

It makes little sense to require students to complete, for example, a semester writing class in order to graduate. Some may be able to gain the important skills in six weeks, while others will need 20. We need to require demonstrated skill in writing, not just seat-time.

A second important learning principle is that some of the most efficient learning takes place when people have a very specific goal, i.e., division, expository writing, researching, CPR, etc. Yet many youngsters report that it's not clear to them what the goals for their classes are, and when they will have achieved those class goals. Students in one school reported to me that they were able to get an A by doing nothing more than print advertisements for the liquor store owned by their teacher's friend. Parents investigating a science class their children reported was "boring" learned to their astonishment that the teacher did not have a clear statement about the class goals. He told them, "Our goal is to get halfway through the science book." That does not say much about skills students should develop in the class.

An administrator reported that the writing of several teachers was so unintelligible that he proofread anything they turned in before he could send it home. A teacher in our school turned in an announcement about an evening program that was incomprehensible. The list could go on and on. We have countless teachers who provide little in the way of specific goals, challenges, or meaningful activity in their classes. Our public schools have many talented, skillful teachers, but their reputations are being tarnished by the incompetence of their peers.

Excellent teachers recognize that not every important and valuable lesson can be readily measured, but certainly some of them can be. These skills can form the core of graduation requirements.

A third important learning principle that competency systems can incorporate is that people learn in different ways. Some students may require a class to learn research skills. Others may be able to pick up those skills by observing others, watching filmstrips, reading some information, and practicing. Some people learn important skills outside of school!

One of the best stories about this concerned an extremely

affluent suburban school district. Several kindergarten teachers noticed that many of their students did not know the different colors. The district spent several thousand dollars developing and then testing a "color curriculum." Finally they were ready to test it. As in many educational projects, they gave the participating students a "pre-test" at the beginning of the school year, before using the color curriculum. At the end of the year students took the same test to indicate how much progress had been made.

Teachers and administrators were disturbed that the student gains were relatively small. This puzzled them because they thought the curriculum was well designed and the teachers highly skilled. On checking, they discovered that the students had scored very well on the pre-test; they had little to learn about identifying colors. What produced the change in several years? Apparently parents of young children, hearing that kindergarten teachers were concerned about the children not knowing colors, worked hard to make sure that their youngsters would know the colors before entering kindergarten. After some discussion, the school district discarded their "color curriculum." It was no longer needed.

Requiring demonstrated competence forces youngsters to test themselves in real life situations. Competence-based graduation asks not "How much time did you spend in school?" but "What have you learned, and how can you prove it?" Students need to demonstrate skills, not just write them down.

The St. Paul Open School Committee understood the weaknesses of a credit system and unanimously rejected it. The next issue became selecting skills which all students would be required to demonstrate.

More than 50 responses to the committee's letter were received. Many of them were thoughtful and lengthy. Their recommendations were strongly, consistently, for three fundamental skills.

First, students need good communications skills, which include both speaking and writing. A number of companies commented on the disturbing inability of otherwise talented young people to speak clearly and coherently. This is not surprising. Of course, young people talk with their friends. However, few of them have been encouraged or assisted in schools or elsewhere to organize, prepare, and deliver a short speech in public. Even more important, very few ever had to try to convince or persuade a group of people not well known to them of anything! Employers also commented on the poor writing skills of many graduates, including those who received high grades in school. National studies identify this as a major weakness in high school graduates. University officials often comment on the poor writing abilities of those who are entering college. This isn't entirely because students have avoided instruction. Perhaps it's a comment on the quality of instruction, and validity of certain instructional methods.

The second major recommendation of employers was that students need strong computational skills. Once again, both business and community agencies described their experiences with pleasant, personable young people who had good grades and attendance records, but who did not know how to compute. They could manage basic arithmetic, but did not know *when* to add, multiply or divide the numbers.

The final community recommendation was that students need the ability to accept and carry out a responsibility when it has been explained and assigned. Employers were disturbed about young peoples' inability to complete tasks. They found many teenagers afraid to ask questions if they ran into obstacles. (How many teachers really encourage students to ask questions?)

The graduation committee carefully considered these recommendations and then surveyed parents, students, and staff in the building. Not surprisingly, staff members tended to stress the value of skills they themselves taught. Other communities in California and Oregon had similar experiences. Social studies teachers stressed the value of explaining causes of various wars, being able to list the Presidents in order and, that old standby, how a bill becomes a law. Science teachers insisted that students should know basic principles of Biology and Ecology. Business teachers recommended that students be able to define "free enterprise system," and identify different kinds of shorthand, etc.

Such skills may or may not be necessary for students, but the teachers certainly viewed them as important and believed they must be included in a competency list. The graduation committee quickly recognized this phenomenon and looked for the skills mentioned by teachers of different academic departments.

Finally a list was developed. While many parents, educators, and state legislators have found the competencies selected to be fascinating, Open School has never recommended that anyone else copy this list. Instead, schools should develop their own list, going through a similar process of surveying community members, students, and staff.

With that caveat, what did the Open School require of its graduates?

1. Consumer skills: Students have to pass a paper-pencil test covering basic mathematics skills: Addition, subtraction, multiplication, division, fractions, decimals, percentages, and measurement. The questions include both computation and application. Students also have to demonstrate their abilities to comparison shop and to get assistance if they have problems with a purchase. Both of these skills require "real world" activities. Neither can be demonstrated just by passing a paper-pencil test.
2. Information finding skills: Students have to demonstrate their ability to gather information important to their needs from a variety of sources. Students are expected to complete a project using this skill.
3. Career awareness: Students have to show that they know how to get and keep a job. They also need to demonstrate that they have some post-graduation plans and have taken steps to acquire skills needed to achieve these goals (i.e., satisfied entrance requirements for and applied to a college or technical-vocational institute; earned enough money for and planned a trip around the country; satisfied requirements and applied for a certain job; etc.).
4. Community involvement and current events: Students have to show that they know how to investigate some significant current community, national, or international problem. They also have to prove that they've been of service to someone else.
5. Cultural awareness: Students have to demonstrate that they know something of both their own background and heritage, and at least two other cultures represented in the St. Paul population.
6. Personal-interpersonal skills and communication: Students have to complete a project in which they work cooperatively with others. They also are required to document a personal health and hygiene program. Students are required to demonstrate

their ability to write clearly and accurately, using the basic laws of grammar and spelling. Finally, they have to demonstrate organizational skills by writing a summary of what they've learned in the last three years and by obtaining a variety of "validation" statements from adults.

These validation statements are a crucial part of the process. They describe the conditions in which the potential graduates demonstrate their skills. By the middle of tenth grade, students meet with a committee consisting of the counselor, the assistant director of the school, the student's advisor, and a parent, friend, or staff member selected by the student. The committee's function is to help plan a schedule of activities to meet graduation requirements, and to approve of the adults selected to "validate" the student's activities. The student reports back to the committee periodically. Ultimately, each student presents the validation statements to the committee, together with an individual statement about his or her major learning experiences in the last three years. The committee then makes suggestions and finally approves or disapproves the student's work. The packets are a fascinating insight into each person's skills, interests, and abilities.

Here are examples of how students demonstrated their competence:

1. INFORMATION FINDING

a. Gathered material about how to build a "thrust" stage, then helped build it. Validation from school architect and carpenter.

b. Gathered information about programs offered by various college and technical institutes to prepare for a nursing position, then applied to several of these programs. Validation from counselor who supervised research.

c. Did an extensive study of the historical background of a play, using both primary and secondary sources. Wrote suggestions for the 11 characters based on this research. Validation from drama teacher.

d. Gathered information and then wrote a research paper about differences among food co-ops in the St. Paul-Minneapolis area. Used both interviews and written material as sources. Validation from home economics teacher.

2. CAREER AWARENESS

a. Held a job for several years at a local fast food restaurant. Became manager of the store. Validation from district manager.
b. Library aide for eight months at Central Library in downtown St. Paul. Validation from supervisor.
c. Worked for a local modeling agency over a two-year period. Validation from agency owner.
d. Researched careers in environmental study, nursing, acting, modeling, computer programming, or the priesthood. Validation from career class teacher.

3. PERSONAL-INTERPERSONAL SKILLS AND COMMUNICATION

a. Exercised regularly by riding bicycle for 50 to 60 miles a week. Validation from parents.
b. Worked in a "growth group" operated by a local counseling center. Validation from the education director of the center.
c. Studied nutrition. Kept track of diet for several weeks, and combined careful eating with regular exercise. Validation from home economics teacher and parent.
d. Regular and active participant in various physical education classes. Validation from teacher.

4. CONSUMER AWARENESS

a. Participated in and helped solve several cases of Consumer Action Service. Validation from teacher.
b. Helped family decide which car to purchase. Did extensive research, wrote out strengths and weaknesses of various models, went with parents to examine and select car. Validation from parents.
c. Did extensive research before purchasing a stereo system. Participated in a consumer class, and did the stereo investigation as part of class work. Also passed a variety of written tests in class. Validation from teacher.

5. CULTURAL AWARENESS

a. Produced several research papers on various cultures, including his own (defined as second generation Polish-American Catholic). Participated in various multicultural

activities, and passed written tests. Validation from
teacher of multicultural class.
b. Did an internship at a community agency providing services primarily to Hispanics. Did extensive study of this
culture, and wrote a paper comparing Hispanic culture to
her own (defined as middle-class Lutheran). Validation
from supervisor at community service agency.
c. Interviewed several senior citizens (including her own 85-
year-old grandmother) who traced family customs and
values for three different cultures. Wrote a paper com-
paring/contrasting experiences and beliefs of each family. Validation from parent and teacher who supervised
the project.

6. COMMUNITY INVOLVEMENT AND CURRENT ISSUES

a. Completed internship at a local nature center, volunteering
approximately 250 hours. Served as a tour guide for more
than 20 elementary school groups, completed a research
project, helped prepare bulletin boards. Validation from
Senior Naturalist at center.
b. Participated in extended study of U.S. Government.
Raised money to go to Washington, D.C. on "Closeup"
program. Read a variety of materials about lobbying and
pressuring members of Congress. Talked with lobbyists
and legislators. Wrote a paper summarizing experiences
and conclusions. Validation from teacher of government
class.
c. Participated in a three-month internship at a local television station. Helped produce a program geared toward
interests and needs of teenagers. Validation from program's producer.

One of the strengths of each student's graduation packet is
that it reflects the individual while illustrating how that person
has acquired and demonstrated fundamental, critical skills.
The process acknowledges that all students need certain skills
if they are to be successful in life. Youngsters are permitted,
even encouraged to acquire and demonstrate those skills in
intriguing ways. This balance is central to the process.

When surveyed, Open School graduates made a number of
comments about this process, including these:

"I showed my graduation packet to several friends attending a traditional school. They couldn't believe how much I'd done. They were amazed that the Open School had such stiff requirements, and felt our demands were far greater than at their school, which has a good reputation."

"This graduation system required me to think, plan, and act rather than be a passive person as my previous high school expected."

"This kind of graduation process is much more rewarding than just sitting in someone's classroom. If you pass the class and get the grades, you get a little credit, and then more. Finally, you get enough and then *they* (administrators, counselor, and teachers) say, 'All right, you've done enough.' Doing it our way, you really work for it. You have to set goals and meet them, and you can do it at your own speed."

"It is lots of work. Right, it's *lots* of work and something you have to want to do. You have to want to put something of you—a part of you—into it or else it is not going to come out well. Everyone can bug you about graduation, but it is only you who can set up meetings of your graduation committee; it is you who has to go out into the community to do something worthwhile for others. It is you who has to do these things. No matter how much someone (such as your parents or advisor) bug you, you're the one who has to take the initiative. It is lots of effort, but I think it is worth the time. You're spending time doing something you know is worthwhile, something someone else says you should know, but in a way you picked, which you think is worthwhile."

"I applied to several very selective colleges (Carleton and Grinnell) and expected some difficulty because the Open School doesn't give grades and so has no 'class rank.' However, the colleges were familiar with our school and liked the individuality of our graduation process. They also looked at my college entrance examination scores and were satisfied that I could do their work. They both accepted me, and one offered me a scholarship."

Other school districts have adopted similar programs. One set of requirements was developed by the Craig City, Alaska, Board of Education. The town is located on one of the Aleutian Islands. In addition to expected requirements in math,

reading, and writing, Craig City demanded several water related skills. For example, all graduates had to demonstrate
their ability to float for several minutes, to provide artificial
respiration, and to use a small boat.

A Denver parochial school applied these principles in a
different way. Starting with the St. Paul Open School's requirements as a base, this school required that students know
about their religion's beliefs and practices. (At least four religions were represented in the student body.) Students were
allowed to demonstrate their knowledge in a variety of ways
(essays, oral presentations, etc.).

An alternative school in Cedar Rapids, Iowa, developed a
lengthy list of required skills. Among other requirements,
graduates had to take and pass the Iowa driver's test, both
written and practical.

Not surprisingly, there were many similarities between the
requirements developed by a Minneapolis public alternative
school and the St. Paul Open School. A particularly notewor-
thy Minneapolis requirement demanded that youngsters identify a medium (painting, photography, weaving, sculpture,
writing, etc.) and then create something of which they were
extremely proud. The product had to be submitted to an
expert in the field for review, and then reworked until it represented the students' finest possible efforts. Such a requirement challenged even the most talented students.

Challenging all teenagers to do their best has been a major
interest of Canadian author and teacher Maurice Gibbons.
Almost 10 years ago, Gibbons suggested that North American
schools adopt a process similar to the Australian rite of passage known as "Walkabout." Gibbons believes that this society needs to refine and substantially improve the ways young
people make their transition from dependent youths to independent adults. Gibbons suggests that all high school students
go through a series of five challenges to show their readiness
to receive additional responsibility. The five areas are adventure, creativity, service, practical skills, and logical inquiry.

This Walkabout concept intrigued many educators; several
hundred schools in North America considered adoption of
these principles. The school which took Gibbons' suggestions
most literally was North Central High School in suburban
Indianapolis. This school established an alternative program

within its traditional one called "Learning Unlimited." The five challenge areas proposed by Gibbons formed the core of its graduation requirements.

Several years after the program had been established, a graduate student compared the attitudes of young people enrolled in the Learning Unlimited and mainstream programs. The survey showed that students enrolled in the Learning Unlimited program for more than a year "demonstrated an increase in positive attitudes toward both school and community while no significant increase was noted for students in the traditional program over the same period of time" (Metzger, p. 6). Unfortunately, very few other schools have tried to apply Gibbons' principles.

Gibbons is not the only educator concerned with developing new ways to prepare youths for entry into our complex society. In his important book, *Basic Skills,* Herb Kohl identifies six skills which he feels children need to acquire "to function effectively and compassionately as adults." These are:

1. The ability to use language well and thoughtfully.
2. The ability to think through a problem and experiment with solutions.
3. The ability to understand scientific and technological ideas and to use tools.
4. The ability to use the imagination, participate in and appreciate different forms of personal and group expression.
5. The ability to understand how people function in groups, and to apply that knowledge to group problems in one's own life.
6. The ability to know how to learn something yourself and to have the skills and confidence to be a learner all your life (Kohl, pp. 110–11).

What would happen if a student began satisfying one school's set of requirements and then transferred to another school? The chances are excellent that most of the requirements would be similar. How many parents would send their children to a school which did not require skills in reading, writing, and mathematics? Additional requirements probably would add to the students' total educational background.

Youngsters certainly would not be harmed by having demonstrated competence in a variety of areas.

"Why go through all this extra foolishness?" A Colorado state legislator looked right at me and demanded an answer. "Why not simply give students paper-pencil tests. It's certainly easier." Unfortunately, this is the direction most states have chosen. The national testing companies—"merchants of measurement"—have rushed in to fill this demand. This legislator had talked with representatives of several testing companies. He was impressed with their products. His question is one many people ask.

I responded by asking, "Senator, is Colorado willing to award drivers licenses to those who only pass written examinations?"

"Of course not. But what does that have to do with high school graduation?"

"Colorado and other states recognize that a driver needs to have a variety of skills and knowledge. Some of that can be demonstrated on paper-pencil tests; some must be performed in a car. In a similar way, I believe schools need to require students to demonstrate their abilities through both traditional testing and real life challenges. We all are aware of the limitations of paper-pencil tests."

Then we discussed standardized tests. Clearly they don't measure everything which is important and can be measured. The former president of the Educational Testing Service, which prepares the College Board Entrance Tests, admitted this in the following statement:

> Major areas of human characteristics and functioning, directly relevant to the likelihood of academic and career success, are omitted from those two useful but incomplete sources of data about a student (grades and test scores). . . . Scores tell you nothing about native potential or about the process by which it has reached its present development. An urgent need now is to increase the breadth of our descriptions so that students can discover for themselves and communicate to others the variety of their talents and opportunities (Turnbull, p. 106).

It would be difficult to construct a clearer statement of why performance of actual life tasks should be required as well as paper-pencil tests.

The second major concern about paper-pencil tests is that high test scores don't ensure success later in life. A number of important studies have examined this relationship.

"Success" is a difficult thing to define, but researchers have viewed it as a combination of achievements, including: satisfaction with one's life, being viewed positively by one's fellow workers, achieving one's goals, participating successfully in a variety of community activities, and receiving awards for one's work.

One important study was conducted by the American College Testing Program (ACT). In this investigation, college graduates were compared to see which ones were successful, and which of the four factors could be used to predict success. Three of the four factors had little predictive value. These were high grades in high school, high grades in college, and high scores on the standardized college entrance test—the ACT. Only one of the four factors predicted adult success: participation in such intense activities as debate, drama, speech, music, and journalism while in high school! (One must admire the ACT for their courage to publish this study, illustrating that their test did not predict adult success!) (Munday & Davis).

Another important study examined the predictive qualities of the other major college entrance examination: the Scholastic Aptitude Test (SAT). This study showed virtually no connection between high SAT scores and later adult success (Hoyt).

The point is summarized by a California Supreme Court judge who reviewed a pile of studies examining correlations between scores on the Medical College Aptitude Test and later success as a doctor:

> . . . Numerous empirical studies . . . reveal that, among qualified applicants, such academic credentials bear no significant correlation to an individual's eventual achievement in the medical profession. (Judge Arthur Tobriner, California Supreme Court, Regents of the University of California, Davis v. Bakke, vol. 553, *Pacific Reporter* 2nd, p. 1151.)

Such evidence only confirms our common sense: Some extremely talented, bright people do not succeed in life; others of limited ability work extremely hard, get along well with others, and achieve prominence and acclaim. When requiring certain skills from our youth, we ought to insist that they demonstrate those skills in truly meaningful, significant ways.

Most standardized tests do not adequately check on information-finding skills. They ask multiple choice questions which probably can determine whether a youngster knows the difference between an encyclopedia, dictionary, and atlas. But a paper and pencil test cannot determine whether a person has the perseverance to go to a library, look through several sources, evaluate opinion differences between authors, produce a thoughtful, well-written report, and turn it in on time.

Another bad idea is requiring that elementary age students pass standardized tests before they can go to the next grade. There are several problems with this approach. Increasing requirements often has the impact of "blaming the victim." How often are teachers fired because of poor instruction? Schools should have effective staff evaluation systems in place several years before holding students back because of their performance. The update chapter describes systems being developed to measure and reward teachers' competence. Is it fair to hold students back until the community is satisfied that appropriate instruction is being provided?

Second, this approach ignores basic principles of human growth and development. Children learn to walk and talk at different rates, with encouragement and assistance, without competency tests. They can learn to compute, write, and read under the proper circumstances. In fact, telling a youngster that he/she is a failure at 5 or 6 may have a permanent impact. The research on this subject is at best mixed, leading me to think that grade by grade competency testing should be required only in some schools, which parents have the option to choose.

Such a system demands constant communication with parents. Many Minneapolis parents complained that no one from the schools had told them about problems until late in April. Requiring competence prior to graduation allows parents to be notified of problems over a period of several years. A single year doesn't give much time, so problems like Minneapolis' can be expected.

A properly implemented graduation system will encourage

students to continue their learning, not settle for the mini-
mums. Open School students used the program's flexibility to
take advantage of learning opportunities throughout the metropolitan area. Many reported that they were learning to enjoy
knowledge for its own sake, rather than simply thinking about
how to acquire a grade.

As mentioned earlier, some Open School students took
courses at traditional high schools. Many teachers at other
schools initially resisted admitting Open School students,
assuming they would not be very responsible. Later, a number
reported that Open School students were among the most
serious, hardworking, and thoughtful in the class.

A recent Gallup poll found that more than 75 percent of
those surveyed believe schools should demand demonstration
of skills prior to graduation. The examples given show that
this expectation can be met *without* spending more money. We
need not spend millions of additional dollars on new standardized tests.

Accountability also requires compassion. This country has
wisely decided all its children deserve an education, even if
some are mentally or physically handicapped. My wife and
millions of other committed teachers work with these young
people, many of whom will be making enormous progress if
by age 18 they can feed themselves and take a bus to work.
Some of these young people clearly will never be able to compute or write. What about them?

The best response seems to be the college response: award
different kinds of diplomas. There could be academic and
attendance diplomas. Diplomas could also represent (as they
now do in New York State) various levels of accomplishment.
But in order to give clear, consistent messages to employers,
colleges, and others, it would be useful to have standards set
at the state, rather than local, level. State standards would
mean that academic diplomas in all parts of the state represent
approximately the same achievement.

Many educators support new graduation requirements
which use a variety of techniques to measure students' skills.
If parents will support more comprehensive requirements,
and educators are willing to implement them, why aren't they
readily available? Answering this question requires a look at
how public education is organized and controlled.

COMPUTERS

We recently purchased a home computer. I'd taken a computer programming course in college 10 years before, but, like any other language which isn't used, I managed to forget 95 percent of what I learned. Both JoAnn and I enjoy using the computer. But it is even more fascinating to watch our four-year-old twins work with it. They convince me that computers have both encouraging and depressing educational possibilities. In thinking about computers, we must consider that schools have poorly adapted to other advanced technology. Unfortunately, the impact of television, typewriters, and video cassette cameras and recorders on our schools has been minimal.

For my children, the computer is a toy. Somehow, it's a different kind of toy, because their Dad spends a lot of time sitting in front of it (far more than he spends, for example, playing in the sandbox or with wooden trains, which both of them like just as much as the computer).

We looked at a number of computer programs for young children before purchasing several. On one disk, there were nine separate programs. (Each program is a separate set of activities.) (Paulson, 1982.) One program asks the kids to find the letter on the keyboard corresponding to the letter on the screen.

Other programs on the disk are more difficult. One game

has the kids count the number of colored boxes on the screen. Another asks them to type their name, or any other word, on the screen. Then they are asked to retype whatever they had entered originally. When the word is spelled correctly, the computer makes a pleasant sound and respells the word in large, bright letters. A different program shows four figures, and asks the viewer to identify one which doesn't look like the others. In each case, the reward for success and consequence of failure are the same: a quasi laugh and a disappointed buzz.

Although our children enjoy these games, they have one particular favorite. In this program, there is a single dot in the middle of the screen. The children push a button in the direction they want the dot to travel—up, down, left, or right. Our children immediately named this "the drawing game." They were delighted to discover that they could change the color of the line they were drawing instantaneously by pushing the space bar.

When we asked our children why this was their favorite game, they thought for a while and then Liz answered, "I can show the computer what to do." David agreed, and added, "The computer likes this game too." Obviously I'm biased, but I find these comments intriguing. They are in complete agreement with the writing of former MIT professor Seymour Papert, author of the classic book about young people and computers, *Mindstorms*. Papert thinks computers have extraordinary potential for learning. He writes:

> The computer will enable us to modify learning environments so that much if not all the knowledge schools presently try to teach with such pain and expense and such limited success will be learned, as the child learns to talk . . . successfully (Papert, p. 9).

Papert believes strongly in computer programs which require the learner to "teach" the computer to do something. The learner must think about her/his goals, and then decide how to explain this to the computer. Papert has developed a language called *Logo* which youngsters as young as four have used. Papert believes that this kind of computer use will be extremely rewarding for young children, and will encourage them to learn quickly and with remarkable ease.

Certainly our children quickly adapted to the computer.

They can type their names, and Liz can type several other
short words as well. David is more interested in pressing certain favorite keys so that he has a row of d's, and a row of f's.
These two kids are an excellent illustration of individual differences to which schools must respond. Here are two young
people, who developed together literally from the womb, and
yet each has different interests and skills—and they're not yet
five years old.

Another program (Hodge Podge) asks them to type a letter
to get a particular picture and sometimes a short song.
David's favorite song is "Old McDonald Had a Farm," which
he sings, "Old McDavid had a farm. . . ." He learned very
quickly that, by pushing the f, he'll get a picture of a farm,
several animals, and the song. Every time we enter this particular program, David begins by entering f. He giggles and
then laughs with joy as the first few notes come out.

We rejected most of the computer programs available for
young children. The majority of them illustrate the response
schools often have made to technology: trivialization. Many
of the computer programs available are basically workbooks
with fancy graphics. They make little use of the computer's
extraordinary potential, and don't expand or enrich the student's creativity. In the majority of programs, students still
have to read relatively uninteresting material and then are
asked to answer a series of questions about it (i.e., fill in the
blank, or answer the questions at the end of the chapter).

The difference between many computer programs and
workbooks is that students who get a correct answer on the
computer get an encouraging response. On many of these
programs, the computer will ask a youngster to type her/his
name in. Then, when a correct answer is given, the computer
will type out, "Nice job, Bill," or something similar. Other
programs produce a pleasant sound for the correct answer.
Some programs will allow youngsters to play a game if they
answer enough questions correctly the first time. Unquestionably computers are more interesting for young people than the
workbooks.

But computers could be used for much more significant
work. A few computer programs help young people understand a problem or issue by putting them in the middle of it.
An excellent example is the program called "Oregon Trail,"

written by Don Rawitsch for the Minnesota Education Computer Consortium. Don's program begins with a family in Independence, Missouri, circa 1847, hoping to cross the country and establish a farm in Oregon. The family has about $500.00. Before starting out, they must make decisions about how much of that money to spend, and what to spend it on. A good classroom teacher will prepare students to use this game by having them study what a wise family took with them (e.g., medicine, a certain amount of ammunition). As the family moves across the country, it confronts obstacles common in the 1830s: disease, drought, broken bridges, and storms. In each case, the student has a range of choices and must make a decision about how to proceed. Each decision has a consequence.

The program teaches a number of important lessons in a truly engaging manner. Students get a feel for the kinds of decisions pioneers had to make. They develop a heightened appreciation for these people's courage and strength. They soon see that an ill-advised or poorly-reasoned decision may produce disaster.

Don and I have often talked about this program's strengths and weaknesses. I've encouraged him to produce a companion, which puts students in the place of the Native Americans whose land was being crossed (and in many peoples' view, stolen) by the pioneers. While recognizing the pioneers' strengths, we must also consider the manner in which this country was "won." We cannot turn back the clock, but we can learn from history and try to create a more just present and future.

"Oregon Trail" offers an important, valuable alternative to a recent American history computer program I saw, which adapted material from a textbook, asked students to read it, and then to answer questions at the end of the chapter. Do we really need computers to replicate this form of learning?

Computers can also help young people think rationally and creatively. Much of Seymour Papert's book, *Mindstorms,* deals eloquently and thoughtfully with this concept. Just as Papert predicted, our children prefer the computer program which calls on their creativity, and which gives them the most opportunity to express themselves. As mentioned above, David and Liz constantly ask to play "The Coloring Game" which allows them to draw their own figures, using various colors. In so doing, they are "teaching" the computer. In turn, the computer is helping them learn logic (If I want my dot to go in a certain direction, I'll push a button on that side of the keyboard. If I want the dot to go up or down, I'll push a button on the top or bottom of the keyboard).

Obviously, there is a place for each use of the computer—encouraging creativity, involving the student in a different place or time, and enticing the student to spend time working on arithmetic. It's silly to say that computers should be reserved for only the most creative, mind-expanding purposes. What worries Papert is that most of the schools will use computers in the least sophisticated ways. Rather than use the computer to change the way we organize instruction and learning, schools will use it to strengthen their present inadequate instructional and organizational patterns.

In purchasing programs for the children, we thought carefully about several of Papert's concerns. The first is what he calls the "QWERTY" phenomenon. This refers to the pattern on the traditional typewriter keyboard, from the upper left-hand corner moving toward the center, "Q - W - E - R - T - Y." Papert explains that the keyboard, like many other school practices, is used primarily because it is traditional. Papert argues that a few more logical keyboards, in alphabetical order, have been produced. Typists have been trained to use the alphabetical keyboards, and their efficiency goes up 10 to 25 percent. Why, then, haven't manufacturers produced different keyboards for typewriters and computers?

Because, explains Papert, we have a circular, self-fulfilling prophecy. The manufacturers produce what they think companies want. Companies want what their typists have been trained on, and what is relatively easy for them to purchase. Typists have been trained on non-alphabetical typewriters because that's what they'll find in most businesses, and on most typewriters available for purchase. It's a classic vicious circle. With slight modifications, we could make better use of available technology. Because of tradition and expectation, we are under-utilizing technology.

Papert fears that the computer will be under-utilized. He believes that the computer may be used to perpetuate the existing school structure, rather than transform it. Many schools are purchasing a few computers and putting them either in a computer lab or scattering them through the building, one per classroom. Papert points out that this is something like purchasing one pencil per classroom, or establishing only one room where pencils are available. Obviously, schools are not organized in this manner.

If schools take the long-range view, they'll recognize that over the child's 10 to 12 year period in elementary and secondary school, thousands of dollars will be spent on her/his education. Assuming $2,500.00 a year, between $25,000.00 and $30,000.00 per person will be available over the next decade. Papert strongly encourages using $1,000.00–$1,500.00 of that money immediately to purchase a computer for every child!

It's easy to think about the long run; but where will the money come from? First, schools can increase their revenues by providing office space for compatible enterprises. Joan Sorenson, a creative principal in St. Paul, has negotiated an agreement with a community agency whereby it has an office in her school, and pays rent. The students contribute to the community newspaper the agency publishes. The agency has a well-lit, comfortable office at less cost.

There are countless ways to save money. For example, in Chicago there are big differences among the administrative staffs of the Catholic and public school systems. The Catholic schools, with 250,000 students, employ 35 administrators. The public schools, with 500,000 students, employ 3,500 administrators. One hundred times the number of administrators, for twice as many students. Do the children in the Chicago public schools need all those administrators?

One powerful application of the computer would be in teaching writing. Explaining how a computer helped to write this book will illustrate some of its possibilities. In writing, I use an outline of ideas. After jotting down a number of possible ideas, I arrange them in the order which seems to make most sense. Examples and other thoughts are added, so the topics become chapters, sections, paragraphs, and so on.

Every writer has experienced the frustration of deciding that a paragraph which is, for example, fourth in one's text, should instead become first, second, or third. That will involve retyping or rewriting several pages, or cutting and past-ing. It's messy, time-consuming and discouraging. Moving sentences, paragraphs, even entire pages, becomes a 15-second task on my computer. I push three buttons, and the move is made.

It also is frustrating to discover misspelled or left-out words and not enough room on the line to fix them. For example, there are six errors in the following sentence: "The miakes are intentionall in demonstraation of comuter poer." That sentence can be changed in 10 seconds to, "The mistakes are intentional in this demonstration of computer power."

The time, attention, and energy presently devoted to correcting mistakes can now be devoted to polishing and strengthening one's prose. Youngsters can become much better writers with *no more effort* than is presently used; they simply will use their time more efficiently.

Some schools are using computers to help students learn to write. Judy Anderson of St. Paul's East Consolidated Elementary School has received national awards because of the computer lab she's established. Judy works with other faculty members to help students as young as 7 and 8 learn to type, and then to use the computer's word processing capabilities. Students use the LOGO language to illustrate their essays. Her students have shown a dramatic improvement in writing skills (see Nathan, *Learning,* 1984).

The impact of computers will be as important as that of television. But there are no guarantees that the computer will help make our society more just or equitable. One disturbing possibility is that computers will broaden the gap between rich and poor in this country. Affluent parents are purchasing home computers. Children (like ours) are gaining because of their direct, continuing access to computers. Children whose families can not afford computers may well fall further behind in the development of skills and creativity.

Home computers probably will become as commonplace as television sets. In some homes, computers (like televisions) will be used for a range of purposes, including learning to write programs, developing academic skills, and playing games. Youngsters in other homes will spend hours playing games as they now spend hours watching hollow, undistinguished television programs.

Computers may follow other patterns established by television. In fact, the parallels already are disturbing. Virtually all elementary and secondary schools have one or two television sets. Theoretically it's possible for television to provide instruction beyond school instructors' knowledge and competence. Unfortunately, televisions rarely are used in this fashion. Instead, they are used as an occasional, interesting supplement to class. Sometimes, programs are videotaped and replayed in classes (i.e., a television dramatization of *A Tale of Two Cities* can be taped and shown in an English class; a documentary on pollution can be used in a Science or Social Studies class). Rather than using the enormous potential of television to greatly increase the range of courses available to students, most schools are using it to supplement the traditional pattern of teacher-directed classes.

There are parallels between most of the television programs and most of the software being produced for computers. The largest market for computer software is not in stimulating, creative educational programs, but in violent games. Parents across the country know how much time can be spent on video games. Television has advanced very little beyond what former Federal Communications Commissioner Newton Minnow described as "a vast wasteland."

Past experiences suggest that computers, like other forms of technology, will have minimal effects on most schools. Many educators already are trying to adapt the computer to the school, as was done with television, movie projectors, and videotape equipment. Each of these discoveries has been used infrequently, with little impact on the overall organization of learning and teaching. Many schools are telling their constituents they can only afford a relatively few computers. Most school computers are being used primarily for the least sophisticated drill and practice exercises.

Our society faces an enormous challenge to use computers to their full potential. A computer is a tool and people need to learn how to utilize it.

Many districts have to compete for the available computers and training opportunities. A recent article in *Electronic Learning* gave an example of this battle (Calkins, p. 34). In one city, an elementary teacher developed enough skill in LOGO so that her programs were distributed throughout the country. She began to help other teachers with the computer language. At the same time, other district officials contracted Seymour Papert to develop LOGO at a few local schools. Central office administrators began to think that the local teacher's modifications of LOGO did not employ the language's full potential, and her workshop was postponed indefinitely. (Currently, she is successfully teaching LOGO at a local science museum and university.) The teacher was not able to participate in Papert's workshop because of the limited space. Other schools, who also couldn't go to Papert's workshop, would have liked to learn from the local teacher whose program had been postponed. Some teachers and administrators wondered if this amounted to censorship—"This is something you can't learn about."

Many districts report arguments among their staff about access to computers. It's no surprise that some wonder if computers are worth the hassle. Several weeks ago at a conference, administrators had a heated conversation about computers. Two of them insisted that, "Computers are only the latest fad. Within several years, most people won't talk much about them. It happened with videotapes—with talking typewriters—and now it's computers." These people may be correct.

People who disagree must act quickly. We should consider adapting schools to accommodate computers. With thoughtful, courageous allocation of funds, computers can be purchased for each student in a school. Computers can help children learn to think and expand their creativity. Computers can help schools develop new courses, and allow for truly individualized, self-paced, self-directed learning. Computers can be used to assess and monitor many necessary skills. Computers can help transform our learning programs. Computers can help millions of children who presently don't have strong applied and basic skills. Computers can stimulate and challenge, they can help people develop their creative and problem-solving skills. Computers can free our finest teachers to provide the most important elements of their position: guidance, reflection, challenge, and encouragement. Fundamentally, computers offer marvelous opportunities, but no guarantees.

PARENTS

"So you're teaching a class on Tom Sawyer and Huckleberry Finn. . . ."

"Yes, and the kids seem to be enjoying it."

"Do you think they'd get much from spending a day on a barge going down the Mississippi River?"

"How soon could this be arranged?"

"Well, I was talking with the owner of Twin Cities Barge at a party the other night. He recently reread Tom Sawyer and I told him about your class. He offered to host the group on one of their larger towboats."

Three weeks later, a sleepy group of 33 students boarded a bus at 6:00 A.M. so they would be at Prescott, Wisconsin, by 6:45. Imagine a clear, mild spring day, with trees just starting to turn green. You've pictured the kind of day we had for this incredible trip through a preserved portion of the St. Croix River which empties into the Mississippi. The St. Croix looks much like vast sections of the "Mighty Muddy" did 150 years ago.

Did that trip make an impression? At a reunion eight years later, four former students came up to me and their first question was, "Do you remember our Tom Sawyer tow boat trip?"

All arrangements for this adventure were made by an interested parent.

"Mr. Nathan, line one."

"Hi, this is Joe Nathan."

"Afternoon, Joe, this is Alice Hausman. Our hospital is looking for students to participate in a disaster drill. Do you think any of the Murray kids would be interested?"

"Sure. Would you tell me more about it, please?"

"Of course. Periodically we test the hospital's capacity to deal with a major emergency—a tornado, bomb, or other widespread disaster. We must be able to respond quickly, set priorities, and make decisions about treatment. If we could get about 30 kids, we'd make them up to appear as if they have a vast range of injuries, from broken arms and legs to fractured skulls. We'll provide a bus to bring them to and from school, give them lunch, and take some pictures if you can have them excused from school."

Three weeks later, a group of seventh graders who had studied the range of careers available in medicine discovered firsthand what a hospital's emergency room and procedures were like. The kids loved the realistic makeup which made them appear to be in truly desperate shape. Several parents reported that their son or daughter talked about the hospital experience longer and more enthusiastically than any other during the entire school year.

All arrangements for this trip were made by a concerned parent.

"Joe, you have an angry parent on line two."

"Hi, this is Joe Nathan."

"Mr. Nathan, what are you doing about all our black kids who spend hours on basketball and don't have five minutes for their homework? Don't you have some responsibilities to help them see beyond rebounds and field goals to life goals?"

"I'm really glad you called, Mr. Simmons. Today we started a program initiated by Mary Sheppard of Macalester College's Minority Program. Her son and daughter attend here, you know. She's arranging to bring in black and Hispanic athletes who can crack a book *and* break a tackle. They'll be talking with students in several classes and hosting visits to the college itself."

"Well, that's a switch. Not too many white folks bring us into their school to talk. Can I do anything to help?"

"Sure, let's set a time to meet and discuss possibilities. Would you like me to come to your home, or would you prefer to meet here at school?"

"Well, could you come over here? I take care of my grand-kids and it's not too easy to get out there."

Several weeks later this parent arranged for us to hold a meeting at the Martin Luther King Center in his neighbor-hood. The meeting attracted about four times as many parents from the immediate neighborhood as had ever made the eight-mile journey to our school. Many of the white parents who attended the meeting had never been in the King Center. Sev-eral expressed surprise at how well they were treated and thanked the black parents for making them feel welcome. The black parents explained that everyone was welcome at the King Center—that's what Dr. King's life was about. Plans were made (and carried out) to have more parent meetings in various communities served by the school.

The parent who made this meeting possible pointed out that the eight mile distance is a mental block: "It's a different world in that tall tree neighborhood (where the school is located)."

One school decided to survey all parents to determine what hobbies and skills they might be willing to share. The results were published in a booklet entitled, *Gold Mine of Parent Resources*. Many of the teachers used the book frequently and encouraged students to look through the pages them-selves. At no additional cost to taxpayers, teachers were able to extend learning opportunities for youngsters.

Another school extended this idea. In a class discussion one day, a teacher discovered that virtually none of the juniors or seniors in the class had much idea of what their parents or guardians did at work. Together, the class developed a list of questions students had about various careers (i.e., salary, op-portunities to use creativity, education requirements, etc.). Then the teacher arranged with a number of parents to have small groups of students "shadow" various parents—factory worker, florist shop clerk, attorney, doctor, carpenter—for a day. Students reported this was the best "career education" lesson they'd ever had.

The priorities committee meeting had just started at our school. "When is the administration going to get concerned about the truly gifted kids who attend here?" demanded one parent. "We have all these programs for kids who are in trouble at home, or just getting by. What about 'good kids?' They need challenge and they *aren't getting it!*"

Other parents agreed. The committee (composed of parents, teachers, and administrators) studied possible ways to improve the school's program for talented youngsters. A proposal was written which a local foundation funded. National experts were brought in to work with the school's faculty. Within six months, a number of new programs were started by the teachers, providing opportunities for talented students to develop and share their skills with other students. The School Board decided to allow children from outside the attendance area to attend this school because of its popularity.

Parents helped spread the word about the school. Within two years, more than 300 students—60 percent of the student body—were coming from outside the attendance area to this school.

One parent was reluctant to visit school, despite several invitations to share her cooking expertise. After some discussion, we learned that she did not have a car and would have to make three bus transfers. Besides, she had a two-year-old at home and didn't have a place to leave him.

A school committee had been discussing this and similar problems. A decision was made to establish a morning day care center for volunteers' children. Students in the child development class got practical experience with young children while their parents had a chance to see what was happening, and to contribute to the school.

Mrs. Ramirez did begin coming regularly to help with cooking classes. One day the teacher gave her the keys to a locked cabinet. Mrs. Ramirez began to cry. The teacher was astonished and worried that she had offended Mrs. Ramirez. After she caught her breath, Mrs. Ramirez explained her tears expressed joy and relief. "You trusted me enough to give me your keys. Can't remember the last time someone 'official' trusted me," she recalled. She remained a valued, trusted volunteer.

One school's magnet status was threatened. Being a "magnet" meant it tried to attract other students with a variety of unusual and strong programs. The district faced budget difficulties and was looking for places to cut. In presenting his minimum budget, the Superintendent included only those expenditures which he thought were absolutely necessary. This minimum budget (of $75 million) did not include the approximately $30,000.00 needed each year for exciting community projects. (The $30,000.00 probably was matched 10 times over by various contributions of people, time, supplies, and cash from parents and other community residents who really liked the school.)

Parents began calling Board members. They pointed out that this was a school which worked: People were leaving private schools to attend, test scores were improving. The school was regarded as a safe place and parents wanted the $30,000.00 allocated for the following year. A large article appeared in the local newspaper quoting district officials. Unnamed officials said the school did not assist district desegregation efforts. The president of our school's Parent-Teacher-Student Association wrote a strong letter to the editor pointing out that the city's racial diversity was well represented at our school. The president insisted that such a program deserved district support.

Within a month, the School Board reversed the Superintendent's recommendation and decided to restore the money.

In our country's most effective schools, public or private, such stories can be repeated and amplified. However, much of what we read in newspapers about parental involvement is negative: "Parents demand that textbooks be removed. . . . Parents insist that their children are not learning in schools. . . . Parents say schools are destroying family values." Many of the parents those articles describe have been infuriated by the lack of response by professional educators to their concerns. Sometimes there are differences about what is appropriate, but in my experience almost all parents are eager to work out disagreements rather than storm Board meetings or go to court.

We have a choice in this country. We can continue to create intellectual and professional barriers around our schools. Educators can continue to resist increased demands for accountability. They can continue to ask for a national consensus on the purpose of schools. They can insist that progress will be made only if schools are given more money. That path will lead to continued frustration, resentment, anger, and confrontations that no one wins—and the children clearly lose. The other option is for us to recognize and develop partnerships with parents and other community residents. We can rethink our roles as "educators" and recognize that schools won't be successful by themselves. And we can act on that belief.

Tom Dewar, a professor at the University of Minnesota in Minneapolis, has written a speech all people working with youngsters should read. (See Bibliography.) Dewar believes the "legitimate roles of the professional" are:

1. Simplifier—help others understand what we are trying to do, and how. Often professionals develop and use code words and jargon which do exactly the opposite.
2. Connector-organizer—help bring people together who can and should help each other.
3. Accepter of the burden of proof—willingly and openly look at whether one's efforts are effective and how they can be improved.
4. Tuckpointer—examine a situation, tell others if anything appears to be wrong, and suggest what possible actions could be taken.

I'd add several roles to Dewar's. First, provider of information about "the system." Often parents don't know whom to contact for help, whether it's in getting tutoring assistance for their child, obtaining a transcript, getting on the Board of Education agenda, or comparing achievement test scores from several schools. Some administrators make information difficult or burdensome to obtain. This makes their decisions more difficult to oppose. Such situations can be extremely touchy. Where does responsiveness to parental requests for help end, and disloyalty to one's supervisor begin? Unfortunately, sometimes they overlap.

Another role is as advocate for and with young people. Youngsters need opportunities to develop and demonstrate their talents and responsibilities. We need to create ways to help them do this, by producing filmstrips, tapes, picture displays, and by obtaining speaking engagements and media coverage. People always will hear about negative actions; we need to be aggressive in spreading the word about progress and accomplishment.

A third related role is facilitator. Often educators find themselves telling parents, students, and others why something can't happen. "We can't do that because of State Department regulations. . . . The other teachers would never accept this program. . . . We need to study that awhile. . . ." In reality, we often know ways around those barriers. Most State Departments are willing to waive at least some regulations if presented with a carefully thought-out rationale and plan. (At one school where I worked, the State waived all graduation and course hour requirements—a substantial action!)

Teachers, like anyone else, usually are willing to listen to new ideas, but their reactions will depend on a variety of factors, some of which we can control. Are the suggestions based on teachers' strengths and experiences, or do they anticipate that the teaching staff is full of incompetent people? (This is not a farfetched comment. Many curriculum projects were developed by university professors in the 1960s and early 1970s who described their products as "teacher-proof!") There are ways to broaden the base of teacher support for improved instruction. These include providing opportunities for faculties to develop the kinds of programs they think are valuable, and complimenting people when their efforts are successful. I'm not suggesting that improvements are easy. However, professionals can either help expedite reforms, or create additional barriers.

As we think about the relationship between professional educators and the people with whom we work, a Lawrence Ferlinghetti poem comes to mind:

'Truth is not the secret of a few'
                                          yet
         you would maybe think so
                                  the way some
                    librarians
           and cultural ambassadors and
                             especially museum directors
                                                    act
              you'd think they had a corner
                                      on it
               the way they
                          walk around shaking
               their high heads . . .
          (Ferlinghetti, p. 82)

Too many schools act as though they have a corner on the
"truth in education market." For many years university professors have produced papers describing how schools should
operate. More recently Mortimer Adler and others from the
Council on Basic Education made a series of recommendations which include (among other things) no opportunity for
young people or their parents to make choices about courses,
except foreign languages.

All my experience tells me that the most effective schools
make use of the expertise and talent of both the people they
serve and the people who work in them. Our finest schools
don't unquestioningly adopt a set of recommendations others
have made. The schools where children learn, themselves
practice and model learning. Such schools recognize that children can gain from experiences outside the school building.
Such schools welcome community members for questions,
concerns, guidance, and assistance.

There will be no complete consensus among parents. Our
schools must recognize and build on this fact. We are a diverse country. Parents want their youngsters to develop
strong skills in such areas as computation, communication,
and reading. However, there are deeply felt and valid differences of opinion in many other areas. There are strong differences among families about the instructional techniques and
learning environment in schools. Some parents want teachers
to be in charge at all times, providing close and constant
supervision for their children. Other families prefer an infor-

mal, relaxed environment with considerable opportunity for self direction. Many parents believe corporal punishment is appropriate, while others view it as barbaric. Some parents want strict dress codes, while others would allow youngsters to wear what they wish.

Differences among families' opinions extend into the range and content of available courses. Some parents agree with Adler's *Paidea Proposal* and don't want their children to have any choice of courses other than which language to take. Others are against such restrictions, and look for schools that provide a choice of courses to help students gain basic skills. Some parents believe teaching about human sexuality is the responsibility of the family and that the school should stay out of this area entirely. Others think the opposite. The question of teaching about creation and evolution has caused upheaval in many thoughtful, well-intentioned communities. Another controversy surrounds the use of textbooks: Many parents demand textbooks that don't criticize this country's actions; others believe that their children should be exposed to a variety of viewpoints.

These are deeply held, fundamental beliefs, and it is foolish to think they can or should be reconciled. Some educators have wasted time arguing that a national consensus must be reached on each of these issues, and similar controversies, before schools will improve significantly. Some school districts have wisely tried to accommodate a range of philosophies by establishing alternative programs, from traditional to progressive. In St. Paul, for example, parents of children aged five to twelve can select from a fundamental school, a "middle of the road" traditional school, and an Open School. What's fascinating about these three schools is that there are both similarities and differences. Teachers from the different schools who attend workshops together report that they learn from each other. Each program has an emphasis on achievement. Obviously there are certain differences in style, but the similarities help illustrate that most parents have the same goals for their children's education: to produce thoughtful, skilled, confident, responsible people.

Parent surveys consistently show that parents are most satisfied with their child's education when it is provided in a setting in which their opinions are respected. If schools are to improve in this country, professional educators and parents must stop pointing fingers at each other, and join hands to work more closely together. This country's schools have been the scene of nasty and unproductive confrontations in the last five years. We should "agree to disagree" about such topics as sex education, interpretations of the Vietnam War, creation versus evolution theories, literary value of books by Kurt Vonnegut, Macolm X, J. D. Salinger, etc. Schools need to reflect the legitimate, honest diversity of thought in this country. Parents, teachers, and community members need to meet and agree on skills they want youngsters to develop. The previous chapter described communities in which this has happened. Equally important, parents and their children need the opportunity to select from the different learning opportunities.

In this manner, we will have fewer confrontations. Should a teacher be able to use Kurt Vonnegut in a class designed to help young people write creatively? Of course. Should all students in the tenth grade at this school be required to read Vonnegut? Of course not. The goal in creative writing classes is clear and imaginative writing; there are thousands of books to help accomplish this end. In the same way, many of our schools should offer young people the opportunity to learn more about sexual expression and birth control. But it is absolute folly to insist that all children must sit in such classes, or complete assignments which violate their families' religious beliefs.

Unquestionably these are very complicated issues, but the public interest cannot be on the side of conformity and compulsion. Teachers, parents, and students should spend more time cooperating, less time confronting. We have a few basic rights in this country, articulated in our Constitution. I believe that no school should be allowed to violate the rights guaranteed therein. With the Constitution as our guide, we can work with parents to develop extraordinary schools. There will be no perfect schools that satisfy everyone. By trying to operate schools that satisfy everyone, we satisfy no one.

Programs that honor diversity and cooperation will be productive, stimulating places for all involved. In establishing such schools, we will truly follow Sitting Bull's suggestion of more than a century ago: "Let us put our heads together and see what lives we can help build for our children."

DISCIPLINE

A September 1983 Gallup Poll reported that for the twelfth year in a row the greatest single concern about public schools is "discipline." The most frequent explanation given for students being withdrawn from public schools is that teachers and administrators are unable to keep order. In no other area is there so much finger-pointing. "If the parents would just keep order at home, students would come to school with the proper kind of respect," insist some teachers. "My child is fine at home," respond some parents. Others say, "We pay you teachers to solve these problems."

The following story illustrates possibilities and dilemmas of public school discipline. It began with a relatively minor encounter on the last day of the 1980–81 school year. The administration, staff, and student council had scheduled a number of special activities. The students had asked for time to sign yearbooks and talk with their friends before scattering for the summer. We'd agreed on a shortened class schedule, an assembly honoring various student achievements, and then about an hour to move around the building, talking with friends, signing yearbooks, eating the ice cream the student government provided, and in general, having a relaxed, positive last day of school.

About 9:00 A.M. a teacher came up to me in the hall and asked, "Isn't that Cal? He isn't supposed to be here, is he?"

I recognized the youngster as a former student at our school

75

who had transferred to another school the previous September. He was articulate, intelligent, and very popular with young women. He was also an absolute master at instigating fights. A number of students called him "the set-up man" because he created so many conflicts. He was the most unashamed liar I'd ever encountered. He would insist that he'd been in a class, demand that the teacher who reported him absent show me the attendance records, and then tell his parents that both the teacher and I were lying when we contacted them about his truancy. Fundamentally, Cal believed the world was out to get him. Unfortunately, his parents agreed and encouraged this attitude.

We had informed all our students that part of the plan for the school's last day was "no visitors." The major change in program would be complicated enough. We didn't want people who weren't part of the student body—and the students agreed. We were not going to make any exceptions. So I walked up to Cal and explained the situation to him. He explained that he was just talking with a few friends and former teachers and would leave in a while. "Now, Cal. The rules are the same for everyone."

While we were talking I'd noticed another youngster I didn't recognize. (One of the major advantages of a small school—ours was 520 students at that time—is that staff members know instantly when someone is in the school who does not belong there.) This student informed me that she was Cal's sister. I asked both of them to leave immediately, explaining that they should be at their own schools and that we already had asked other visitors to leave. They agreed to leave and not come back for the rest of the day.

Less than two hours later Cal was back in the building. At that point, I warned him that the police would be called and he would be charged with trespassing if he came back into the building. He acknowledged that he understood. We walked together to the nearest door. I watched as he walked away. Unfortunately, Cal came back into the building less than 30 minutes later. I told him that he would have to come with me to the office and that the police would take him from the building.

"Aw man, I was just fixing to leave," he pleaded. I pointed

out that he'd made a series of poor decisions and his chances had run out.

Suddenly he became belligerent. "Are you going to make me go?"

"Only if you force me to. Wouldn't you rather be charged just with trespassing, rather than trespassing and resisting arrest?"

For the first time that day, Cal made a wise decision and walked quietly to the office. As we were walking toward the office, I saw his sister back in the building and told her to come with us. Then I called the police. The next hour was among the very worst in my 11 years in schools. The police did not come for more than 45 minutes. Meanwhile, Cal and his sister continued to plead for one more chance and the opportunity to leave. My decision to keep them until the police arrived may have been among the worst I ever made. As time went by, all of us became more irritated. Finally, they decided to leave, despite what I had told them. I tried to restrain them. There was a scuffle right outside my office, with Cal, his sister, and I pushing and shoving each other. I called for help, and several other staff members helped me push them back into my office.

The events of that scuffle became the subject of court proceedings which stretched out for the next eight months. I filed assault and trespass charges against both Cal and his sister. They filed assault charges against me. When the county attorney determined that there was no reason to charge me, Cal's parents went to the Superintendent and then to the School Board to complain about my actions. After investigating the case, the Superintendent recommended to the Board that no action be taken against me. He wrote me a letter explaining he was glad the Board had followed his recommendation. I was too! Cal and his sister were found guilty of trespassing and not guilty of assault. Each was fined $25.00.

The case cost me far more than $25.00! First, there was the amount of time I spent writing reports and meeting with various attorneys. Next, there was the time I spent worrying about what was going to happen.

Finally, there were several newspaper articles about the case. When the parents went to the school board, they spent almost an hour describing in great detail how I "allegedly" assaulted their children. A reporter called me the following day to get a statement from me. I explained to the reporter that I'd been advised by the county attorney to make no public statements about the case. She reminded me that if I had no comment, the paper would have only the students' point of view to print. I suggested that the story be deferred until after the court proceedings finished, when I would be able to give a statement. The reporter said her editor wanted a story now. "Well, I believe that my actions were in accordance with School Board policy and St. Paul laws, and that the court will rule that way. You can quote me on that." She did—accurately.

Then we talked about the use of names in the article. She was planning to use my name, but not the youngsters'. The newspaper had a policy of not printing the names of minors involved in court cases unless they were ordered to stand trial as adults. After considerable discussion, the reporter agreed with my view that printing my name without the students was unfair. So all names were left out, although most people familiar with our school knew the identity of the unnamed administrator in the story.

The following fall, Cal's parents decided to enroll him in a private school (his fourth school in four years). Cal lasted several months there before leaving to attend another public school in town.

Among other lessons from this story, I learned that nothing is effective in every case. Equally important, it's clear that I *don't* have all the answers. As many educators note, it's far easier to write articles or books about effective disciplinary techniques than to solve all the discipline problems in a school.

Another incident demonstrates helpful discipline guidelines. On the first day of school, about 10 members of a class were very disruptive. The teacher who had been in the district for many years became angry and decided to teach the students a lesson. This was his first year at this particular school. He told the class that he was keeping everyone for half an hour after school that day. He agreed with some who protested that they had not misbehaved but said this was the best way to have better behavior for the rest of the year.

More than 60 percent of the students at this school rode a bus (meaning they live more than a mile from the building). The Assistant Principal's phone began to ring literally every few seconds later that afternoon as students went home or called their parents for rides after being kept in the teacher's room after school. The Assistant Principal and teacher were angry with each other, the parents were angry with the school, and the students generally loved the whole thing: Adults angry with adults! A great game.

The best advice I know about discipline specifics has been pulled together by a California educator named Lee Canter. Canter calls his program "assertive discipline." Using his techniques, the incident just described probably never would have happened. Canter says that before the school year starts, teachers and administrators need to agree on a clear, specific discipline plan for classrooms and common areas such as hallways and cafeterias. The plan must include specific rules and consequences for misbehavior. The plan also should include consequences for positive behavior. Canter strongly recommends that this plan be shared on the first day with students and sent home to parents.

How would the above incident have been different if Canter's advice had been followed? The teacher and Assistant Principal would have discussed rules and consequences. It's unlikely that the Assistant Principal would have authorized keeping an entire class after school the first day because of a few students' misbehavior. Next, the school rules would have been sent home to parents, so they would have had a chance to read and respond to them. Unquestionably some of them would have raised concerns. However, Canter's experience (which corresponds to my own) is that most parental reactions to the plan are, "It's about time schools did something like this." Finally, it's possible that the misbehavior would have stopped more quickly if the students had known the consequences, rather than been told suddenly, "OK, that's enough—you're all staying after school."

Our district brought one of Canter's associates to St. Paul last October to work with several hundred district teachers and administrators. The evaluations of her presentation were excellent. Followup questionnaires indicate that when teachers and administrators follow the Canter guidelines, the program significantly reduces discipline problems, leaving more time for learning and teaching. Some teachers will be more effective using these guidelines than others. Why? Because an interesting classroom is less likely to be disrupted than a dull, boring, or hostile one.

Most parents, teachers, students, and administrators acknowledge the value of a positive, caring teacher. Even the best instructors have an occasional problem; but they have fewer than those who demonstrate dislike, boredom with, or even hatred of students. Such teachers constantly "put down" youngsters and often employ the two least effective classroom techniques: lecturing, and "read the chapter, answer the questions at the end." These techniques have some value, when used in conjunction with others. *Nothing* should be used day after day, hour after hour.

In the real world of schools, there are excellent, adequate, and lousy teachers. This fact places the Assistant Principal in a fascinating position. A traditional public Assistant Principal is expected to be an ogre by 90 percent of the faculty. The teachers want students to be afraid of the threat: "If you don't stop what you're doing, I'll send you to the A.P.!" Many Assistant Principals become cynical, frustrated, bitter people. They believe that too much of their time is spent dealing with the symptoms of problems, rather than the causes. They'll readily admit that the worst teachers create most of their problems, and can often make a bad situation worse.

How does this happen?

A student will be absent for several days, perhaps legitimately, perhaps not. A good teacher will try to encourage the student on his or her return: "Good to see you—let's go through some assignments later in the hour." A poor teacher will make the student regret returning to class: "Oh, you finally decided to come back, huh? Well, there's no way you can make up what you missed—you're too far behind. You're destined for a D or worse. Better get the counselor to transfer you out, if anyone else will take you! Of course, your brother missed a lot of school, too. What's the matter, did the electric company turn off your heat at home?" Teachers have admitted making each of these statements to various students. Such comments may be perfectly acceptable and even humorous to some. In my experience, however, they tend to discourage and deflate youngsters.

Another dilemma arises when there has been a misunderstanding between a student and teacher. The teacher may think the student said one thing, when the youngster said (or meant) something entirely different. This happens more often than seems possible. It's amazing how two people can hear entirely different things.

Once a community organizer and I met to discuss a proposal he was writing for a local foundation. He wanted to obtain funds to start a "rent-a-kid" program, which would provide jobs for youth and low cost assistance for senior citizens needing help with minor household jobs. We discussed the value of producing a slide film about the program. Other communities could see it and learn from this organization's experience. The organizer asked me how much I thought it might cost to produce (including camera, film, processing, and a person to help the young people write and produce a polished product). I estimated between $500.00 and $1000.00. Then I said that I'd be willing to donate some time to help produce the filmstrip. That's not what the organizer heard me say. Several weeks later I received a copy of his proposal. Imagine my surprise when I read in the proposal that I'd offered to donate $1000.00 toward production of a filmstrip! There's no doubt that the organizer was conscientious and honest. We simply heard my comment in two different ways.

Similar incidents happen in schools all the time. Once a teacher sent a student to me because he heard the youngster talk about how he was going shooting after school. This youngster had been involved in more than his share of problems. The teacher thought that the student might be talking about either a big fight or a drug ring. In fact, the young man was going out with his father to a target range. The parent was teaching his son to shoot a pistol.

Everyone makes mistakes and has misunderstandings. The finest educators admit to theirs. Their quiet, open apologies and willingness to proceed as before are important lessons to all young people with whom they come in contact. If we think about our own lives, we'll remember how much more we learned from those who encouraged us. Weren't our favorite teachers those who demanded our best, but made us feel they really cared about each of us? Didn't the most effective teachers maintain an orderly learning environment, not with threats and brutality, but with clear expectations, consistent consequences for behavior, and a kind word or note when we made progress?

Many teachers (and some parents) believe that the best route to learning is through rigid, dogmatic teaching. "Sit down and shut up. Good posture accelerates learning," some say. A substantial body of research supports the common sense notion that young people (and older people as well) do not learn as much in a threatening environment as in a supportive one. In fact, research by Les Hart about the brain provides some fascinating insight. Hart explains in his classic *How the Brain Works* that heavy-handed, intense criticism from teachers appears to have just the opposite effect on many people than the teacher intended. Faced with a teacher yelling directly and vigorously, many students will withdraw. The brain will "shift," much as a driver does when going from third down to first or second gear. The brain becomes much less receptive or efficient until the environment appears to be less threatening. Hart does not recommend that we end all criticism of students. He does suggest that we remember how we corrected our children as they learned to walk: patiently, with a great deal of support and constant encouragement.

Part of the research for my doctoral dissertation helps illustrate the influence of school structure on discipline problems. Students who graduated from the St. Paul Open School were asked to rate the qualities of their academic preparation and their feelings about the school staff and overall atmosphere. Their reactions were compared to those given by students from a traditional senior high school with excellent facilities.

Students from the alternative school generally rated the academic preparation they received slightly better than did traditional school students. However, it might be argued that alternative school students had lower expectations. (Nevertheless, standardized test scores showed the two graduating classes to have exactly the same rank—considerably above the national average for people their age.)

What about the students' attitudes toward their teachers? On each of nine questions, the alternative school students rated their teachers higher than did the traditional school students. Alternative school teachers were regarded as caring more for individual students, treating students more fairly, encouraging them to think more often for themselves, and trying harder to understand students.

As the Assistant Director at the alternative school and later as the Assistant Principal at the traditional school involved in this study, I was expected to deal with major discipline problems. There were fewer to handle at the alternative school. Unquestionably each school had a range of teachers, from poor to excellent. Students with family problems attended both programs. The key variable seems to have been the different structure. The specifics of that structure are important to identify. The first is that, at the traditional school, students were expected to accumulate credits toward graduation, while at the alternative school, they were expected to demonstrate competence in various skills. The alternative school allowed youngsters to progress at their own rate, and to learn from a variety of people in various locations. It equated graduation with achieving clearly needed skills. In the traditional school, there was no overall minimum skill level required for students in any area.

Theoretically, students at both schools had schedules reflecting their interests and abilities. However, the alternative school choices were wider, even though it enrolled 300 fewer students than the traditional school. Alternative school students could and did take courses at other high schools and more than one-third of them had taken and passed a college course before graduating. Less than 1 percent of the traditional school students could make that claim.

Another major difference was how the two schools provided counseling. Each alternative school student had an advisor, and no advisor had more than 30 "advisees." The advisor was expected to meet at least every two weeks with each advisee to review progress, work out problems, and react to new developments. Each traditional school student had a counselor, but the counselors' loads were more than 300 students each. This meant less individual attention—many of the traditional school students saw their counselor only once a year. Unquestionably the traditional school counselors had some special training the alternative school advisors did not.

This meant that the alternative school staff referred special problems to the one certified counselor on the staff. Alternative school advisors tended to screen out minor problems. The alternative school counselors handled less registration paperwork than their colleagues at the traditional school.

The alternative school was able to achieve this different ratio by making part of each teacher's responsibility that of working with advisees. "Support" staff such as the Director (Principal), Assistant Director, librarian, and social worker also had advisees, which enlarged the pool of advisors and increased direct contact between staff and students.

These differences between schools meant that, at no additional cost, students attending the alternative school received more individual attention than those attending the traditional school. Open School staff were able to make more effective use of their time. The school had fewer discipline problems because it was able to serve its students better. The Open School's structure helped reduce some of the frustrations and misunderstandings that can lead to large problems. My research showed that Open School graduates were more satisfied with their teachers' attitudes toward them than were traditional school graduates (Nathan, 1981).

Of course, not everyone will benefit from attending a school comparable to St. Paul Open School (and many fine teachers would not want to work in such a school). At certain points in our lives, most of us need more direction and supervision than at other times. Some of us learn better by working with a group, others gain more by working individually. Perhaps most importantly, each of us has at least one thing we can do really well, and at least one thing that we try to avoid as much as possible. Many factors influence discipline, besides a particular school's structure. A central issue, and an important problem for private and public schools, is the quality of instruction.

About five years ago, a nationwide study of 1,000 adults, "Project Talent," asked them to reflect on their high school years. The results were summarized as follows: "The evidence of these interviews suggests that high school education as a whole serves no very useful purpose" (Gagne, p. 2).

A 1979 Gallup Poll asked students throughout the country

about their school experiences. About 50 percent felt they were not being challenged enough (Proctor, p. 5). A recent Minnesota Youth Poll of more than 850 teenagers confirmed that an overwhelming percentage of teenagers, while agreeing that education was important for their future, described their academic experiences as "a waste of time" and "boring" (Hedin and Simon).

Taxpayers and students alike have a right to expect that schools will offer stimulating, challenging, useful courses. These courses and learning opportunities will require hard, sometimes repetitious work. But students deserve the opportunity to learn skills they will need and require in their lives. Youngsters need to gain knowledge to enrich and extend their horizons and ambitions. All too frequently, students report that their classes appear to have little to do with the world beyond the school. The curriculum is dull, and many teachers make little effort to help youngsters understand the value of what they are doing. As any parent knows, a bored youngster is more likely to get into trouble than a busy, stimulated one.

Effective teaching will not always be entertaining. However, it will engage youngsters in thoughtful, productive activity. Our finest teachers think carefully about their course content and student needs. They utilize the interests and skills of their students to build interest in the lesson. Our best teachers use a variety of instructional techniques to retain students' attention and to stimulate their desire to learn. Educators need to think carefully about the valid expectations their students have. I believe that each youngster has a right to expect that people in schools will care about him or her as an individual and look for positive qualities. We talk a great deal about the worth of the individual in this country. We need to act on those beliefs, and recognize that many teachers stifle rather than stimulate, discourage rather than encourage. We have too many instructors who confuse threatening with teaching, lecturing with learning.

School people ought to remember why our society created schools: to help individuals achieve their potential, and to help build a more just, equitable, productive society. Recognizing this, people in schools must consider how much of their time is spent advancing those goals. How often do school administrators allow themselves to get bogged down in paperwork and other "administrivia" that contributes little or nothing to better education for youth?

Related to the purpose of schools is the question of an administrator's audience. How many times have administrators explained, "Well, I didn't want to do that, but the teachers would accuse me of not supporting them if I didn't suspend the kid." We hear this too often. Responding to an administrator's "audience" is more difficult than it may seem. Obviously, administrators are expected to follow laws and district policies and procedures. However, most districts (including ours) give administrators some discretion. A classic example was the issue of wearing hats in our school.

Our Board of Education's dress code stipulated that students should not wear clothing that would endanger themselves or others. The Board also required that students follow "legitimate directions of teachers." Some teachers regarded the wearing of a hat in their classrooms a direct insult. Some of the parents also thought students should not be allowed to wear hats in the school, agreeing it signified disrespect and lack of a serious attitude toward learning. Other parents and staff thought this was not an important issue; they felt the school should have as few rules as possible, and enforce them consistently throughout the building.

During my first year in this school, hats became a major issue between several teachers and me. The Principal talked with me about it. He told me that I was to send students home for the day if they insisted on wearing a hat despite their teachers' direction to remove it. He felt that if the student refused to obey the teacher, he or she should be dismissed (sent home for the rest of the day, and readmitted after a parent conference). I talked with the students who insisted on wearing hats, and asked them to keep them off in classrooms where they were unacceptable. The students usually complied. In two instances, however, I did send home youngsters because they absolutely refused to remove their hats. My action troubles me.

The most respected rules come from parents, students, and staff who represent the school's community. They should be enforced in a calm, consistent manner. Asking young people for their opinions about rules helps not only them, but us.

One of the best suggestions for an improvement in our school came from several youngsters who pointed out that school dismissal was exactly what certain students aimed for. Instead, we started an "in-school suspension program." Under this plan, young people guilty of certain kinds of misbehavior were isolated in the school. They completed course work under a staff member's supervision, but were not allowed to spend any time with their friends during the school day. They went to restrooms when other students were in class. They ate alone. This treatment, suggested by youngsters, was enormously effective with many students guilty of minor but consistent misbehavior. We never assigned a student to in-school suspension for more than two days; if behavior didn't improve we looked for other solutions.

In establishing the "ISS" program, we were guided by excellent suggestions made at a conference called by the National Institute of Education, which stressed the value of clear guidelines and of working with staff on discipline issues. Teachers and administrators worked together to develop clear, reasonable rules for classrooms and common areas. Generally, those rules were respected (Garibaldi, 1979).

School rules should prohibit only actions which clearly endanger accomplishment of the school's purposes. Often, there are too many rules; banning hats strikes me as "much ado about nothing."

Many readers will disagree with me, and they should have the opportunity to teach in or send their children to, schools more closely reflecting their values, so long as those values don't violate Constitutional guarantees and rights. This is the beauty of offering a range of choices: Parents can select schools with which they are most comfortable. Teachers can pick a school which matches their instructional philosophy. Administrators can be more effective when staff, parents, and students agree about basic school goals and the climate for learning.

However, there will always be differences of opinion, regardless of discipline policy, and administrators need to remember that *no one* in a school deserves automatic support. This statement is considered heresy by many teachers and administrators. Perhaps the first thing an Assistant Principal hears upon entering a new school is, "The teachers here expect you to support them." Sometimes a choice must be made between loyalty to justice or to other staff members.

In one case, a teacher sent a student to me who had complained that a certain volunteer was making indecent advances toward her. The teacher insisted that the student work with the volunteer, whom she regarded as a fine person. The student alleged that the volunteer had propositioned her, and she offered to call in witnesses. Several other students confirmed the first youngster's account. Then I asked to talk with the volunteer. The teacher became extremely angry, accused me of "not backing her," and threatened to involve the Teacher's Federation representative since she felt I was not enforcing the District Discipline Code, which stated that students who refused to follow a teacher's legitimate direction would be sent home for the day (the student had refused to work with this volunteer). I sent a note asking the teacher to see me during her preparation period. "When I was at another school," I began, "we had some university volunteers who solicited young women for prostitution. Perhaps I'm being overly cautious, but you wouldn't want something like that to happen here, would you?"

"Of course not, but Sam is not that kind of person. You have a lot of nerve!" Her face was flushed and angry.

"Perhaps I'm being overly cautious, Mrs. Schmidt. However, several of the young people say that Sam propositioned them. Sam says he was just playing around. I don't think this is an appropriate way to joke with students, and he's agreed to stop immediately. If he doesn't, we're going to ask him to stop coming into the building. How would you suggest we proceed?"

The teacher said she'd like to discuss the situation with the volunteer and would talk with me the following day. She also said she would clear up the situation with the other teachers she'd already complained to about my "lack of support." The following day she reported that she had talked with the volunteer and obtained his promise to find another way of joking with the students. She had apologized to the student whom she sent in to me for disciplinary action. We talked about misunderstandings, and I complimented her on her willingness to investigate the situation and apologize to the student.

Of course, these confrontations don't always end so happily. Another situation produced bitterness which lasted several years. We had a teacher who'd been in the system a long time. He often told younger staff members that the school had been a better place to teach in before blacks arrived. He was physical with students, sometimes slapping them in the face and, at least once, jabbing a student in the stomach.

Not surprisingly, parents complained about him. I tried unsuccessfully to help him understand that students of all races had a right to attend our school, that diversity added richness to the school, and that his comments were inappropriate.

After one flagrant jab in a student's chest, we had it out. He suggested that we talk with the Principal, since I obviously didn't believe in supporting teachers. He complained bitterly that I didn't back him up, especially when he referred black students to me for disciplinary action. He charged that I'd encouraged parents to complain about him. (This was partially true. When parents called me to ask what could be done, I suggested that they discuss the situation with the Principal.) The Principal of course supported me. The teacher developed some health problems and decided to retire early. He made his hatred of me clear to all who would listen until the day he walked out of the building for the last time.

Unquestionably an Assistant Principal can go too far in trying to respond to students' complaints, as is evidenced in the following story. A young Science teacher sent several students to me because they would not stop talking when the class was watching a movie. After listening to them, I offered to move them each to another class. When I gave them transfer slips, I soon heard from the teacher (who refused to sign them). "Hey Joe, aren't you giving these kids the message that if they complain, you'll move them? What they need to understand is that people are quiet during the movie. And it was an extremely good one—would you like to see it?" I had enough confidence in the teacher to believe that the movie was appropriate for the class. I admitted my mistake, called the students back in and explained why I felt that moving them would be a poor decision. They laughed, agreed that they'd hustled me, and promised to behave better during movies. They created no further problems that semester.

Administrators must recognize that they make mistakes. If fact, things usually work out better if we admit mistakes and go on from there, rather than try to "tough it out."

An effective discipline program must also provide a variety of ways for youngsters to "shine" and succeed. All of us want to make a difference. We want others to know we've been on the earth. Our schools must provide opportunities for students to make a positive difference. An earlier chapter described youth participation programs that produced remarkable academic and attitude improvements. One of these programs was called peer counseling. Under the careful supervision of a faculty member, students learned several vital lessons. First, they discovered that other people their age shared similar anxieties and concerns. This was news to many. Many of the young women discovered that they were not alone in feeling ugly because they didn't look like Brooke Shields. They learned that others worried about never finding someone who would love them. Many of the youngsters had been afraid to tell their friends about their fears of a nuclear war. In the relaxed, supportive peer counseling environment, these deep anxieties came out, and young people comforted each other.

A second important lesson involved seeing the world from other peoples' perspectives. Students thought about, for example, how they might act between Monday and Friday so that their parent or guardian would be inclined to allow them to go out with friends on the weekend, and perhaps even chip in a few dollars for a movie or whatever. Many of these teenagers had done very little thinking before this class about the ways adults made decisions. Resource people came into the class at the students' request to help them learn more about reliable sources of information on everything from suicide to drugs. Unquestionably youngsters were already sharing information on these topics. Peer counseling helped make that information more accurate.

Fundamentally, this class improved students' abilities to help each other. Young people who were viewed as leaders, but who weren't attracted to activities such as student council, loved the class. We saw dramatic changes among several young people who began to understand ways they could continue to be viewed as leaders by their peers while gaining praise and acceptance from adults.

In another school, the staff faced a major problem with young women fighting. After a peer counseling program was established for the students involved in the fights, the disruptions ended, dramatically and completely. Young people learned other ways to resolve disagreements and retain their reputations. They also learned how others had "set them up" by playing, "He said, she said, you said, they said." Peer counseling is the best way to handle what otherwise can take years to straighten out.

A reporter once asked me how I would answer critics who feel that programs such as peer counseling have no place in schools, who say that the only legitimate role of the school is to teach reading, writing, and computing. In response, I recalled a young woman who was referred to me because she had put her head down on her desk during a test. The teacher thought she might be looking at some answers. He discovered that she was crying and sent her to me. My customary procedure in such situations is to offer a Kleenex and wait. The problem usually comes out quickly. It certainly did in this case: The young woman's mother was dying of cancer, and the entire family wondered how they would survive her death. The father had started to drink, and the brother was hanging around with older guys who were suspected of several robberies. It was just too much for this student, and she was unable to concentrate on the test.

With the parents' permission, the young woman became involved in the peer counseling program. She enjoyed the program and was selected for the advanced class. A year later, she was helping younger children at an elementary school as part of her course work.

The fact is that this student was not ready to take that test. Tragedy crosses race and economic lines. There's no guarantee that divorce, alcoholism, and death won't touch our young people—and for some, it will be immobilizing. If we care about young people learning to compute, we must also be willing and able to help them deal with disaster. If they don't learn to cope, they may not learn to compute either. We must remember the gruesome statistics on teenagers taking their own lives. Suicide is the second leading cause of death among teenagers in this country.

So I answered the newspaper reporter, and the critics, by saying that we must help youngsters deal with their anxieties, fears, and problems if we want them to develop skills and confidence. Most young people are frightened, lonely, or depressed at some point. Many will be able to overcome their problems with support and assistance from friends or family. Others will need help from the schools.

Solutions to difficult discipline problems do not lie in blaming each other. In our finest public and private schools, administrators, teachers, parents, students, and other concerned members of the community have created:

a clear list of expectations and consequences for positive and negative behavior;

opportunities for all youngsters to gain praise for their talents and skills;

a series of courses and learning opportunities allowing young people to gain needed skills, move at their own pace, and receive appropriate counseling;

a climate in which everyone can and does admit their mistakes;

and finally, the fundamental, overriding assumption that *all* youngsters can and will learn in this school.

As with many aspects of teaching and learning, it is easier to write about an effective discipline program than to create and maintain one. People who are successful should be encouraged and prized. That rarely happens in most public school systems. The realities of discipline help build the case for a better system of schools.

TWO GOOD PUBLIC SCHOOLS

"Look Joe, doesn't it really come down to getting the best people working in our schools? People make the difference, and if we can get good administrators and teachers together, we'll have effective schools—right?"

"Ann, even the best public school people are unable to use their full potential in our system. Sometimes it feels like we're running with a 50-pound pack strapped to our backs. We do our best, but eliminating the weight certainly would improve our efforts. Even Olympic athletes couldn't run four-minute miles with all the baggage we have to carry."

This conversation with a concerned state legislator compelled me to describe the nature of that 50-pound pack, and to identify barriers more money can't knock down. While we agreed on the importance of articulate, confident, skilled citizens, we disagreed about the likelihood of public schools producing them. So I began to think hard about the fundamental barriers to widespread excellence in public schools.

Past experiences help illustrate six fundamental obstacles in our public schools: 1) Pressures toward standardization; 2) Institutional overload and complexity; 3) Lack of incentive for innovation; 4) Restrictive teacher contracting arrangements; 5) Overreliance on teacher certification system; and 6) The seniority system.

Education library shelves hold thousands of reports about

attempts to improve public schools. Many conclude that, despite huge expenditures, most schools don't become much more effective. The Ford Foundation produced one of my favorite reports, *A Foundation Goes to School,* on the results of $34 million spent over a decade. The conclusions: 1) The easiest changes to create and sustain are the least complex; 2) Most of the changes don't last long after Foundation money is exhausted; and 3) A charismatic, talented administrator is necessary for most reforms, and when that person leaves, the reforms languish.

Another recent report suggested that people apply for Federal school improvement grants for the same reasons they go to garden parties: prestige, connections, and something to do. The investigators illustrated why millions of dollars in Federal funds never accomplished their stated purposes (Farrar, 1980). These reports, and hundreds of others, help us understand why it's so hard to improve our public schools.

Unquestionably public schools have many dedicated, committed teachers and administrators. However, in most school systems, their efforts are constantly frustrated and inhibited.

In 1981–82, a non-partisan, nationally recognized citizen's group in the Minneapolis-St. Paul area studied past school reform efforts and talked with frustrated parents and educators. After six months of deliberations, the committee issued its conclusions:

1. The incentives in public schools are too weak to force widespread adoption of outstanding existing programs and promising alternatives to current practices.
2. "Many legal, contractual and regulatory barriers hamper the public schools from pursuing the innovative approaches necessary to adequately respond to the diversity of student needs" (Citizen's League, 1982).

It is more appropriate to criticize the system rather than particular individuals within that system. Experiences in several different schools help confirm the wisdom of Yale University's Seymour Sarason, who wrote more than a decade ago: ". . . The major problems in our schools inhere far less in the characteristics of individuals than it does in its cultural and system characteristics . . ." (Sarason, p. 229).

The two public schools described here did not share the same educational philosophy. One would be considered "traditional," the other "progressive." Each, at a certain point, had a number of students waiting to enter the program. Students' test scores were above national averages and showed consistent improvement. Both schools attracted children from throughout St. Paul, Minnesota, and the student bodies of both reflected the city's racial and socio-economic mixture.

Each school's strength lay in its ability to use principles identified earlier in this book. Both viewed parents and young people as resources. Both tried to respond to parent and student interests and priorities. Both worked hard to make learning an enjoyable experience. Teachers at both schools tried to specify clear goals for their classes, and to include enjoyable experiences in their lesson plans. Teachers at both schools were sure the young people with whom they worked could learn, and maintained high academic expectations. Each school aggressively communicated with various constituencies, and tried to use strengths and interests of its staff. Finally, each worked hard to insure that staff and students felt safe and secure within the building. Yet the programs and structures of the two schools were different in many ways.

Both schools attempted to respond to parental requests and student needs. They frequently struggled with the first obstacle to excellence: *Intense pressures from the Central office and Board of Education to conform and standardize.* The first school, a junior-senior high school when I was assigned to it in December 1977, was a traditional public school in an affluent, highly educated neighborhood near the University of Minnesota St. Paul campus. Ninety-five percent of its students were white (compared to a district average of about 78 percent). Within three years, the school's percentage of minority students went from 5 percent to 25 percent.

The school's Principal was well known throughout the district. He was a senior Principal, former outstanding college football player, and talented chemistry teacher. He insisted on running a "tight ship."

Walking into the building for the first time, I tried to reassure myself. This was my first experience as an Assistant Principal, having worked for seven years as a teacher and administrator at a progressive alternative public school. Some of the open school staff warned me that the traditional school staff would never accept me.

Nevertheless, I was looking forward to my new assignment. I had heard that the parents were eager to work with the school staff and that many of the students were talented and creative. When I arrived for my conference with the Principal, he surveyed me warily and began, "I think you should know right off that I called the Deputy Superintendent last week and asked him not to assign you here. I don't think it's fair." Well, the man was direct! He continued for 15 to 20 minutes, pointing out that the faculty expected to be backed by the administration, that the school had many good teachers, and that he expected me to follow his directions. He also explained his suggestion that I be assigned to another school: He felt I should have the opportunity to work in a larger structure, with several Assistant Principals from whom I could learn. In this school of 875, I would be the only Assistant Principal.

Gradually, many of the parents and I got to know each other. Some of them knew I'd been at an open school and were curious about my shift to a more traditional program. They mentioned that their youngsters said the school had a new A.P. who was young. (I was 29, the third youngest person out of 42 on the faculty.)

With the Principal's permission, we had a few meetings, to discuss parent concerns. Several emerged. First, many parents thought their children were bored, particularly in the junior high classes (the school enrolled grades 7 to 12). Students took English 7, 8, 9, Social Studies 7, 8, 9, and Math 7, 8, 9. Parents wanted to see more challenge in those classes.

A second concern was student fighting. Parents heard stories from their children about fights several times a week and wondered if there weren't ways to reduce this disruption. A third concern was about specific teachers who appeared to have little commitment to quality instruction. They accused several teachers of rambling, or telling sports or war stories for most of the class, or simply assigning chapters to be read with question-answering at the end.

The Principal had made it clear that I was to stay out of staff problems, so the third concern was not something I addressed, at least initially. However, our meetings with parents regarding lack of challenge certainly gave us enough to think about and work on.

One excellent teacher complained that she wanted to write notes home to parents about students' successes, but had been unable to obtain stamps to do this. Of course she could buy her own, but on principle, she refused. The school paid for postage about bad news (dismissal, suspension, failure, etc.). Why not good news? Agreeing, I bought about $25.00 worth of postcards, told her, and watched the news travel through the faculty in two days. That probably was the best $25.00 I ever spent on school supplies, though with various grants we've probably spent $25,000.00 by now.

Several English teachers responded to the parents' complaints by saying that they would be willing to offer well-developed electives, if the Principal would authorize it. Several parents met with him to discuss this offer. I'll never forget his wry smile the day the parents came in: "Well Joe, I see someone has some ideas for in-no-va-tion (he stretched it out) in this school." Nevertheless, he authorized two new junior high English courses for the following semester, one in debate and the other in writing. Parents and teachers were ecstatic.

Over a five-year period, the school developed many electives, focusing on development of important skills such as writing clearly, reading with greater attention to detail, researching, and public speaking. The courses included: Great Books, Newspaper Writing, and Public Service Communications (which involved researching and producing slide films about various subjects). Each of the courses stressed skill development.

Because of a $19,000.00 grant from the Northwest Area Foundation, we were able to bring in several fascinating people who encouraged and inspired us. One, a 78-year-old dynamo, was Judge Mary Kohler. Kohler had been a juvenile court judge in San Francisco. She was frustrated by the number of repeaters she saw. Getting together with some of her friends, she asked if there was something that could be done. One friend had heard about a few projects in which students tutored other students. Kohler was excited by the idea and quickly pulled together a project in which a number of under-achieving, low income youngsters taught each other.

The dramatic results were reported in a *Saturday Evening*

Post article and subsequently in her book, *Children Teach Children* (jointly authored with Alan Gartner and Frank Riesman). Students receiving tutoring made considerable progress. However, those students who were responsible to provide the tutoring, made incredible progress themselves, both in academic and social skills! The experience led Kohler to found the National Commission on Resources for Youth (NCRY). In the last 15 years, NCRY documented and encouraged projects in which youngsters provided service to others. (See my chapter on effective learning, page 20.)

Judge Kohler mesmerized people. She told stories, she whispered, she appealed to the very best in each of us, and the response was incredible. Young or old, teachers loved her. She helped them understand their own importance and the value in helping youngsters feel productive and capable. Several days after Kohler's speech to our faculty, one of the physical education teachers, who'd been at the school for more than 15 years, came into my office. He explained that many of the student-athletes came to him for advice, and that Judge Kohler's ideas about peer counseling intrigued him. "Teenagers give each other a great deal of advice, whether we like it or not," Judge Kohler had reminded us. "Since this happens regardless of what we do, it's our responsibility to help guide and strengthen this advice. We can help youngsters learn how to think through their problems, and where to get accurate information about their questions on the future, drugs, and sex. You can be sure that they'll find some answers. Peer counseling helps increase the chances their information will be correct."

Gradually, this teacher developed a peer counseling class. At first, the school offered it one hour a day. The demand was so large that within two years, five sections of the class were offered. Fights decreased as students learned peaceful ways to resolve disagreements and rumors. In several discipline cases, I turned to the peer counseling class for advice, which was excellent. The teacher was so committed to the class that he spent his own money on a trip to California to meet with Barbara Varenhorst, who had developed an outstanding peer counseling program for the Palo Alto Public Schools. Peer counseling was one of several electives offered within English and Social Studies. Parents had to approve before their son or daughter was admitted.

Another option was debate, a class many parents had strongly requested be reintroduced into the curriculum. The junior high debate teacher was an extraordinary man. He was pleased when we began to discuss the possibility of offering debate as an elective in English. "Joe, you know I don't like many of those 'open school' ideas of yours," he'd begin. "However, I do believe strongly in carefully designed courses which meet kids' needs and help them develop skills. And I believe kids should have a few choices, because they're not all alike."

It was impossible to argue with that position. We agreed. So did the parents, and gradually we developed four electives in English, along with a basic required course in composition, spelling, and literature.

This teacher also created a class on cancer which received national recognition. He had cancer and knew he would live for only another 18 to 24 months. However, he loved teaching and refused to leave until he was physically unable to help youngsters. The students called it the "cancer class." The youngsters read a variety of materials about cancer, talked with experts and produced a filmstrip which several local hospitals are now using as an orientation for their cancer patients. Students interviewed by newspaper reporters described what they learned in this class:

"Well, we learned a lot about cancer. That's important, because most of us know people with the disease. Before it was pretty scary. Now at least we know something about it. It's easier to deal with something you know about."

"Sure we learned about cancer, and about research. But most of all, we learned about courage. Mr. Merritt was a real hero. He showed me what success is in life: it's not necessarily becoming an administrator or 'king of the world.' It's finding out what you want to do, learning to do it well, and continuing for as long as you can."

Profound words, indeed, from 14-year-olds. Quite a class.

Over the next several years, our school developed a number of electives, supported by parents, students, and staff. One of the program's strengths was that staff members were encouraged to develop programs based on their own interests and talents. Parents felt their children derived real benefit from being in a debate or creative writing or newspaper class. They believed, correctly, that there are many effective ways to develop writing, research, and speaking skills. The point is that all youngsters need to develop these skills, not that they necessarily should take the same path to this goal. In fact, using the youngsters' interests increased the possibility that the goals would be achieved.

Response from the community was excellent. Our school was designated a magnet program, allowing parents from throughout the city to send their children there. Within two years, more than half of the students at the school were from outside the school's neighborhood attendance, attending because they wished to be at this particular school. Some parents were taking their children out of private schools, believing that this was a public junior high school in which their children would be challenged to achieve, and in which parent concerns would be carefully considered.

However, during the 1981–82 school year, our Superintendent of Schools issued a new directive about junior high course credits. He was responding to strong pressure from the Board, which was concerned about test scores and the complaints of some parents about proliferating elective courses in which youngsters apparently acquired few skills. The Superintendent also was concerned about reports from high schools that many youngsters entered tenth grade without basic writing, computing, and reading skills. Some experts suggested that the way to handle these problems was to have a standard curriculum for everyone. The Council for Basic Education's *The Paideia Proposal* recommended that "All sidetracks, specialized courses or elective choices must be eliminated. The course of study to be followed in the twelve years of basic schooling should, therefore be completely required, with only one exception. That exception is the choice of a second language" (Adler, p. 21).

The Superintendent directed junior high schools to offer one basic course in English and one in social studies, with no electives in these areas without his approval. The effect was chilling. Some parents complained, but the

Board and Superintendent were convinced their plan had value. Thus, a program of community-supported electives was destroyed. It happened not because parents at the school were complaining, not because youngsters at the school were receiving low test scores, but because of other forces outside the school.

Recently, friends told me about their frustrations with a textbook decision. The school district had established a textbook committee to make recommendations about which books to purchase. The textbook committee made suggestions to the Teachers Advisory Board, which passed ideas to the Superintendent, who in turn made the final recommendation to the Board of Education. Textbooks are reviewed about every five years and this process takes almost an entire year.

During one recent year, the textbook committees made their suggestions after meeting for months. About the same time they reached a decision, the Board of Education decided not to buy any new textbooks because the budget was very tight. So a decision was made not to forward the committees' recommendations on to the Teachers Advisory Board and so on. About a month later, the Board decided to spend about $100,000.00 to purchase replacement texts. By this time the school year had ended. Several administrators and teachers asked if it would be possible to purchase some of the recently recommended texts, since the Board-approved material was at least five years old. The answer was no.

New texts could not be purchased because the adoption process had not been completed. By this time, it was summer and the Teachers Advisory Board members were scattered. It appeared to be too difficult to reconvene the group until fall. Thus, thousands of dollars were spent on five-year-old books, when more up-to-date texts were available. The textbook adoption process was designed to satisfy the community and its teachers. Sadly, this process ended up being counterproductive.

Another experience with textbooks produced disappointing results for a different reason. The committee was selecting books for a senior high school current issues class. Teachers readily agreed on the value of adding a number of books to the list approved for use with a contemporary problems class.

The teachers recommended several books, and also suggested that the funds allocated for texts be used during the five year period, rather than all at once during the first year. The instructors reasoned that an unforeseen world crisis might develop in the future. They wanted flexibility to purchase timely material.

Several senior teachers warned against this procedure. They explained that unspent money often was a convenient target for cuts. They were right! Within a year, the unspent textbook money was withdrawn. Those schools which tried to be careful with their funds were penalized.

Such experiences encourage people to scheme and waste. Teachers and kids are the real losers.

Pressures toward standardization are not unusual in public education. There are solid, logical reasons for them, as Donald Willower points out:

> . . . Forms of routinization . . . speak to the massive logistics of educational organization. They make the enterprise more manageable, that is, they function to channel, order and regularize the manner in which the organization attends to and processes its clients (Willower, p. 392).

But Willower recognizes what is lost by adoption of such procedures:

> Routinization reduces the likelihood of instruction geared to variations in client characteristics, since procedures that accommodate unusual or unique client requirements are apt to be disruptive (Willower, p. 392).

Robert Benjamin, an award-winning journalist who traveled around the country looking for unusually good schools, commented on the effect bureaucratic demands have on most public school principals:

> They have their eye on the mandates of the bureaucracy, rather than on the academic needs of their students and teachers. This is encouraged by the structure of large public school systems: The higher educators advance, the further they get from the classroom. It is enforced by the relatively small degree of autonomy accorded principals by their ad-

ministrative superiors: They are expected to be mere managers, and most have settled for that (Benjamin, p. 188).

The tension between central office demands and parent/student requests places school staff in a difficult position. Unquestionably public schools have many dedicated, committed teachers and administrators. However, in many school systems, they are frustrated and inhibited.

In all fairness, this frustration is often shared by central office administrators. They find themselves bound by increasing, often conflicting demands from Boards of Education, courts, legislators, Departments of Education and parents.

Several stories help illustrate the next major institutional barrier, as defined by Daniel Levine at the Center for Study of Metropolitan Problems in Education: *Organizational Complexity and Overload.*

Our junior high school was successful in obtaining a grant to improve programs for gifted students. After discussions with parents and students, a decision was made to hire a professional artist to work with one of our teachers and several talented students. The artist would train the teacher so that, in following years, he could conduct similar activities. District policy required that all grants go through the central accounting office. It was not acceptable simply to open an account at a nearby bank, write checks, and provide periodic documentation that the money was being spent in an appropriate manner. *This is a fundamental problem!*

We identified a group of professional artists, and in late November, 1979, I called the District Business Office to learn the procedure for paying them (about $4,000.00). The first step was to submit a resolution to the Board authorizing this payment. Several days later I sent a note to the Secondary Assistant Superintendent with a sample resolution asking that it be placed on the next Board meeting's agenda. I didn't hear anything for several weeks and noticed that the resolution was not considered at the next Board meeting. So I called the Assistant Superintendent's secretary. She told me that there was a "Board Meeting Agenda Request" form and promised to send me some.

More time went by, and then it was Christmas vacation.

Shortly afterwards, the forms arrived. I filled them out as well as I could and delivered them on January 10 to the Assistant Superintendent. At the next Board meeting, on January 22, the Board approved a resolution authorizing the District to enter into an agreement with a local arts organization, COMPAS (Community Program in Arts and Sciences).

Two weeks later (February 1) we submitted a form requesting partial payment to the arts organization so they could begin buying materials. February 15 the Legal Affairs Office secretary called to ask for a copy of the agreement between our school and COMPAS. I didn't hear anything for three weeks and assumed that the artists would be paid soon. (Bad assumption.) On March 7, the Business Office called to say that a copy of the agreement was insufficient; I needed to bring in the original. The Attorney must sign it before the Business Office would process the payment request. I delivered the original agreement to the Business Office that afternoon and was assured everything was in order.

On March 17 a business office envelope arrived which pointed out everything was *not* in order. They had returned the request for payment form I'd submitted on February 1. Attached was a note saying that the Principal's signature was not enough. I was listed as the project director, so my signature was required. (This does make sense. Otherwise, a Principal could charge something to a grant without the director knowing anything about it. It just would have been nice to know that both signatures were required when the form had been sent in a month earlier.)

That afternoon I called a business office official. I angrily reviewed events of the last several months, and asked, with considerable vehemence, "When will I get a manual telling me how to do all this?" He replied that, "Everyone who needs to know already does." (I wasn't sure where that left me.)

The official promised to look at the request when I brought it in. The Principal and I decided to talk directly with the Superintendent. When we met the following day, the Superintendent agreed that this kind of thing could be very frustrating. He described similar frustrations earlier in his own career and said he had hoped to eliminate such problems when he was named Superintendent. He explained that what kept him from his goal was that when Principals were given more dis-

cretion some of them abused it, laws were violated, and inevitably more power became centralized. He promised to ask the
Business Office to straighten out our specific problem.

That afternoon I talked with a high Business Office official.
How soon did he think the artists could be paid? (It was now
March 19, almost two months after Board authorization and
six weeks after the original payment request had been submitted.) The Business Office Director wasn't sure. At that
moment I got an insight into how a volcano feels just before it
erupts.

"The Superintendent wants this paid! He said so this morning!"

"If he wants me to do something right away, he knows
exactly where I am. Incidentally, I've been getting comments
from some of the staff in my office that you're harassing
them."

"Well, we've certainly talked a lot!" Then I listed our
numerous discussions.

He promised to look into the situation and hung up. Subsequently the Principal and I met with one of the Superintendent's deputies. He wanted to know if I had been threatening
people. I offered my version of events. "Well, Joe, now you
see what happens when you anger people in the bureaucracy."

"Do you think it would be helpful to develop a manual of
procedures?" I asked quietly.

"Look at yourself—don't blame others for your problems."

"Well, some other building administrators tell me they've
had similar problems."

"Don't go stirring any more trouble. We'll take care of the
bills."

End of conversation. The artists were paid within a week.
As time went by, I came to understand the various forms and
procedures. The Business Office people and I get along well.
The question is: Do we need all the forms and procedures?

This was not the school's only brush with bureaucratic
complications. Murray Junior High School had been available
to parents from throughout the city for several years. Its enrollment had increased steadily, demonstrating that many parents wanted the kind of program the school offered. Many,

although certainly not all, of the staff were young, with two to five years of experience.

When the District found itself in financial difficulty, half of the school's 22 teachers were laid off. Under union contract, the youngest teachers were laid off first. Because the school had so many young teachers, it suffered significantly more cuts than most other district programs. No one knew until late August what teachers from other schools in the District would be transferred to Murray to fill the many gaps and what the new class schedule would be.

Ultimately, a schedule was constructed. Teachers who were willing to spend the summer planning lessons didn't know until a week before school opened whether they'd be working with seventh graders or eleventh graders, or what specific classes they'd be teaching. Many of the new teachers were assigned to the building only a day or two before students arrived, so they missed planning and orientation meetings with parents and other teachers. These and other complications appear to be inevitable, as contractual arrangements become ever more rigid, angry teachers demand grievance hearings, and frustrated Board members demand more centralized control of what's happening.

Why weren't assignments made earlier? Central office staff gave a variety of explanations, including time taken with grievances filed by staff members who felt they'd been laid off unfairly; time required by the union contract to give more senior staff the opportunity to review available openings and select their preferences; inability to forecast exactly how many students would be returning to school, leading to uncertainty about how many teachers to rehire. Yes, things had become incredibly complicated; perhaps there were just too many factors involved.

David Seeley, former Assistant U.S. Commissioner of Education and later director of New York City's Public Education Association, recently wrote, "The present educational bureaucracy is antilearning: it must be turned upside down to redirect education to its primary purposes . . ." (Seeley, p. 211). He's right!

Another incident illustrates this dilemma. During my second year at Murray Junior High, a group of parents and staff met to discuss ways to increase understanding among racial groups within the school. A variety of activities were developed to help youngsters learn about one another. People representing various cultures spoke in Social Studies classes, parents sent in ethnic recipes for cooking classes, and the Parent-Teacher-Student organization held meetings in different parts of town more convenient than our school building, located in the far northwest section of the city.

At one meeting, a student mentioned that he'd read about cohesive ethnic neighborhoods in Chicago. He and others were fascinated by the notion that in some areas, signs were written in Lithuanian, German, Chinese, Polish, and Spanish. After considerable discussion, we decided to take 80 students to Chicago. This was about 10 percent of the school. The Principal and I met with the Assistant Superintendent to review district procedures and obtain his support for the project. A number of fundraisers were held (bake sales, car washes, etc.) and necessary arrangements were made. Parental support was enormous, with some volunteering to help chaperone, others contributing money for scholarships, and others helping to make arrangements in Chicago.

Ten days before the group's departure, the Principal received a late afternoon phone call from the Assistant Superintendent. Apparently there was a misunderstanding between the Superintendent and Assistant Superintendent. The Superintendent insisted that this trip required Board of Education approval. Despite our attempts to follow approved procedures, we apparently had not taken the final required step. The Superintendent was trying to decide whether to place the matter on the Board's agenda for the following day's meeting. Recently the Superintendent had been criticized by the Board for bringing up items at the meeting which were not on the agreed upon agenda. The Board members wanted a chance to study relevant reports and recommendations before making decisions. In order to allow time to process and deliver information to Board members, supporting information had to be in the Superintendent's office eight days before a Board meeting.

Our Principal reminded the Assistant Superintendent of his assurance that all procedures had been followed. If Board approval was required, it would have to be on the next day's agenda. The Board met only twice a month and the next day's meeting was the only one scheduled before the trip. Delaying the trip would produce enormous complications. Some students would lose deposits, as they had made special arrangements to be absent from after-school jobs. A coach accompanying the group had rescheduled a game so that he wouldn't have to miss it. A number of staff would be unable to go on the trip, if it was rescheduled. The Principal asked the Assistant Superintendent to share this information with the Superintendent and, if need be, with the Board. He was promised that his concerns would be communicated.

Late the next afternoon (the day of the Board meeting) the Principal received a phone call saying that the Superintendent had decided not to place the trip on the agenda. Apparently several Board members had reiterated their concerns about not following established procedures to the Superintendent. He had decided that placing an additional item on their agenda would be a direct affront. The trip would have to be delayed or canceled.

The Principal called me into his office. "What should we do, Joe?" We reviewed several options, including enlisting parents to call the Superintendent or Board members, calling Board members ourselves, calling the Superintendent, going to the Board meeting, or forgetting the whole thing. Just then, a Board member walked into our school, to return a textbook she had found in the neighborhood. The Principal reviewed the situation with her and asked for advice. She decided to tell the Superintendent that she wanted it on the agenda for that night's meeting. The Principal said, "I have a meeting of the State Principals' Association Board tonight. If it's on the agenda, Joe will have to represent the school!" He told me that since I would have to appear in front of the board, the decision was mine. "Thanks a lot," I smiled. I called several parents and students, briefly explained the situation, and asked them to meet me at the Board meeting. They agreed.

The Board meeting went well. The Superintendent felt he had not been given enough time to review our request and declined to make a recommendation to the Board. The students were brilliant, pointing out the detailed planning and preparation they'd conducted, and how the trip fit in with many other class activities. The Board voted six to one in favor of the trip.

The following morning the Principal received a phone call

ordering him and me to the Superintendent's office in 30 minutes. The Superintendent pointed out how procedures had been violated. He supported the trip, but felt he'd been put in a tough spot. We agreed.

Fortunately, the trip was a complete success. The students were cooperative, mannerly, and responsible. We stayed at a hotel on Michigan Avenue, directly across from Grant Park. A few students decided to stay up late on the first night and made more noise than was necessary, so I got them up at 5:00 A.M. and took them out for morning exercises in the park. That stopped the late night noise.

We visited several ethnic centers in Chicago. For some, the highlight was Chinatown. Others gained most from their visit to an Afro-American museum, or to the futuristic offices of Johnson Publishing Company, producers of *Ebony* and *Jet* magazines.

A world far different from Minneapolis and St. Paul opened up for many of the students. Some were fascinated by discussions with people in neighborhoods where little English was spoken. There was time to visit and attend a dance with students from a large, integrated suburban senior high school, Evanston Township. Many youngsters had their first Greek meal through the incredible cooperation of the Parthenon restaurant, which seated all 85 of us, and served a delicious six-course dinner for $6.50 a person. From time to time the students and I see each other. They often mention the Chicago trip. It's sad that more such trips aren't planned.

Another St. Paul public school encountered its own set of problems with the district. This school had been started in 1971 because of a massive community effort to establish a public "open school." Parents and potential teachers from St. Paul met weekly from fall of 1970 through spring of 1971, developing proposals for funds which the Board of Education reviewed and ultimately agreed to submit to various government agencies and foundations. The Superintendent met with the community group in late 1970 and gave them four tasks:

1. Develop a coherent philosophy for the school.
2. Demonstrate that there are at least 500 sets of parents who will send their children to such a school.

3. Determine where the program might be housed.
4. Identify outside resources to provide "startup costs."

The community group completed the tasks by spring, 1971, and in March the Board of Education authorized acceptance of grant funds which permitted the district to begin the St. Paul Open School in September, 1971.

Some people will question whether it was advisable for a public school district to operate such a program. However, unlike other "open schools," the program in St. Paul was carefully evaluated, and found to be extremely effective in helping some students gain basic and applied skills. The school had 500 students, ages five through eighteen. Each student had an advisor, who met periodically with the student and her/his parent or guardian. These conferences helped youngsters and their parent(s) identify goals for the year and develop plans to meet those goals. The plan often involved taking classes, doing independent studies, and for older students, spending some time in the community as an intern or apprentice.

The Open School required potential graduates to demonstrate competence at a variety of tasks before graduating. There were a few students who decided to challenge that system. They quickly learned that students who did not demonstrate their skills and submit validations to the school committee would not receive diplomas.

A fundamental assumption of the Open School was that the most effective program would be developed after extensive discussions among parents, students, staff, and administrators. The school established more than a dozen committees, whose members represented each of the constitutencies and made recommendations to the Principal on everything from budget allocations to staff evaluation.

The school believed that the entire continent ought to be used as a classroom. Each year dozens of students spent part of their time as interns or apprentices with various community agencies or businesses. Many older students took some of their courses at another high school or even a local university. Within several years, almost one-third of the graduating students had accumulated some college credits.

The school's unconventional procedures often clashed with those of the district. As mentioned earlier, only textbooks approved by various district committees could be purchased with district funds. Teachers who hoped to use several different books in a literature class found that they had to ask students to check them out from the library or purchase their own. (At one point, one class had contacted 27 libraries to get enough copies of *The Adventures of Tom Sawyer!*)

Another use of the community was via cross country trips. Students conducted a variety of fundraisers and often camped out or stayed in university dormitories as they traveled across the continent. Spanish classes participated in month-long exchanges with a Puebla, Mexico, school. A Civil War class spent eight months studying the war from textbooks, encyclopedias, and movies, and then went on a trip to Gettysburg and Harper's Ferry. A group of 12- to 14-year-olds read a number of Laura Ingalls Wilder's books *(On the Banks of Plum Creek, Little House on the Prairie, Little House in the Big Woods)* and then visited the locations about which Wilder wrote.

From the beginning, such trips irritated some people in the district. During the school's first year, a $500.00 mini-grant from the district was awarded to a teacher who planned to build a large raft with a group of students and then travel down the Mississippi River to St. Louis. The students located a company willing to lend them two motors to help guide the raft, another company to donate the lumber and a third to contribute barrels. Despite the pleas of parents involved, the corporate support, and the willingness of the staff member (me) to contribute weekend time to the effort, the district felt the project constituted an unreasonable liability. The district's attorney feared that an accident might produce a lawsuit.

Gradually more restrictions were put on Open School field trips. In its earliest years, the school was allowed to lease buses or vans, and use school staff and parents holding appropriate licenses to drive the vehicles. After a few years, on advice from its attorney, the Board insisted that the school hire drivers supplied by the companies owning the buses or vans. Obviously this added to the cost of such trips.

One can understand the district's concern. Its insurance costs were increasing. School Board members attended conferences with other Board members from around the country who talked about huge settlements they had paid out because of accidents for which courts decided they were liable. Moreover, there were several accidents involving the Open School. Even before the building had opened for students, a parent's life was lost in a tragic accident. The parent was helping paint the building's kitchen when he apparently lost his balance, fell off a ladder, and hit his head on the hard floor. The district might have decided at that point to delay the school's start, or even to withdraw support. To its credit, it did neither.

During the school's first year, another accident hospitalized several teenagers on a field trip. Six years later, another Open School field trip under the direct supervision of two paid staff members resulted in fatality. Students at a camp were swimming without permission or authorization and one of them drowned.

Clearly district administrators did have reasons to be cautious about field trips! During this same seven-year period, there were several accidents involving other schools and programs, so the Open School was not the only program producing concern. Why did the Board of Education allow field trips in spite of the potential dangers? Probably because they recognized the enormous values of these projects. The trips extended and enriched a variety of classes, from Geography and History through Map Reading, Budgeting, and Cooking. Many youngsters wrote to Board members, or made a presentation to them, illustrating what they had learned.

Despite the accidents, the Open School was an attractive alternative to hundreds of parents in St. Paul. They liked the emphases on skill development and responsibility. They were heartened by an award the U.S. Office of Education presented to the school, as "an outstanding innovation, worthy of national replication." Many of the citizens of St. Paul would have been more than satisfied with local replication—a second such program available to the people who were on the Open School's lengthy waiting list. When the school was established, it had more than 1,200 students competing for the 500 spots. The waiting list grew rapidly to almost 1,500.

The school's advisory council suggested that another similar program be opened to accommodate the waiting list, not wishing the present school's enrollment to extend beyond

500. A number of parents and staff volunteered to help establish the second program. But, despite hundreds of parental requests, and the advisory council's recommendation, the Board of Education decided one Open School was enough. In so doing, the Board rejected offers of assistance and support.

Parents in other school districts met similar frustrations. A local reporter examined parental attempts to establish "open schools" in the early 1970s throughout the Twin Cities area. He concluded: "Alternatives have not caught on in a big way mainly because the people in power—administrators and school board members—have been reluctant" (Pinney, p. 3A).

The reporter helped identify the next major barrier to educational excellence: *The ability of public schools to resist adopting promising or proven programs.* This is a widespread problem, as three national experts on educational change discussed in their book, *Dynamic Educational Change.* They reviewed several hundred reports about reform efforts and noted,

> Public educational institutions are in a unique position with regard to ignoring forces for change. They enjoy the "protected status" of a public agency with a conscripted client and are less subject to the immediate pressures of the marketplace (Zaltman et al, p. 30).

The American marketplace has not always served all our citizens well. The affluent have far more choices than low and middle income persons. The same grocery chain may have better produce in its suburban stores than its inner city stores. Nevertheless, consumers may have an impact. For many years, automobile companies ignored consumer demands for smaller, more fuel-efficient cars. Eventually, however, they were forced by competitive pressures to produce them.

The situation, as Zaltman reports, is different in public schools. Low and most middle income parents have been forced to accept what the public schools offered. Their only alternative, placing their children in private schools, is difficult.

Poor parents have been unable to force schools to become more effective with their children. While the national dropout rate is about 25 percent, it is more than 40 percent in some cities, and approaches 50 percent in some low income areas. As Cincinnati reporter Robert Benjamin concluded after visiting schools throughout this country, "America's public schools typically do not equip the children of the poor for anything more than a second-class role in this country's society. The failure is systematic. . . . The public schools most everywhere amplify—more often than they mollify—the economic and social inequities of American life" (Benjamin, p. 3).

Should, or could, school boards and administrators respond favorably to all parental or community requests? Of course not! Obviously some are contradictory (i.e., don't offer sex education, do offer sex education; don't use textbooks which depict women and men in non-traditional roles, do use such textbooks, etc.).

A second factor preventing positive responses is budget. Dollars will go only so far. Administrators and School Boards must make choices. They can't pay all teachers at least $20,000.00 a year (as Minnesota Education Association members demanded in the fall of 1981), reduce class sizes, retain athletics and other extracurricular activities, and purchase large numbers of computers.

A third problem for school boards has been the incredible range of demands placed on them. Interest groups have developed to support expenditures in almost every conceivable area. Many Boards have learned that in trying to respond positively to all citizens, they've satisfied almost no one.

Some programs and practices are more effective in teaching reading, writing, and math than other programs. Certain schools have done a better job helping a variety of children develop the skills they will need. Despite the limitations of budget and conflicting demands, school boards theoretically could establish priorities and fund those programs and projects which have demonstrated results. But, there are powerful forces inhibiting these decisions. Primary among these forces is another major barrier to widespread excellence: *The seniority system of retention, payment and assignment of staff.*

Both the traditional and open schools in which I worked had excellent, adequate, and ineffective teachers. However, in the public schools, there was no relationship between the quality of instruction and the retention of staff when some teachers needed to be laid off. Teachers were laid off on the basis of experience, not skills. An excellent statement about this system appeared in the traditional school's student newspaper on May 21, 1982.

UNFAIR!

Has one of your favorite teachers been cut? Most likely so. In fact 427 teachers were cut in St. Paul and 12 were cut at Murray. Some will be rehired. Among the 427 teachers cut were some excellent ones with little experience. Among those remaining teachers, there are some poor ones with a lot of experience.

Experience is important, but so is the ability to teach and enjoy kids. Not always do the three go together. Should experience be the only way of deciding who is cut? NO! An evaluation of each teacher would be a better way of deciding who is cut. (Fretheim, p. 3)

A 15-page essay couldn't say it better. In our school, the cuts made because of declining enrollment in the district included the following staff, among hundreds of other talented people:

- A young Science teacher who was constantly requested by parents and students alike because of her careful preparation, variety of experiments, and high expectations of all students. She helped plan and organize a four-day environmental-multicultural trip for more than 70 students with community cooperation three years in a row.
- A young Reading-English teacher who volunteered to work with many of the most troubled youngsters in our school. He taught a class in which students planned, wrote, and produced a filmstrip about the value of tutors in schools. Many of his students showed dramatic improvement in attitudes toward learning, school, and themselves.
- An outstanding Math-Science teacher, who planned a variety of field trips and was strongly commended by students and parents for her positive, challenging, strict classroom environment.
- An enthusiastic, creative Woodshop teacher, who was particularly good at helping shy youngsters develop skills they didn't know they had.
- An eager, creative Foreign Language teacher who doubled

enrollment in language because youngsters learned so much, and enjoyed themselves in the process.

Only one of these people returned in the fall of 1982 to the St. Paul Public Schools. The rest were lost, while many less able people stayed on, because the School Board and State Legislature had agreed to teachers' organization demands that layoffs be made on the basis of seniority, with no regard whatever to individual skills.

In some districts, race is considered when firing, so that declining enrollment won't result in all white faculties. In some districts few minority teachers were hired until the last decade. While allowing schools to retain a racially diverse faculty, this provision still does not guarantee that the most effective instructors will be retained when cuts must be made.

Evaluation of administrators and teachers is possible, and a few places are doing a fine job. Most do little evaluating after the first two to three years. For the last 10 years, St. Paul has not had a formal procedure for staff evaluation after a teacher receives tenure, although one is presently under consideration. One of the central tasks of a more effective system of schools will be establishment of an evaluation system which serves central purposes. First, it will identify staff strengths. Next, it will specify areas where improvement and growth are needed. Finally, it will help provide sufficient information and documentation so that if needed improvements are not made, the person involved can be fired.

At this moment, many of the brightest young people are not being attracted to the teaching profession.

High school seniors planning to major in education scored well below the average for U.S. college bound seniors in 1976. . . . Education majors in 1975–76 tied 17th place in math and 14th place in english of the 19 fields of study in which entering freshmen enrolled as reported by the ACT program. . . . Five thousand forty-six Minnesota high school seniors taking the SAT in 1980–81 were asked to indicate their intended areas of collegiate study. Of the 28 vocational areas listed, students intending to go into education had lower SAT scores than all other occupations except three, and lower scores than all other fields but two (Citizens League, p. 24).

Certainly test scores are not the only indicator of excellent teachers. Teachers need intelligence, compassion, creativity, patience, and commitment. Standardized tests don't measure any of these factors adequately.

Another, related problem for schools and students is that people with strong technical skills are not being attracted to education. In 1980 the supply of qualified Beginning Math teachers met less than 80 percent of the national demand. This country has only 10,000 Physics teachers for its 16,000 school districts—less than one Physics teacher per district (McGuire, p. 18).

Presently many of the best teachers are quitting education in disgust. A 1981 national study of 22,000 people showed, "Teachers who score highest on measures of academic ability are most likely to leave teaching early . . . [and] those who score highest leave teaching in the greatest numbers and those who score lowest are most likely to stay in the classroom" (Vance and Schlechty, p. 22). Excellent teachers see too many poor teachers earning thousands of dollars more than they are because of seniority. Our finest teachers have been attacked too often for the "sorry state of American education."

Instead of attracting bright young people and retaining their most talented senior members, our public schools are losing them. This is a loss not only to the profession, but to our nation's children, and ultimately to the country's future. If talented teachers are not attracted and retained, can we expect quality instruction?

I've been a member of the Minnesota Federation of Teachers for almost 10 years. I believe strongly in the rights of working people. However, the first obligation of our schools is to help young people. Like many others, I am convinced that the seniority system used to retain, assign, and pay educators does not serve our youth or this nation.

Staffing was viewed as critical in both the traditional and open schools discussed in this chapter. After extensive negotiation, the district allowed the Open School advisory council to recommend about half of the staff be hired from outside the district. Thus the original staff represented a mix of 50 percent present and 50 percent new teachers. The school quickly lost control of its staff. As people decided to leave (often to take administrative positions), their jobs were taken by other district employees. Some were supportive of the school's philosophy, others openly hostile to it. Nevertheless, the Open School found it impossible to prevent the district from placing whoever it wished at the school, in both administrative and teaching positions.

At Open School staff meetings, several faculty denounced the school philosophy. They would have been happier, and more effective, in schools with different philosophies. However, in several cases, there were no other openings. It was either accept a position at the Open School, or face unemployment. Teachers were allowed to select positions on the basis of seniority, and all the faculty with more seniority had chosen to go elsewhere.

Similar frustrations were reported by parents at a traditional-fundamental school. They reported an inability to retain staff who shared their school's philosophy. This is a classic example of how unusual and effective programs, serving clear constituencies, can be hindered by a district's contractual arrangements.

Seniority assumes that the best way to keep quality is to retain people on the basis of their years of experience. Seniority systems were developed because teachers feared they would be evaluated unfairly, and discriminated against by administrators who disagreed with their methods. Though examples of these instances are plentiful, I believe we have better alternatives to meet the needs of youngsters and talented, hardworking teachers.

As more cuts are made, remaining teachers will become older and more expensive. In many school districts, there are few teachers with less than 10 years experience. Public schools end up with fewer, more expensive teachers who have ever larger classes. Is this what we want? Seniority and salary problems are well known to everyone involved in education. They have discouraged thousands of talented young people from entering the profession, eliminated thousands of effective teachers, and angered mature, excellent instructors.

These problems are well known to millions of parents and community members. In 1981, pollster George Gallup asked a representative national sample about seniority in education and received unusually unified answers. The question concerned the basis by which teachers should be laid off if a school district needed to save money. Seventy-eight percent said teachers should be kept on the basis of performance; only 17 percent said they should be retained on the basis of seniority! (Gallup, 1981). Despite considerable opposition, the seniority link in the public school system chain remains. It inhibits lasting, meaningful improvements.

There is a final barrier to public school excellence: *Excessive reliance on teacher certification systems.* It's worth comparing requirements of college professors with those governing instructors in our elementary and secondary schools. Do we require medical or law school professors to complete a teacher preparation program? Of course not! Teacher education programs are notorious for their poor quality. A variety of recent studies have pointed out that between one-third and one-quarter of recent teacher preparation graduates have been unable to pass minimal writing or computation examinations.

Colleges frequently bring in professionals to provide instruction—journalists, insurance agents, computer programmers, politicians, etc. None of these people would be allowed to teach courses in the public schools. They would have to obtain certification first!

Students suffer in another way. As cuts are made, more teachers are instructing outside their area of primary expertise. For example, a teacher may hold certification in English, Social Studies, and Physical Education but have taught exclusively in only one of those fields. After seniority cuts, the person may end up teaching something she/he has seldom, if ever, taught! The person may not have enough seniority to retain her/his job as an English or Social Studies teacher. Thus, after cuts are made, the physical education teacher with the least experience might have 11 years seniority, while the youngest Social Studies teacher might have 15 years experience. More and more school districts are encountering this problem. Can we expect the quality of education to improve as people teach outside their areas of expertise?

I'm not suggesting that anyone can teach well. But holding certification in a certain field is no guarantee of high quality instruction. The update chapter describes several valuable alternative routes into teaching.

As Seymour Sarason wrote more than a decade ago, the fundamental problems of schools are more those of the system than of individuals who work in that system. We have developed potent teaching and organizational techniques, but public schools have resisted their widespread adoption.

The fundamental barriers to widespread excellence are:

1. Enormous bureaucratic pressure toward standardization.
2. Institutional complexity and overload.
3. Lack of strong incentives for responsiveness and achievement.
4. Contractual arrangements preventing staff assignment on the basis of philosophical compatibility with programs.
5. Use of the seniority system to retain and pay educators.
6. Unwarranted reliance on teacher certification procedures.

A case can be made for seniority, bureaucracy, and centralized decision-making, but experience suggests that their disadvantages outweigh their benefits. The present system of public education acts as a leash around the necks of millions of youngsters and teachers, limiting and frustrating them.

These are difficult, controversial judgments, but necessary ones. We've tried to improve student achievement by building better facilities. It didn't help. We tried to satisfy teachers' demands for better pay, hoping this would improve test scores and student attitudes. It didn't. Universities tried to develop curriculum materials which were teacher proof. They weren't. National legislation was passed providing millions of dollars for school reform. Most of the improvements died after the money ran out. It's time to rearrange the system by which educational opportunities are made available to young people and their families.

A just society should not provide better educational opportunities for its affluent people. A wise society should not accept a 25 percent national drop-out rate. A thoughtful society should not tolerate the future suggested by a 1979 Carnegie Report, based on current trends: "One third of our youth illeducated, ill-employed, ill-equipped to make their way . . . "

Lincoln said it well:

The dogmas of the quiet past are inadequate for the stormy present. As our case is new, so we must think anew and act anew. We must disenthrall ourselves, and then we shall save our country.

VALUABLE STRUCTURAL CHANGES

This country has many ideas for education improvements. Some reforms have made schools adopting them more effective. The challenge is to encourage widespread adoption of these strategies. Each of the ideas suggested below has worked.

The first suggestion is to stop construction of buildings devoted exclusively to schools. Every building which serves as a school or educational center for youngsters learning ought also to host other agencies and businesses.

New York City pioneered this concept. With assistance from the New York City Educational Construction Fund, more than a dozen buildings have been completed which house combinations of profit making groups, social service agencies, schools, and apartments. The Bergtraum High School for Business Careers is directly underneath an American Telephone and Telegraph service center. Many of the school's 2500 students have internships in the companies on top of or surrounding the school. Park West High School has 3500 students and a 395 apartment building for low and moderate income families.

Shared facilities are also appropriate in much smaller towns than New York. Springfield, Massachusetts, established its New North Community School almost 10 years ago. In addition to a school for 1000 5th and 6th graders, the

121

complex houses a public library, senior citizen center, pre-school recreation program, and various community agencies. The school's principal, Mary Dryden, notes that "we're able to serve people here from ages 3 to 93!"

Rural areas can make better use of their school buildings. The hamlet of Malta, Illinois, rents several rooms in its elementary school to a community college. Several small Michigan towns have social service agencies and town librar-ies in their local school.

Boston has 18 elementary schools which share space with social service agencies. The Quincy Community School houses more than a dozen social service agencies and occupies an entire city block. One corner of the block is occupied by a high-rise apartment building for senior cit-izens. Contact between the young people and seniors is encouraged. It's good for everyone involved!

In St. Paul, a community center was recently constructed next to and is connected by tunnel with a large older school, Washington Junior High. The center houses 11 agencies, including a nursery school/daycare center, senior citizen activity program, community college program, medical clinic, delinquency prevention program, and monthly com-munity newspaper. The building operates under a "joint powers agreement" between the city government and school district.

Another community center was built next door to an ele-mentary school. The center contains a number of social ser-vice agencies, while the school has a pool which has been opened to the entire community.

Wichita, Kansas, used the same general idea several years ago in constructing a new public library. The library is in a public school between an elementary program and daycare center/nursery school. Books in the library are available to the school children and the general public. The building's administrator reports that the community's use of its library has been excellent.

Shared facilities have many advantages. The financial ben-efit is obvious. Heating, cooling, security, and construction costs are reduced for each agency when it shares a building. A 1983 American Association of School Administrators study found that more than 60 percent of the urban school districts studied were laying off teachers and other personnel in order to help pay heating bills (AASA, 1983). Joint occupancy of a building would provide more money for instructional purposes.

Business people should consider advantages of moving certain facilities into school buildings. Bankers would gain by having automatic teller machines in secondary schools. Young people have a great deal of money but often don't get in the habit of saving it. An automatic teller machine in their school could encourage thrift. Some school districts are considering contracting with fast food restaurants to locate in their buildings. This has been done in one Florida district where the restaurant provides both employment and food. Real estate agents, doctors, dentists, artists, counselors, and other service groups might find advantages in relatively low rent available in vacant or underused space. Businesses can make real contributions to improving education not just by providing grants, but by sharing space.

A related advantage is found in the increased learning opportunities which are available. Young people from the St. Paul junior high school help out at the next door nursery school as part of their classwork in child development classes. Senior citizens who come to the North End Community Center often spend some time tutoring youngsters at the junior high. Several youthworkers from the community center have guided the school's peer counseling programs. A number of young people have written articles or taken pictures for the *North End News,* their community's newspaper which is published monthly at the center.

What are the barriers to constructing such buildings throughout the country? For one thing, organizational patterns differ. Before Wichita constructed a cooperative library, the school and city librarians had to resolve the fact that they used different systems to catalog the books. Another issue was, Whose librarians would staff the facility, those hired by the city or those hired by the school district? Would they be paid on the same salary schedule, or continue with their respective employers' salary schedule? Ultimately, the Wichita decision was to hire both city and school librarians, each reporting to the business administrator.

St. Paul recently considered developing a similar library to make the best use of limited city and school district funds. Librarians insisted that many adults would feel less comfortable coming to the library. This has not been Wichita's or Springfield's experience. In some discussions, I suspected that the real problem was the fear that somewhat fewer city and school librarians would be needed if the two organizations cooperated. This may be true and must be faced squarely. Libraries, like schools, exist primarily to help citizens learn and expand their knowledge. The purpose of a library or school is only secondarily to provide employment for librarians, teachers, and administrators. Sometimes people lose sight of that fact.

During its 1984 session, the Minnesota legislature took two actions recognizing the value of shared facilities. The first changed a statutory debt law to provide more incentives for shared facilities. The second asked the Commissioner of Education to review results of shared educational facilities around the country and publish a report which will be available to educators and citizens around the state.

People who want more information and don't want to wait until the Minnesota study is completed should contact the Educational Facilities Laboratory, 680 5th Avenue, New York, N.Y. 10019. Their book *Community School Centers* is the best statement of the rationale and mechanics of operating a shared facility.

A second reform strategy enables parents to choose from among public schools with various philosophies and sizes. Mario Fantini's *Public Schools of Choice* is a major statement of this philosophy. Fantini points out that the opportunity to choose is a central American freedom. Consumers are not told which car to buy or where they must live. Food stamp recipients are not told where to shop. The government does not tell parents where to send their children for daycare or nursery school.

Many school districts have tried to provide parents and students with certain alternatives. Virtually every large city school district offers some "open" and "fundamental" programs, as well as the mainstream schools. Some public schools offer Montessori programs, based on the Italian educator's ideas. Some rural or suburban school districts offer "in school alternatives" which depart from the traditional and offer parents and their children some choice.

Choices could be expanded significantly within public schools. In many school districts, students only have one program they may attend. This is particularly true in rural or suburban areas, where there is only one elementary and secondary school. The state of Vermont provides a useful alternative. For a number of years, the state has allowed towns to decide whether to have their own school, to join with other towns to form a unified school district, or to offer parents choices in nearby towns. 95 of the 246 towns in Vermont fall in the last category, and allow parents to select from a number of elementary or secondary schools (McLaughery). The town board pays tuition to the schools selected by parents. Each town must have a written policy about whether transportation is provided to all students or only to handicapped students. Vermont schools have quite different characteristics—some more traditional, others more progressive, some more, others less receptive to parent involvement.

Middletown Springs, Vermont, is located in the west central part of the state. In the 1982-83 school year the town had 61 students in grades 7-12. 26 of those students attended school in Mill River, 17 in West Rutland, 12 in Poultney, 3 in various private schools, and 3 in other schools.

Many of the people with whom I talked during a weeklong visit to Vermont endorsed the choice program. They said it has caused few problems and increased parental support for schools. The chair of the state Board of Education, Vi Luginbuhl, said that parents like the opportunity to match their children's learning styles with different kinds of schools.

During its 1983-84 session, the Minnesota legislature passed a landmark bill increasing choices for certain students. Lawmakers agreed that some districts have outstanding programs. The legislature asked the Minnesota Commissioner of Education to draw up guidelines which would allow students from one district to transfer to another district which offered a state-approved "program of excellence."

During legislative hearings, the Minnesota Commissioner of Education, Dr. Ruth Randall, testified that she would favor permitting students to attend public schools outside the district in which they live without paying tuition. Presently students' education is free only in the district where they reside, unless the local board authorizes payment from its district to another (this is sometimes done for handicapped students). Students are permitted to pay tuition to attend public school in another district, and some students do this. The Commissioner's recommendations would significantly expand students' choices.

Recently, Denis Doyle of the American Enterprise Institute in Washington and Chester Finn of Vanderbilt University proposed a statewide public school choice system. They believe that educational finance reforms logically demand financing which is not based on local wealth. As programs throughout a state are more equally funded, more choices will increase parent satisfaction. Their paper illustrates ways to implement what Randall is suggesting (Finn and Doyle).

Dr. Randall has recommended other ways to expand choices using technology. The legislature has funded several programs which use computers, two-way cable television, and videodiscs to provide several programs some districts find it difficult to afford. Several districts are cooperating to produce an advanced trigonometry course which students will take using both computers and videodiscs. In other parts of the state, school districts will be using cable television to offer advanced language and science courses which they could not offer by themselves.

In some parts of rural Minnesota, neighboring schools have decided to cooperate by making different courses available to students from participating districts. In one area, for example, a secondary school offers courses in Spanish to students from several districts, while another school offers advanced science courses. In another area, cooperating schools offer different vocational classes. One secondary school specializes in auto mechanics, another in electronic repair. In these cases, the schools are less than 10 miles apart, though they are located in separate districts. The schools find it more cost effective to bus students to other schools part of the day than to duplicate each other's course offerings.

Public school options are not just for rural areas. Many districts offer choices within public schools, choices based on instructional method, curriculum focus, or a mixture of the two. Dr. Mary Anne Raywid of Hofstra University studied more than 2500 secondary alternative programs located throughout the country (Raywid, p. 13). In about ⅔ of the 1200 secondary schools which responded to Raywid's study, alternative programs cost the same as or less than traditional programs in their district. Schools report that attendance and attitude of most students improved significantly after they began attending the alternative program.

Another national study was completed recently of magnet public schools. Magnet schools "can be a means of renewing the interests and motivation of teachers by organizing their efforts around a common academic goal and developing inter-disciplinary curriculum planning, writing and quality improvements" (Lowry). A number of cities, including Houston, Cincinnati, Dallas, New York City, St. Paul, Minneapolis, and Boston, have developed exciting, specialized magnet programs.

Some magnet schools cost much more money than the average school in the district. Others do not. They certainly are helping the young people who attend them. But an important question is what impact the magnet school has on other schools in the district. Many Chicago teachers are deeply critical of the way magnet schools have been carried out in their city. Magnet schools have pulled out many of the brightest, most able students and teachers from neighborhood schools. The magnet programs have extra financial resources, eager students, and capable teachers. No wonder neighborhood school staff resent the situation!

A more effective way to provide choices has been pioneered by Community School District 4 in New York City. This East Harlem area has no neighborhood public junior high schools. Instead, students have a variety of choices. Many of these programs were created by groups of teachers, encouraged by the area superintendent. Several of the programs focus on a particular academic or curricular area. Program specialties include math, computer literacy and science, or performing arts, or liberal arts, and, in one case, a marine-based curriculum. Despite being located in an extremely poor area, the district finds itself deluged with applications from parents living in more affluent areas.

Previous chapters illustrated concerns about these public alternatives. In many cases, these programs have been altered, even distorted, by school district mandates. Parents in many places have been frustrated because the programs in which they wanted their children enrolled were full, and the district was unwilling to start another, similar program.

Sometimes desegregation orders prevent youngsters from attending a program. For example, in St. Paul there is an outstanding elementary school named Webster Magnet. It is located in the neighborhood with the highest concentration of Black families in the city. White students living outside the attendance area are able to transfer into the program to help meet desegregation guidelines imposed by the state Department of Education. However, Black and other minority students from outside the immediate neighborhood cannot transfer into Webster.

Across the river in Minneapolis, many Black and Native American parents are angry because of similar problems. In some cases, they are not even allowed to attend the schools closest to their homes because the program does not attract enough White students. So, people of color see their children bussed away from their neighborhoods. Isn't it ironic that a desegregation program intended to prevent this situation has actually forced it!

The St. Louis, Missouri, desegregation plan expands choices for many young people. How does the plan affect Black students, whose advocates filed the original lawsuit?

Black students who have not been disruptive in schools are allowed to transfer into suburban schools. Any Black student who wishes to transfer into the suburbs must agree to a check on his/her behavior. The director of the desegregation program acknowledges that some students have been denied admission to suburban public schools on the basis of previous behavior. Black students who want to attend various magnet schools in the city may apply to attend. Several neighborhood schools have been closed and changed into magnet schools.

Some Black students who have applied to attend these schools have been unable to attend because the schools have been magnetized and may not be overwhelmingly Black.

What about White students? The program expands choices for both urban and suburban Whites, but with a significant difference. Suburban Whites are allowed to transfer into the city to attend any of various magnet schools. Thus, White students with affluent parents (who can afford to live in the suburbs) have a significant expansion of their educational opportunities. White students who live in the city may select from among various urban magnet schools, but are not allowed to transfer into the suburbs. Thus White students from wealthy families are able to choose between the suburban and urban schools. Low income Whites are limited to choices inside the city. Despite being widely acclaimed as a metropolitan desegregation program, the St. Louis plan appears guaranteed to produce increased resentment and conflict.

Not all districts are willing to respond to parental suggestions and recommendations. In one small town, parents tried for 3 years to convince their school board to establish a classroom or school within school for elementary grades which had allowed students to (1) read real books, rather than watered-down text and workbooks, (2) work at their own pace, rather than having essentially the same lessons as other children their own age, (3) use the community as a place from which to learn. After 3 years of rejection by the school board, the parents opened a private school. They were deeply committed to public education but were even more committed to what they viewed as appropriate education for their children.

On one Native American reservation, parents found their public school staff to be unresponsive. Some of the (White) townspeople openly regard Indians as subhuman. Some English, home economics, and social studies teachers refused to accept community suggestions for curriculum improvement. American history books did not include contributions from Native Americans to our culture and described westward expansion as a great civilizing movement, without reviewing the strength of Indian cultures or mentioning that treaties were violated in the process. English teachers insisted that

there were no worthwhile Native American authors and home
economics teachers wouldn't incorporate into their curriculum certain recipes which reflected local culture.

The hostility toward Native Americans produced a bad
educational environment. Native American students were
being suspended from school much more often than Whites,
and tension was increasing among the White and Indian
students.

Finally, the reservation parents decided to establish their
own school. Test scores, attendance, and graduation rates
went up dramatically. While the parents do not regard this
school as perfect, they view it as much better than the one
where their ideas were ridiculed and rejected.

Sometimes rural districts do try to establish programs to
meet needs of all their students. In one town, a superintendent
and director of an alternative program sadly described what
had happened to their alternative school. The district had
experienced declining enrollment for several years. 5 years
earlier it had established a small alternative program for
approximately 75 teenage students. About 3 staff people
work full-time, and several others part-time with these young
people. In the last 3 years, 40-50 percent of these staff
members have been cut each year. Both the alternative school
director and superintendent recognize that the program's
quality has declined, but wonder what to do, when they are
caught in a situation where seniority must be followed in
making staff cuts.

In one city nationally known for providing alternatives,
parents recently met to talk about how things were going.
While pleased that they had choices, there were numerous
concerns. Parents from the Montessori program reported several problems: the program was located in a building amidst
other programs and the principal did not have a keen interest
in or orientation toward their program. Few of the teachers
had any upper level training in the Montessori approach or
interest in pursuing it.

Open school parents felt the district was handing down a
number of curriculum directives which violated the program's philosophy. The school also had a substantial waiting
list, and the district appeared to be ignoring people who

wanted to get into the open program.

Parents whose children attend a continuous progress model were dismayed because the most important element of the program—having the kids move along at their own ability levels—was not happening. Parents felt the district was advertising things which weren't really happening.

Contemporary school parents were equally unhappy. They felt that all students whose parents didn't select any other model were dumped into the contemporary program. They had been promised that parent input would be sought. Instead, they felt it was unwelcome.

Parents from all the programs said they had tried to meet with administrators and school board members. They returned depressed or angry. Generally they were told to be satisfied with what they had, that it was better than most school systems.

Parents and teachers in an eastern state encountered problems when they tried to use noncertified staff in their public alternative school. One of the parents was an Academy Award winning actor who offered to teach a drama class. The local teachers' union protested to the state department, which ruled that the actor could not teach the class.

Concerned teachers encountered other frustrations in public schools. In one urban district, a building principal and teachers received ten computers and a mandate to use the computers only to teach students a certain computer language. Teachers would not be allowed to use the computers to help students learn to write (via word processing), could not use the computers to keep records or generate tests, and could not allow other teachers to use the computers unless they participated in central-office approved training programs. While the central office concern that computers not be misused or underused is understandable, the teachers felt they were being treated like stupid children.

In another urban district, several alternative school teachers had conflicts with other teachers after a contract was settled with the school board. The contract stipulated working hours: teachers were to be in the buildings 20 minutes before and after school. Administrators could not require teachers to be in buildings after that unless they were paid additional money.

While some teachers thought this was appropriate, others felt that the contract was inconsistent with the legitimate role of a teacher. Some of these teachers regularly stayed after school for 45-60 minutes to talk with students or prepare for the next day. They were harshly criticized by teachers who said "staying after school makes the rest of us look bad— don't do it or we'll file a complaint!" Those staying after school were in a quandary. How could they stay on good terms with other teachers while continuing to do their job as they felt it should be done?

Other alternative school teachers shared another frustration. Several faculty members of one "open school" readily confessed they wanted to work in the school because it was close to their home, or because they were coaching at a nearby building. They would have preferred to work in a program with a different philosophy but their seniority was too low to obtain an assignment in a school which fit their teaching style.

A group of parents described their frustration with a school board's insistence on controlling principals. One "fundamental" school established by a Black parents'/ministers' group in cooperation with a school district had a strong Black woman principal removed and reassigned to another school. One of the parent group's major concerns had been to have more Black role models in administrative positions. A White male principal with no strong commitment to the school's philosophy was assigned to the building. Another school with a very liberal philosophy found itself assigned a succession of principals who publicly criticized the school's curriculum, parents, and students.

Those who insist that options should be limited to public education must find some way to deal with these issues. The fundamental problems with limiting parents' choices to public schools are:

1. Distinctive public schools often are not allowed to hire faculty who believe in the school's philosophy. Particularly in areas where enrollments have declined, younger teachers have been cut and replacements sometimes do not share the school's

philosophy. They accepted the assignment for other reasons.
2. Public schools are bound by certification requirements. They generally must use people who meet state requirements, regardless of other background, experience, and expertise.
3. Principals who do not share or strongly disagree with a program's philosophy sometimes are assigned to buildings by central office administrators.
4. A program's effectiveness is no guarantee of its continued existence. In many districts, alternative programs were closed when budget cuts had to be made, despite waiting lists, above average standardized test scores, and strong support from the families they served. There is no focused pressure for school districts to replicate successful programs. As former Dean of the UCLA School of Education John Goodlad concluded after studying 1000 classrooms around the country, "The cards are stacked against deviation and innovation" (Goodlad, 1983).
5. Affluent parents have significantly more choices than low and moderate income families. They can select neighborhoods in which to live and decide whether to send their children to a public or private school. They can select "public" schools in affluent suburbs which are not available to low income children. The unjust gap in choice for rich and poor cannot be eliminated in a democratic capitalistic society, but it can be reduced.
6. The best public programs may be full. Not all students from low income families will be able to attend the school which their parents believe is most appropriate for them. Meanwhile, high income families can move to areas served by their favorite schools, or pick a private school.

Public schools need not develop *all* the choices which they offer to parents. Another way to proceed is for school districts to extend the contracting system. Many school districts purchase food, equipment, and transportation services from a private company. They should consider purchase of instructional services.

Manhattan's District 4 encourages and empowers professional educators to create effective programs for low income youth. The Ombudsman program in suburban Chicago is another example of educators who have created a program to work with alienated, disruptive students who might other-

wise drop out or be expelled. Ombudsman staff contract with
district officials to work with a certain number of students
and provide a highly individualized program where students
move at their own pace and must demonstrate competence
before graduating. Ombudsman has a strong seven-year
record of improving students' self-concept, increasing test
scores, and raising attendance rates.

Another privately controlled program contracts with public school districts, something like the Ombudsman program.
Smokey House Project is located on 5000 acres of hillside and
valley in southwestern Vermont, 25 miles from Rutland. In
operation for more than a decade, the project staff work
exclusively with extremely angry, disruptive students.

These students are expected to help Smokey House in
various ways, and in so doing they gain employment skills.
Students learn how to build houses, how to gather maple
syrup, how to maintain and improve forests, and other
extremely practical skills. At the same time, the students
learn to plan and work with others in a group. Their outdoor
experiences help convince them it's important to have reading
and computation skills. They discover how careful reading
saves time when trying to determine how others put up a
building.

Smokey House has been judged a nationally outstanding
innovation by the U.S. Department of Labor. Public school
superintendents in Vermont speak highly of it and willingly
commit funds to help support it. None of the staff is a
certified teacher.

This teacher partnership idea intrigued a recent college
graduate in St. Paul, Jessica Shaten. She established a company, Math Unlimited, which contracts with various groups
including corporations to provide math instruction to their
employees. Shaten suggests that school districts allow teachers to establish their own partnerships (Shaten and Kolderie).

In one suburban district, a group of teachers have created
their own Advanced Placement American History class
which is transmitted via cable television to several neighboring districts. These teachers are intrigued about the possibility of going into business for themselves, creating other
courses which they could then market to various districts. The

Minnesota legislature recently authorized the Department of Education to study several structural improvements in education, one of which may be the teacher partnership concept.

Minneapolis has pioneered partnerships with alternative schools which it does not control. More than a decade ago several social service organizations developed programs to help students who either had dropped out or felt they had been pushed out of the schools. Organizations sponsoring the alternatives include the Urban League, Plymouth Christian Youth Center, Loring-Nicollet Community Center, City, Inc., and Na-way-ee, a Native American organization. The alternative schools are small (35-65 students), located in old houses or storefronts, and have a number of caring, committed, noncertified teachers.

Since the early 1970s, the Minneapolis district has provided a certain amount of money for each of these students, a state-certified counselor who works with the programs, plus lunch and access to the district's audiovisual library. The alternative schools agree to maintain graduation requirements comparable to the public schools, and their students receive a public school diploma.

A North Central accreditation team recently concluded that the schools were doing an excellent job of helping these students increase basic and applied skills along with improving their self concept (North Central). The Minneapolis program illustrates another way to approach the issue of choice. Some people have argued against allowing private schools to receive tax funds until the private schools meet the same requirements as public schools in such areas as teacher certification, seniority, tenure, and programs for handicapped students.

Another way to think about this issue is to reduce the number of requirements for public schools! We should not back away from our commitment to handicapped students. However, it would be desirable to reduce some of the mandates on public schools in such areas as teacher and administrator certification, seniority, and hours spent on a particular subject. The cooperative arrangement between the Minneapolis Public Schools and Federation of Alternative Schools shows that some students can learn in schools which do not meet all the requirements now in place for public schools.

In some parts of the country, public school districts choose not to develop certain programs required by their legislature. In such cases (usually with handicapped students), districts contract either with a private school or with another school district which in turn develops a program. This is happening in the Minneapolis-St. Paul area. A number of suburban school districts send handicapped children into one of the two cities to take advantage of large special education programs.

The Ombudsman program offers another example of how some school districts are providing services to their students outside the schools they control directly. The Ombudsman director retains complete control over his budget and staff. School districts give him a percentage of the per pupil allotment and a certain number of students with whom to work.

Such arrangements offer many advantages. The program is designed for many youngsters whose needs clearly are not being met by large public schools. Ombudsman has been able to retain its distinctive features. Excellent staff members have been hired and paid well. The young people like the program far more than previous schools. Standardized testing shows that the youngsters are making substantial progress.

Unfortunately, Ombudsman-type programs are not available to everyone who wishes to attend. The school district, not the parents or students, decides who will be assigned to Ombudsman. How does a student become a candidate for referral to Ombudsman? It appears that the student wanting to go there should begin to disrupt and disturb as many people as possible. When the district tires of trying to deal with the youngster's disruption, then and only then will the student be offered the opportunity to attend Ombudsman.

Presently, many school districts are not under major pressures to deal with disruptive students. Most boards of education and superintendents appear to be far more concerned about raising test scores than meeting needs of disruptive students. Pacific News Service reporter Elizabeth Lafferty studied this issue with the support of the Fund for Investigative Journalism. She reported, "Under widespread attack on the issue of educational performance, school systems ironically stand to 'improve' their average test results through the de facto weeding out of many problem students who, in dropping out, simply disappear from enrollment lists."

About ten years ago the Gary, Indiana, School District tried to improve students' scores by hiring an outside company (Behavioral Research Laboratories) to work with its employees. The program did not succeed. I think it failed for two reasons:

First, the teachers had no incentive to make BRL look good. They resented the company's statements that they had not been working up to their potential. They disliked textbooks that BRL insisted that they use and were irritated by payments to the company.

Second, the company gave the teachers very little opportunity to use their own creativity and knowledge of the youngsters. The company brought in a very tightly organized curriculum and told the teachers to use it. Many of the teachers resented the attitude and approach of the company.

The differences between the Gary, Indiana, and Ombudsman programs are extremely significant. Ombudsman staff volunteer to participate. The Gary teachers didn't. Some Ombudsman staff have financial incentives for improved performance. The Gary teachers didn't. Ombudsman staff help to shape their program. The Gary teachers didn't. It's no surprise that Ombudsman is successful, and the Gary program wasn't!

Contracting for services is a strategy which has many advantages and only a few disadvantages. Those problems are significant. Contracting still does not allow parents to place their children in the schools they regard as most appropriate. In some cases, contracting of the sort Ombudsman does may encourage students to disrupt their schools.

Another reform strategy is for a central school district to provide far greater flexibility for its own programs to manage funds. This proposal is known as "school site management." Schools would be given a certain number of dollars, and they would choose how to spend it. For example, some schools might decide to hire 1 or 2 fewer teachers and purchase computers or a bus with the money they save. Some "site management" schools have established "mini-grant programs" in which individuals or small groups of teachers may apply for $300-$1000 to try some special project.

Many businesses are investigating the advantages of the "quality circle" idea which is used extensively in Japan. During college I had the opportunity to spend a summer in Japan and watched several of these programs in operation. A number of American companies are now finding that they can improve employee morale and the quality of their products by listening carefully to suggestions from people who are closest to the production line.

The concept is simple—and reasonable. People responsible for carrying out a program often have ideas about how to cut costs or increase efficiency. Moreover, people all over the world like to have their opinions considered. People like to feel that their suggestions are considered. No one of us knows as much as all of us.

In a few places, districts have tried to provide incentives for building staffs to reduce absenteeism, thus cutting substitute costs. Statistics were compiled on the average number of days absent in a particular school over the last several years, and an average was computed. If a school staff was able to reduce the number of absent days, it received the savings to spend on various supplies and equipment.

These attempts to provide more authority and accountability at a building level are commendable. They offer excellent opportunities to build on the expertise and talent of fine teachers.

Unfortunately, they have many of the same limitations as other ideas suggested earlier in the chapter. Parents still are unable to select the programs which they find most appropriate. School site management programs, like all other such reform efforts, operate only as long as a central decision making group (the superintendent and board of education) allow. As educational research shows, the most effective, efficient programs are not always the ones maintained in such a system.

There is one final suggestion which will be appreciated throughout the country, though it contradicts "professional wisdom" of the last 20 years. This country has seriously underestimated the value of small schools.

What advantages do small schools have? Regardless of their location (city or small town), smaller schools have higher achievement results on standardized tests, far less violence, and far greater involvement of young people in various activities.

Unlike larger schools, many small schools will not have both a debate club and speech program, newspaper, yearbook, and literary magazine, and a vast number of athletic programs. However, careful research shows that a far higher percentage of students at small schools than at large schools have participated in these valuable activities.

Certainly large schools are able to offer a greater number of courses. But a vast range of courses is not the most important aspect of schools where young people learn to achieve—and gain skills. Virtually every American president has come from a small town and attended a small school. Did this prevent achievement? Obviously not.

There are a number of valuable books on this subject. The most helpful to me have been Barker's classic *Big School, Small School,* Scher's *Education in Rural America,* and Sale's *Human Scale.* The World Health Organization summarized research on this subject by explaining:

> So many wise books and reports have appeared in recent years on the principles which should be followed in organizing institutions for children that little discussion is called for here. All are agreed that institutions should be small in order to avoid the rules and regulations which cannot be avoided in large establishments.

This research will come as no surprise to many people in rural areas who protested against school consolidation. They recognized the value of schools to their communities and the children who lived in them.

Opponents of small schools sometimes argue that the schools are too expensive to maintain. Certainly it's difficult to have a strong K-12 curriculum for 5-10 students. However, the economies of scale which many professionals forecast for huge schools have failed to materialize. Far more money has been required for security, repair of damaged property, and administrative services. The expected savings usually were not realized.

In this chapter I have discussed a number of suggestions for improvements in education through structural changes within the public schools:

1. Establish community service centers, rather than school buildings. Combine other agencies and businesses in the same building, allowing financial savings and cross-fertilization of staff and physical facilities.
2. Provide a range of carefully evaluated, distinctive public school programs from which parents, students, and staff may choose.
3. Establish contractual arrangements between school districts and outstanding educators. Provide these people with funds and the flexibility to establish and maintain programs as they see fit.
4. Provide opportunities for greater involvement of staff, parents, and students by establishing "school site management" programs. Make sure that the councils developed have power to make real and significant decisions.
5. Retain small schools.

Each and all of the proposals made would allow taxpayers' money to be spent in a more cost-effective manner. Several of the proposals would provide stronger incentives for excellent teaching. Parents and their children would have more choices than at present. These are important, worthy goals and should not be dismissed.

Americans justifiably are skeptical of "quick fixes." Nevertheless, our country has produced a number of creative solutions to educational problems. Many of these approaches are no more expensive than traditional ones. This country can have more productive, effective schools without spending additional money.

RESPECTING FAMILY CHOICE

The Anderson family has four children, ages eight through seventeen. Robin, seventeen, is independent and thoughtful; she has done well in school, getting good grades and being elected to leadership positions in the student council and band. She hopes to be a professional musician. Having demonstrated her competence in the locally required life skills, she now has the option either to attend college or apprentice with a local musician. Fourteen-year-old Karl is not organized, at least about academic matters. He spends almost half an hour each morning in the bathroom, combing his hair and attempting to make himself look like the latest rock stars. Karl and his parents agree that he needs close supervision if he is to make much academic progress. He attends a nearby private school of three hundred students, ages thirteen through eighteen. Twelve-year-old Ben really likes sports. He's attending an outstanding public magnet school which requires all of its students to participate in at least one sport and do at least two hours of homework each night. Sally Anderson, the eight-year-old, loves animals. She's attending an elementary school at the local zoo which uses animals as a key motivator in helping students learn mathematics, reading, writing, ecology and art. The zoo school is so popular that it had a waiting list for some time. Zoo authorities now have opened a second program in response to parental interest.

The Jackson family lives several miles from the Andersons. Mrs. Jackson is raising the kids by herself after her husband's death in an automobile accident. Things have been tough. Warren, at sixteen the oldest of the Jackson children, is eager to get on with his life. He's almost finished demonstrating competence in the required life skills and plans to start a full-time computer programming course run by a major multinational computer company. The corporation promises jobs to outstanding students, and Warren intends to be one of them. Warren's twelve-year-old sister is not sure what she wants to do after graduating. Right now, she's happy attending the neighborhood public school with her friends. Her nine-year-old brother attends the same school and seems to do well. As a single working mother, Mrs. Jackson appreciates the fact that the school maintains a variety of interesting programs from 7:00 A.M. through 5:00 P.M. The school shares facilities with a neighborhood youth center, a bank, and day care program, allowing it to provide a range of services.

The O'Toole family lives near the Andersons and Jacksons. Kevin and Marge O'Toole have a large family: seven children. Until recently, Kevin worked in an assembly plant, but he was laid off, and the family finances are tight. The O'Toole children have attended a variety of schools in their town, but all began with the parish schools for kindergarten through fifth grade. The O'Tooles believe the school gives their children a strong foundation in values and academics. Last year Marge O'Toole joined the staff of a new, parent controlled school which has purchased fifty computers for its one hundred students. Three of her children attend this school, which has attracted students from throughout the city. Several of the school's teachers are parents and former public or private school teachers. They are willing to work with larger classes so there is money for computers and a bus which takes children throughout the metropolitan area on field trips.

In thinking about school reform, we need to begin with families. The ideal educational opportunities described above are available today only to those citizens who can afford them.

In the 1980s, Americans face fundamental questions about their educational systems, including

- Do our public schools challenge all our students?
- Do our public schools prepare students for the future?
- Do cost efficient methods exist to improve public schools?
- Are the incentives sufficient to have widespread adoption of these methods in our public schools?
- Do our public schools attract and retain the finest teachers?
- Is our society well served by continued funding of ineffective schools?
- Must this society accept far more attractive and effective educational programs for the rich?

Those who see room for improvement should consider reforms which change public schools' fundamental structure. Two basic changes have been suggested recently: tuition tax credits and vouchers. Tuition tax credits allow families to deduct tuition paid to private schools from their income taxes. Vouchers provide a certain number of tax dollars for each child which the family can award to any school it chooses—much as World War II veterans were funded to further their education and training under the G.I. Bill. The first probably would make things worse; the second probably would help produce more effective schools.

Tuition tax credits (TTC) discriminate against the poor. They offer little to low income families, who are least able to opt out of public schools. Families on welfare or with low paying jobs pay relatively little or no income tax and would receive minimal benefit from a plan which subtracts tuition from taxes. These tax credits would be significantly more beneficial for middle and upper income families. Such a program seems to discriminate against the poor.

A second problem with TTC is that they add nothing to public support for education funding. In fact, these credits will reduce tax revenue, thus increasing the competition between education and other government programs. Families whose children attend private schools will have no direct incentives to support funding for public schools.

The third problem with TTC is that they probably would not stimulate the development of new schools and learning opportunities. The present tax deduction plans in TTC proposals call for no more than $500 in tuition to be allowed as a credit against federal taxes. In most states, public schools are spending at least $1500 per pupil. In some affluent school districts, per pupil expenditures are more than $3000.

As explained earlier, schools can be far more effectively operated without additional funds. Some private schools (especially those associated with religious groups) are doing a fine job while spending less than the public school average. However, it is difficult to foresee many schools able to function solely on the $500 per pupil tax credit.

While not encouraging establishment of new schools, tuition tax credits would help middle and upper income parents remove their children from public schools. Thus, these credits would make the public school population primarily low income.

A voucher program, another proposal for changing the fundamental structure of public schools, need have none of these basic disadvantages. Vouchers could stimulate additional learning opportunities. They could significantly expand the range of choices available to low and moderate income families. They could encourage many bright, able people to become educators or stay in the field. Finally, vouchers offer an opportunity to develop coalitions of families who send their children to private and public schools. Since all children would be eligible for the voucher, a much greater percentage of parents would have a substantial interest in the amount of funding for education.

Many Americans support the voucher concept. A September 1983 Gallup poll found that the general public, by a 51-38 percent margin, favored vouchers, and that Blacks favored vouchers by a 64-23 percent margin (Gallup, 1983).

Academic recommendations and debate are valuable. Equally important is the experience this country has with educational choices. The most fascinating voucher program exists, almost unheralded and unnoticed, in New England. For more than 100 years, Vermont has permitted tax funds to be spent paying tuition at certain private nonsectarian schools. There are four broad classes of schools in Vermont: public schools which meet all state requirements; private schools designated public schools in towns which have not established their own school; private, nonsectarian schools which meet certain state requirements (less stringent than the first two groups of schools); and finally, private schools associated with religious groups (principally the Catholic church).

The first three groups of schools (including private, nonsectarian schools) are eligible to receive tuition payments from the local boards of education. The tuition payments will be approximately the average of state-certified public high schools (during the 1983-84 school year, about $2850/student). Private schools are allowed to charge additional tuition beyond the state average public school cost if they have not been designated as the town's exclusive high school. Some of the approved private high schools charge extra tuition, others do not. 95 of the 246 towns in Vermont have decided to allow families to use tax funds to make decisions among schools (McClaughry, p. 25). These towns permit families to use tax money to attend private nonsectarian schools.

The state contains a range of educational activity, in part encouraged by this legislation. Several private secondary schools develop basic and applied math, communication, research, reading skills, along with world-class skiing skills! Graduates of Burke Mountain Academy, in northeastern Vermont, have won major international ski competitions and participated in the Olympics. The headmaster, Warren Witherell, has been a national swimming and water-ski champion, author of a pioneering book about teaching people to ski, and a private school teacher. He never took education classes which would lead to state certification, nor does he intend to! Yet people from throughout the United States and Canada compete eagerly to be admitted to the Burke Mountain Academy. Graduates have done extremely well not only in world ski competition, but at liberal arts colleges in the country (Dartmouth, Yale, Harvard, Middlebury, etc.). Witherell insists that his major purpose is not to develop world-class skiers, but to show young people they can accomplish more than they ever imagined if they commit themselves to a task and practice self-discipline. The atmosphere at the 65 student Burke Mountain Academy is extremely friendly, much like a large, healthy family.

Another tax-supported private school, St. Johnsbury Academy (grades 9-12), attracts students from all over New England, as well the immediate area. The atmosphere is intense and "preppy." All male students must wear ties. Officials at this school agreed with other private school administrators that the regulations and officials at Vermont's Department of Education do not inhibit them in any way.

Several St. Johnsbury Academy students talked recently about why they had selected the school. "Having a choice lets you improve your education," explained one 15 year old, whose town of McIndoe Falls will provide tuition to St. Johnsbury, Blue Mountain High School in Danville, or other private schools. A student from Waterford said he felt that he'd get more individual attention than at a public high school which some of the other people from his town are attending. A 14 year old from St. Johnsbury said she'd visited the high school in Concord (9 miles away) before deciding she wanted to stay in town for high school. All of the students agreed that there was a great deal of discussion before students made their decision about which school to attend.

Several other Vermont private schools are much more informal than St. Johnsbury Academy. The Community High School in Montpelier works with students who did not feel comfortable with large traditional high schools nearby. The school is located in the back of an old house (the other end of the spectrum from the imposing buildings of St. Johnsbury Academy). Ironically, Community High School receives tuition from nearby Barre Town but not from Montpelier, where it is located.

Another small school working with students uncomfortable with the traditional school structure is the Shaker Mountain School in Vermont's largest city, Burlington. This school has small classes and uses the entire North American continent as a place to learn. Shaker Mountain students frequently help plan and go on trips across the country, doing odd jobs to support the trips (and learn about employment in this country). Shaker Mountain and Community High School students report that their teachers care a great deal about them. As one Shaker Mountain teenager explained: "The teachers here believe in us so much that we start to believe in ourselves. Lots of people come here thinking they aren't much good. We learn math, writing, and reading at Shaker Mountain. But we also learn that we count."

Another program which contracts with public school districts is Smokey House Project, described in the chapter on Valuable Structural Changes.

Vermont officials who work extensively with low income families say the choice system has helped students. First, around the state, schools have developed which are designed to work with alienated, angry students (some but certainly not all of whom come from low income families). These schools do a better job with certain students than the large public high schools. The second advantage for low income students is in providing choice among public schools. Several advocates pointed out that sometimes one member of a family will have a bad experience in a school, and the family will get a bad name. Having choices among public schools allows younger members of the family to avoid going to a school where some staff members expect certain behavior from members of the family. It also allows students to transfer to another school at the end of a particularly difficult year.

Vermont's experience suggests that extending choices for parents would be neither a disaster or a panacea for our schools. Although popular, the choice system is by no means pervasive in Vermont. None of the major Department of Education officials or politicians felt there was a strong state-wide push to expand the choice system. The Commissioner of Education, Dr. Steve Kaagan, believes that tuitioning "happens more often than one might imagine," but that "the opportunity to decide what school one's child attends is not as important as the opportunity to influence what happens in that school." He places a much higher priority on increasing meaningful parent involvement in schools than in trying to expand the tuitioning program. Several superintendents said that while they would prefer that tax money not go to private schools, the system has been accepted in many parts of the state and doesn't cause their districts any problems. They liked being able to attract students into the districts and felt that residents liked the opportunity to choose because "Vermonters just don't like to be told what they have to do."

Transportation is handled at the local level. The Vermont legislature mandates that local districts provide transportation for handicapped students. Districts are free to provide transportation to other students, but if they do it for some regular education students, they must do it for all. Many but not all districts provide some form of transportation.

Contrary to my expectation, there are relatively few examples of parents or teachers starting schools which then rely principally on tax funds for support. Some of the people who might start such schools have been content to establish "home schooling" programs. Others who have started schools live in areas (such as Plainfield, Montpelier, Burlington, North Bennington, or Putney) where the town board established its own local school and will not tuition students to private schools. The executive director of the Vermont NEA feels most teachers do not seriously consider the possibility of starting their own school.

The teaching profession in Vermont suffers from many of the same problems it faces in other states. State officials say that in 1984 Vermont ranked 43rd among states in its average teacher salary. This is an improvement from 1982, when it ranked 50th in terms of average teacher salary and 39th in family income (U.S. Department of Education). The state director of the National Education Association believes that many excellent teachers are leaving the profession because salaries are so low. The Vermont Commissioner of Education agrees with her assessment, calling it "shameful and unwise to pay teachers so little."

Though Vermont makes the most extensive use of the "tuitioning" system, it is used occasionally in other New England states. The Maine Deputy Commissioner of Education recently reported that "We never called them vouchers but they served the same purpose." In more than 30 Maine towns without high schools of their own, students have been allowed to attend any of several public, private, or parochial high schools with the town paying their tuition. Board members in School Attendance District 63, a regional elementary school district, were dissatisfied with the area's consolidated high school of 1300. They regarded it as "too impersonal" and asked for and received permission to attend private schools. Nevertheless, 304 of the 317 high school students in the district continue to attend the large public high school (*Education USA*).

Is Vermont so different from most other states that its experiences are not really relevant? In their 1983 book on the United States, Neal Peirce and Jerry Hagstrom say that

> There are values which set Vermont apart in America: pride and independence, stemming from the pioneer heritage, tolerance, which grew out of respect for others' privacy, conservatism, usually in the best sense—to conserve a way of life that lets the individual be what he would, for good or ill. . . . (Peirce and Hagstrom, p. 193)

Aren't these values fundamental to the American dream and promise? I think so. Therefore, the important question is not, Is Vermont so different from other parts of the country that its experiences aren't useful? The question is, Shouldn't other states seek to be more like Vermont?

A more widely known experiment occurred during the mid 1970s in the Alum Rock section of San Jose, California, where the federal government tried to test a public-private educational system. Unfortunately, families were not allowed to choose from among public and private schools. Educators were not allowed to establish schools outside the public school system which would then be available to interested families. In most respects, the Alum Rock program did not provide a true test of the voucher concept because of the limited choices parents had. Results of the Alum Rock project were mixed. Most families chose the schools located closest to them. However, parents strongly supported the opportunity to choose from various programs. Administrators and teachers liked the chance to create distinctive programs.

The educational choice plan proposed here takes into account veterans' suggestions and criticisms of earlier plans. First, each family would receive a paper redeemable for a certain amount of money. These funds would be paid by the state Department of Education to an educational institution chosen by the family. The legislature in each state could establish the size of the voucher. In Minnesota, for example, the legislature guarantees each school district approximately $1450 per pupil unit. A kindergarden youngster represents .5 pupil unit, an elementary age youngster 1.0 pupil unit, a junior or senior high student 1.4 pupil units. A child whose parent or guardian is on welfare represents 2.5 pupil units. Students classified as handicapped are reimbursed by the state as if they were 2 or more pupils, depending on the handicap. Some persons may disagree with these weighting factors.

There are substantial differences among state expenditures on schools. One way to further equalize opportunities would be for the U.S. Congress to establish the size of vouchers, and fund them out of its income tax revenue. This would eliminate education's dependence on local real estate taxes and allow local governments to lower that tax. National funding of vouchers is not necessary or critical to this proposal, though it is worth considering.

Second, educational institutions could choose whether to participate in the voucher program. Some probably would not. Such schools would be unwilling to accept vouchers as the complete cost of educating students, or to alter their admissions policies.

Schools receiving voucher payments would have to accept these funds as full payment for a child if the family income was less than 130 percent of the federal povery level. This chance to earn more than the poverty level without losing the benefit of fully paid education would provide some incentive to get off welfare.

Some schools might enroll children who are using only vouchers, while in other schools certain students would pay additional tuition. Such a mix exists in many private schools which enroll both scholarship and tuition-paying students.

The headmaster of a prestigious local private school recently suggested an interesting variation. His school charges a tuition of $4400 to those parents who can afford it, using the standard college financial statement as a measure. More than 20 percent of the students at this school are on scholarships. The headmaster felt that his board would be reluctant to accept a voucher for the full cost of students' fees if financial statements showed the families could afford more. However, the school might be willing to enter the voucher program if it were able to continue using their financial aid form and charge additional fees to higher income families.

It is easy to abuse provisions such as these. Any voucher plan must uphold its fundamental purpose, to increase educational opportunities for those who presently have few if any choices.

Schools with a mix of tuition and voucher students would have to accept a representative racial and socioeconomic sample of applicants. For purposes of illustration, assume that each school has 500 openings, 250 of which are reserved for voucher students and 250 for tuition students. Inspectors would periodically check to insure that openings for voucher students were being filled with students representing the diversity of the applicant pool.

Schools accepting vouchers would be subject to government health, safety, and Bill of Rights guarantees. We must be explicit about these constitutional guarantees. They include free speech, due process requirements, and prohibitions of discrimination against people on the basis of their race or religion. Some schools may choose not to accept such standards. I believe they should not be eligible for tax funds.

STANDARDS FOR SCHOOLS

One of the most important questions about schools which receive tax funds is, What standards should be established which must be followed? There are several valid but contradictory guidelines regulators should consider: (1) Allow individual parents/educators enough freedom so that they can create distinctive, creative programs which will meet the needs of students they serve; (2) Protect children against dangerous and inappropriate instructional and curriculum approaches; (3) Protect the rights and needs of the society which is helping to support schools and has certain expectations of them; (4) Insure that all participants in a competitive situation have a fair chance to attract students; (5) Insure that guarantees of appropriate service exist for those who are extremely expensive or unusually difficult to work with.

Harvard's Richard Murnane argues that the impact of extending educational choices "would depend to a large extent on the details of the regulations defining the program" (Murnane, p. 221). The Vermont response to details is helpful because it has operated successfully. Vermont standards fall into several areas: curriculum, staff, buildings, and schedule. Public school buildings must meet certain health and safety requirements. They must employ staff who have completed approved university programs. The schools must offer classes in certain areas, including basic communications skills, citizenship, history, government, physical education, principles of health, English, American and other literature, and the natural sciences. Schools must meet a certain number of days. Finally, schools must either offer a program for handicapped students or pay tuition and provide transportation to a program acceptable to the parent or guardian.

The two kinds of private schools must meet standards which are somewhat different from those for "public schools." The "designated" private schools must meet all requirements of public schools except that they are allowed to hire noncertified teachers.

A nondesignated private school must meet the following major standards: (1) Offer courses in basic communication skills, including reading, writing and mathematics, citizenship, history, government, physical education, principles of health, English, American and other literature, and natural sciences; (2) Keep records of pupils' attendance and notify the Department of Education within seven days if a pupil leaves or is terminated; (3) Assess each pupil's progress at least once a year and maintain records of that assessment; (4) Develop and make available to others a statement of the school's objectives; (5) Maintain a faculty with appropriate training and experience; (6) Have each of its teachers and administrators subscribe to an oath supporting the Constitution and the laws of Vermont and the United States; (7) Require that all students have certain immunizations; (8) Obtain approval from the state for its operation once every five years.

Vermont's experience demonstrates that a program such as this can work without destroying public schools or the fabric of society (two claims sometimes made about the impact of expanding educational choices). None of the Vermont Education Department officials interviewed during a recent trip to the state felt there had been a significant problem of fraud.

However, the Vermont plan has several troubling features. Private schools are allowed to charge extra tuition in addition to funds from the state. Thus some private schools are not accessible to low income people. Vermont also does not require that graduates of private schools demonstrate skills prior to graduation (although public school students must meet this requirement). And Vermont does not prohibit racial or religious discrimination in private school admissions (although state officials do not recall this having been a problem).

Another approach to extending educational choices is being considered in Minnesota. A bipartisan coalition of legislators introduced an educational family choice bill which would allow low and moderate income families to use funds allocated by the legislature to select among public and private schools which agreed (1) To admit all who applied. If there were more applicants than openings, a lottery would be held. Schools would be allowed to decide that some openings would be available to state-supported students and other openings would be available to parent-supported students; (2) Not to charge any additional money to those who were bringing tax funds with them; (3) Not to discriminate against students; (4) To have no admission test for students.

There are several other important features in the bill. Families would not receive cash. They would get a piece of paper which the school they select could send in to obtain money from the state. The amount of money would depend on the child's status (using the Minnesota System previously described, in which secondary, handicapped, and low income students generate additional dollars). Transportation would be provided within the district of residence.

This plan would eliminate from participation some exclusive private schools, as they would insist on an admissions test. However, the proposal has received strong support from a broad coalition of Blacks, Hispanics, Native Americans, and low income Whites. It has been endorsed by a statewide network of people who work with low income families. Directors of the Community Action Programs have agreed that extending educational choices would benefit rural and urban low income families. Several suburban public school superintendents have also testified in favor of the plan. Dr. Michael Hickey, Superintendent of the St. Louis Park Public Schools (and winner of numerous awards for his work) explained:

> One of the most important factors in making education more effective is the exercise of free choice by individuals, and responsibility for that choice in meeting educational goals. The kind of restructuring which is needed in public education can best be brought about by empowering individuals to play a more direct role in shaping educational systems to make them more responsive now and in the future. (Hickey, 1983)

The Minnesota bill has been heard in both House and Senate Committees and is scheduled for additional discussion around the state during 1984. No vote has been requested by proponents or opponents.

One of the most difficult details of an educational choice plan is whether "for-profit" educational institutions should be allowed to receive tax funds. Richard Murnane of Harvard has compared tax supported nursing homes run by different kinds of organizations. He concluded that nonprofit nursing homes run by religious organizations appear to "provide high-quality services in an honest manner." However, they have little incentive to expand services to meet demand. They often have long waiting lists. For-profit facilities have responded to increased demand by creating more programs, but also have been more likely to provide low quality care (Murnane, p. 221).

A recent article in *Across the Board,* a magazine for corporate officials, compared several prisons being operated by profit-making companies. Since 1975, RCA has operated a small state training school for Pennsylvania juveniles, making a profit described as "modest." "The school has brought only good press; it has remained uncontroversial and according to juvenile delinquency experts, is very well run" (Krajick, p. 23). The article points out that the federal government has recently signed contracts with a number of for-profit companies to maintain detention centers for illegal aliens.

Experience with profit-making schools is limited. Profit-making vocational schools received tax support under the G.I. Bill, but the majority of veterans chose to attend universities or vocational programs operated under nonprofit status. The previously described Ombudsman program in suburban Chicago is a "for-profit," and has received strong praise. Some of the most successful nursery schools in the Minneapolis-St. Paul area are operated as part of a profit-making operation. They have not offered the kind of low quality programs predicted by some who referred to the potential for "Kentucky Fried Children" when they opened.

The observation of Anthony Travisono, director of the American Correctional Association, makes sense. Commenting on plans to allow businesses to run prisons, Travisono says "Complex problems require complex solutions. It is true that the profit motive could cause a conflict of interest, but for that very reason, people are going to watch private industry very closely, probably more closely than they watch the public sector" (Krajick, p. 27).

Given the opportunity, some entrepreneurs probably would operate schools with more concern for profit than quality. However, there are relatively few people who have opened profit-making schools catering to affluent families. They have significant competition from already existing schools. Under these circumstances, it's unlikely that many people will be able to make a substantial profit while offering an attractive educational program.

As in the G.I. Bill, a voucher plan would give families the option to leave if they are dissatisfied. Given this ability and the presence of public and private schools, it's worth allowing people to use their ingenuity to open profit-making schools. They should have the opportunity to compete for people, following certain standards.

Neither the Vermont or Minnesota plan is perfect, but both

have valuable features:

1. Expansion of choice to some private schools.
2. Specification of areas in which schools must provide instruction.
3. Protection of a school's ability to hire noncertified teachers.
4. Protection of a school's ability to determine appropriate instructional methods.
5. Monitoring of a student's progress and periodic reporting to parents.
6. Requirement that students be admitted without racial or religious discrimination.
7. Health and safety requirements for buildings.
8. Requirement of appropriate immunizations prior to admission.

A year's study convinces me that an even better plan would also incorporate the following requirements:

9. A clear, consistent policy on discipline, including dismissal and expulsion.
10. Opportunities for parents and community members to inspect financial records.
11. Demonstration of skills prior to award of a diploma.
12. Additional financial incentives for schools to take low income, handicapped, and disruptive students.
13. Sufficient appropriation to provide transportation within an area to be determined by the state legislature.
14. Information available to all interested parents and community members about the school's faculty members, curriculum, and facilities, and a list of graduates who can be contacted for their views on the school.
15. Agreement of participating schools not to charge additional tuition to those whose family income is less than 130 percent of federal poverty guidelines.

GETTING APPROPRIATE INFORMATION TO FAMILIES

It's often hard to make decisions. Since deregulation of airlines, banks, and telephone companies, many more choices are available. It's tough to know which long distance phone company to pick, which Individual Retirement Account is right, and the best way to get from New York to Chicago.

Some people argue that choice is inappropriate in education because it will be difficult for many parents to make decisions about appropriate education. This section describes experiences where people have made educational decisions.

A number of public school districts in urban areas established alternative programs in the late 1960s and early 1970s. R. Gary Bridge and Julie Blackman of the Rand Corporation investigated several in California, Minnesota, and New York.

When educational choices are available, parents "vary widely in their awareness of their school alternatives and in the accuracy of their information about the rules governing choice." Specifically, people with higher incomes and more education know more about the choices. However, "over time, the differences between parents' information levels are reduced as parents gain more experience with the choice system, given that the rules of the system stay relatively constant" (Bridge and Blackman, 1978, p. xiii).

The researchers also concluded that parents differ in how they make decisions. More educated parents rely more on printed materials from schools, and less educated parents rely more on information from personal contacts, particularly contacts with school personnel (Bridge and Blackman, p. xiii).

These conclusions are completely consistent with experiences in St. Paul. When the two alternative programs in which I worked were developed, written materials were sent out throughout the city. Presentations also were made in a number of community centers, churches, etc. Both schools worked hard (and were ultimately successful) in attracting a racial and socioeconomically diverse population.

Affluent people relied on printed materials, and low income people were much more likely to rely on personal contacts. When parents from low income areas were asked why they wanted to enroll their children in certain schools, the answer was likely to be "because I heard from my friends, pastor, social worker, etc., that this is a good place." More affluent parents responded to the question by saying that they agreed with a brochure they had seen about the school.

Some experts have called the information issue "a fatal flaw" in choice systems (Olivas, p. 133). Michael Olivas,

Director of Research for the National Educational Service Centers, Inc. of the League of United Latin American Citizens, agrees with Bridge and Blackman that low and high income people have different sources of information. Olivas insists that the informal, verbal communication systems of low income people will be overloaded, unable to handle a great deal of complexity which must be a part of any choice system. Arthur Wise and Linda Darling-Hammond of the Rand Corporation ask whether parents will have enough information to make wise decisions about different schools and answer, "Probably not" (Wise and Darling-Hammond, p. 12).

Recent research has examined whether public school teachers want educational choices for their own children. A 1983 *Detroit Free Press* survey of public school teachers across the state made it clear they like having choices. In fact, the poll found that the percentage of public school teachers sending their children to private schools was twice the state average. 20 percent of the public school teachers polled send their children to private schools, while only 10 percent of Michigan students overall are enrolled in private schools (Macnow, p. 1). The *Chicago Reporter*'s review of 1980 census data showed that 38 percent of the Chicago public school teachers living in the city send their children to private schools. Another 18 percent of the teachers have children in public and private schools. Thus 56 percent of public school teachers living in Chicago have some children attending private schools. Only 20 percent of Chicago parents who are not teachers enroll their children in private schools (Grimes, p. 2). As part of the *Chicago Reporter*'s examination of private Black schools in Chicago, the reporter checked with the Illinois Advisory Committee on Non-Public Schools. Dren Greer, chair of that group, estimates that "40 percent of all private school parents are public school teachers" (Washington, p. 1). These public school teachers regard choice in education as valuable.

Isn't it ironic how many researchers (and others of the middle and upper class) search out the best possible schools for their own children while insisting that poor people must be protected from themselves?

Studies by the National Center for Neighborhood Enterprise and Virgil Blum show that test scores and attitudes toward learning of students from low income families improved dramatically when the youngsters enrolled in independent or parochial inner city schools. This is perhaps the best refutation of the attitude that poor people can't make wise decisions. They want choices, like everyone else!

Vermont provides a variety of choices described above. Parents in small country stores, in gas stations, in interviews said they traditionally received written and verbal information about various schools. Lynn Wood, a former member of the Vermont State Board of Education, pointed out that in northwestern Vermont, a number of schools have started going out to community meetings to tell people about themselves (Wood, 1984). Many of the young people with whom I talked at Shaker Mountain, Community High School, and St. Johnsbury Academy said they heard about schools from their friends, and talked about the choices with their families.

In St. Louis, desegregation money has been used to print large posters and fliers which are distributed throughout the area. These fliers describe the programs and specialties of various schools. They have been distributed through libraries, community centers, churches, and mass mailings. Meetings also have been held in low income communities to describe and discuss the choices available to families.

In Minneapolis, the district has printed a 96-page booklet describing various alternative programs available to parents. This booklet is supplemented by a one-page brochure about various alternatives. The printed material has been distributed throughout the city. Several of the schools have held public meetings in community centers to describe their programs and encourage applicants.

A summary of New York State's decade-long experiment with vouchers for handicapped students found that a variety of families were actively involved. "Parents of all races and income groups appeared eager to take advantage of the voucher option." The same study found that approximately 55 percent of the students enrolled in voucher schools were minorities. While patterns and percentages varied, "no all white 'segregation' academies were established'' (Hunt, p. 14).

Recently the predominantly blue-collar town of Worcester, Massachusetts, decided to offer alternative programs to desegregate their schools voluntarily. They found that more than 80 percent of parents returned surveys asking them to choose among programs with various philosophies. Many White and Black parents chose schools outside their neighborhoods (Glenn).

It's Pollyannish to suggest that everyone immediately will make wise decisions. Bridge and Blackman make excellent suggestions about how to develop an effective information system. They recommend sending printed materials to all families and following up with personal contacts directed to less socially advantaged families.

In 1970 the Center for the Study of Public Policy in Massachusetts recommended that an independent agency be established to collect and disseminate data. Schools wanting to receive funds from the state would have to describe their philosophy, curriculum, specialties, graduation requirements, staff characteristics, and methods of monitoring and reporting students' academic growth. Gathering this data seems like a good role for either a state department or an intermediate unit. The intermediate units are called various names: Board of Cooperative Services (BOCES) in New York, Educational Cooperative Service Unit (ECSU) in Minnesota.

Under certain circumstances, vouchers might be used to extend far beyond what we presently describe as "schools." Youngsters should demonstrate competence in basic or life skills before having certain opportunities. Having achieved proficiency, students should be allowed to use their voucher funds for a greater range of learning programs. One possibility would be the reestablishment of the apprentice program, first used hundreds of years ago. Young people might contract for training directly with artists or technical people. It's easy to envision apprenticeships in everything from computer programming and repair to carpentry, violin playing, and auto mechanics.

An important part of any voucher program is the way information about available programs is shared with families.

Printed information should be provided in such locations as public libraries, community centers, banks, shopping malls, government centers, churches, temples, and synagogues. Additional information should be made available on radio and television programs. Information must be accessible to all interested.

Local areas should be free to establish other appropriate guidelines. For example, in some states citizens might want periodically to test students in voucher schools. (Many private and public schools already use such tests to give parents information about their children's progress.) It's vital that uniform testing procedures are adopted. In our town, for example, students with the lowest natural intelligence and those who've immigrated within the last three years are not counted in district averages. This affects those averages. States may wish to develop forms to provide clear, concise information to parents.

Parents consider many factors when deciding about their children's school, among them proximity, experience with certain teachers, written information, and hearsay. Some parents allow their children to make the decision. Experience suggests that students will select a school on the basis of programs available to them and attractiveness of that program to their friends.

Under this plan, teachers would achieve their stated goal of being treated like professionals. Teachers would have the opportunity to "practice" individually, in small groups, or in large groups, as do doctors and attorneys. Teachers would have far more control over their working conditions, and could allocate the available funds as they deem appropriate. Instructors could choose their own administrators, as do doctors and attorneys. They could contract with universities to assist in the training of new teachers—or perhaps establish their own teacher training programs. These programs might be affiliated with universities, or independent. The training programs would have to satisfy local or statewide standards.

This plan is somewhat different from any yet proposed. However, the work of such dissimilar authors as Milton Friedman, John Coons, Denis Doyle, Steven Sugarman, and Jonathan Kozol has been of great assistance (see Bibliography). Their thoughtful, compelling arguments are valuable to all interested in a voucher program.

The philosophical diversity these authors represent is fascinating. Friedman is one of the most eminent conservative philosophers in our country. After working at the National Institute of Education and liberal Brookings Institution, Doyle is now director of education policy studies at the conservative Washington "think tank," American Enterprise Institute. Coons, Sugarman, and Kozol are all liberal activists and scholars. Coons and Sugarman are professors of law at the University of California. Kozol is a former public school teacher in Boston and author of a number of prizewinning books. Kozol, Coons, and Sugarman support only those programs which meet certain guidelines to protect consumers and enforce equity.

Why should private schools be interested in a voucher program, as opposed to the tuition tax credit plan? Most important, because vouchers would bring them far more money. TTC plans call for no more than $500 tax credit. Public schools in this country receive $1000-3000 per pupil from tax revenues. Under a voucher plan, these funds would go to schools selected by families (as long as the schools met conditions previously discussed). Thus, the private schools would receive two to six times the $500 involved in a tuition tax credit program.

In fact, tuition tax credits would not necessarily increase private school income. The tax credits would ease some families' financial burden of paying private school tuition. The major way for private schools to increase their revenue would be to increase the tuition they charge.

Additional funds received under a voucher program provide limitless opportunities. Some schools would upgrade their facilities. Others might contract with public schools or other institutions to provide services (some private schools already have such contracts with museums, zoos, and computer companies).

In many cases, private schools would raise teachers' salaries. Many of them have relied on deeply committed teachers willing to accept minimal salaries. For the first time, these schools would be able to afford more appropriate salaries for effective teachers.

Vouchers would allow more private schools to act on their often stated beliefs about the value of serving a variety of students. (The National Association of Independent Schools filed a "friend of the court" statement in a recent U.S. Supreme Court case. NAIS strongly opposed providing tax-exempt status for schools which discriminated against students on the basis of race.)

Vouchers would enable private schools to serve more students. This would be a great attraction for many private schools. Like their counterparts in public schools, some private schools have space which could be used without adding significantly to their costs.

Our national experience with the G.I. Bill should help us examine effects of a voucher program. Most accounts of the G.I. Bill suggest that it had three major results: (1)Provided opportunities for many people who never before had considered continuing their education; (2)Encouraged individuals and groups to provide new education or training programs; (3)Resulted in some limited abuses by unscrupulous people who promised more than they could deliver. Despite some abuses, most veterans regarded the G.I. Bill with great enthusiasm and were pleased with their educational experiences.

Many of the arguments being raised against vouchers were also expressed against the G.I. Bill. However, the idea worked well then, and it is worth considering now. Certainly we can learn a great deal from G.I. Bill experiences.

At this point, it's appropriate to consider the major criticisms of most voucher proposals. Some people believe expanding educational choices *eliminates the "safety net" which protects handicapped students.* They fear that few people will want to work with handicapped students and that allowing transfers out of public schools will leave only the most difficult students for the public schools to deal with. Both are important concerns.

Who worked with handicapped students before the Federal "Education for All Handicapped Students Law" (PL 94-142) passed? Frederick J. Weintraub, Assistant Executive Director of the Council for Exceptional Children in Reston, Virginia, says that schools for handicapped children were "frequently established by parent associations. . . . Professionals, both in their private capacity as individual citizens and in their corporate identity on boards of clinics, hospitals, and universities, also established schools for handicapped children." He also notes that parochial schools have "a long history of running educational programs for handicapped children," as do certain religious orders (Weintraub, p. 50).

Some of the private schools established for handicapped students—particularly deaf, blind, and retarded students— began receiving federal and state funds in 1965. This occurred under Part B of Title I of the Elementary and Secondary Education Act. This is another precedent for "private" schools to receive tax funds. Weintraub estimates that by 1977, approximately $1 billion of public funds (federal, state, and local) were being spent annually in private education for handicapped children (Weintraub, p. 52).

Historically, there have been people who cared about handicapped children and acted on that concern. Many of these committed people provided services despite severe financial problems; more than one such person has commented bitterly that they'd love to have half of the financial resources that public schools in many states now receive to provide services to handicapped students. It's ironic that some public school advocates wonder if anyone would serve handicapped students if parents had choices. In fact, most public schools did not choose to serve the students until forced by court and congressional action to do so.

Not all handicapped children received appropriate services before PL 94-142. Affluent parents could pay for programs. Poor parents could not afford much of what was available. Rural handicapped students generally had to leave their homes to attend residential programs or received no help.

Not all the private schools provide high quality programs for handicapped students. In some schools, there is little review or scrutiny of what is happening. Some psychologists have a conflict of interest when referring students to a private school since they are either employees or board members of the school. However, the incidence of poor performance is low. Attorney and handicapped students' advocate Michael Rebell recently summarized results of more than a decade's experience of vouchers for handicapped students in New York. New York City alone contracts for 5000-7000 students a year to attend nonpublic schools. Rebell estimated that 5-10 percent of all schools on the authorized list of private schools were found to be unsatisfactory. He also noted that reports by state Department of Education officials on public school programs alleged more extensive deficiencies than did reports on private schools (Rebell, p. 463).

Weintraub concluded that advocates for handicapped students no longer bother with discussions of whether tax funds should go to "private" schools. "In education of the handicapped we are beyond the question of public support of private schools. The questions we now face are, When is a school private or public? What standards should be required and how should they be enforced?" (Weintraub, p. 54).

Obviously, providing parents with choices does not completely answer these questions. But it can empower parents and help provide a more appropriate education. Parents of handicapped students are no different from other families. They want choices! Rebell found that New York "parents of all races and income groups appeared to be eager to take advantage of the voucher option" (Rebell, p. 463).

Lee Dietz, Executive Director of the Vermont United Cerebral Palsy Association, says that many families "consider it a plus to have choices." When moving into the state, they "often decide to live in a place where they'll have choices among schools."

One concern about vouchers is that *they destroy the public schools*. When pressed, critics say this means that many parents will take their children out of the public schools, leaving the poorest and least desirable students.

People who believe vouchers would destroy public schools should consider the experience of Minnesota and Vermont. Tax deductions for school expenses have been permitted since 1955 in Minnesota. Although public schools make some charge for participation in extracurricular activities and for unusually large home economics or industrial arts projects, most of the money Minnesotans deduct is for private school tuition. Presently the legislature allows a deduction of $500 for elementary students and $700 for secondary. This will increase in 1985 to $650 for elementary and $1000 for secondary. The U.S. Supreme Court ruled this system constitutional in its 1983 *Mueller v. Allen* decision.

Teachers union officials have threatened doom, gloom, and destruction if such programs are implemented around the country. Writing about the *Mueller v. Allen* decision, Albert Shanker, President of the American Federation of Teachers, thundered, "I can't think of a worse decision—or a worse time for it to come" (Shanker, p. 8A).

When questioned, opponents find it difficult to show how the Minnesota plan has hurt its public schools. A higher percentage of Minnesota public school students graduate than in any other state, and Minnesota public school students score above national averages on standardized tests. Even opponents of the tax deduction plan acknowledge that Minnesota students' performance on standardized tests "has made public-school supporters less concerned about the tuition deduction than might otherwise be the case" (Paulu, p. 5).

Despite opposition from those who advocate public school monopoly on tax funds, the Minnesota program has not produced a mass exodus from the public schools. About 11 percent of Minnesota's 900,000 kindergarten through twelfth grade students attend private or parochial schools, almost exactly the national average.

Vouchers would broaden the support for increased funding for education, because more people would have a direct personal interest in the amount of funds per student allocated by state legislators. Thus, vouchers could increase the per pupil allotment, benefiting both public and private schools. The Minnesota Education Association's chief lobbyist admits that "people who are non-public advocates are also public school advocates. They'll fight for bills on each side. The guy who is in there fighting for a voucher bill or to boost the amount allowed for the tuition tax deduction is also fighting for money for public education" (Paulu, p. 5).

Vermont has been using the system described above for more than fifty years. Ninety percent of the children in Vermont attend public schools. Vermont's students score above national averages on standardized tests, and its graduation rate is better than the national average. Where is the evidence that options have destroyed Vermont's schools?

The impact of extending educational choices will vary, depending on a community's attitude towards its schools. Nathan Glazer, a sociology/education professor at Harvard, says that in relatively homogeneous rural areas where parents are roughly satisfied with their schools, "one can expect no large effect. And there are large areas of American society in which these conditions prevail" (Glazer, p. 91). (Even in homogeneous areas of rural Vermont, however, parents exercise choice when they have it.)

Glazer believes that in large cities the two groups responding most to choice will be "Blacks trapped in ghetto circumstances . . . and upwardly mobile Blacks." Glazer does not expect much urban "White flight" as he thinks it already has occurred.

Recently one of the national groups studying education strongly endorsed the value of expanding educational choices for students from low income families. The Committee on Vocational Education and Economic Development in Depressed Areas suggested that each student ages 14-18 receive a grant which could be used to obtain vocational training in public or private schools anywhere in the country. Grants would range in size, depending on family income. The largest grants would be equal to 100-120 percent of national average expenditures per student for secondary vocational education programs. They would "give low-income students a larger choice in vocational programs than they currently have" (Committee on Vocational Education, p. 80). This group's membership is significant: it includes the director of the Organizing Department of the International Association of Machinists and Aerospace Workers, the chief administrator of the New York City Schools Office of Occupational and Career Education, the state director of the Oklahoma State Department of Vocational and Technical Education and the former Commissioner of Education in California. Such people can not be dismissed as uninformed, radical opponents of public education.

A Gallup Poll of the Public's Attitude toward School, published in September 1982, provided important information on this issue. Gallup asked a representative national sample, "Suppose you could send your eldest child to a private school, tuition free. Which would you prefer—to send him or her to a private school or to a public school?" The answers of those who now send their children to public schools were: public school, 47 percent; private school, 45 percent; don't know, 8 percent (Gallup, 1982, p. 47).

Vouchers would do for low and moderate income people what suburbs and private schools have done for affluent people: give them a real choice. Have all public schools lost out in this competition? Of course not. Despite the barriers described earlier, there are some excellent public schools. A voucher plan could encourage far more careful, widespread examination and, ultimately, *adoption* of effective instructional and organizational practices by public school officials.

Experiences in New York state support this view. After a decade of litigation and research, attorney and handicapped students' advocate Michael Rebell concluded that "a voucher alternative tends to improve, rather than 'destroy' the public school system, since in terms of both numbers of students served and quality of programs offered, the competition from the private sector appears to have led to substantial improvements in the public sector" (Rebell, p. 465).

A related criticism of vouchers is that *they eliminate the "safety net" which provides low income, minority, and disruptive students with at least minimal education.* Earlier chapters examined the quality of the public school safety net and found numerous holes. Given the opportunity, many people would rush to offer educational services to young people. Youth workers in churches and social service agencies in low income neighborhoods are furious with the schools for their disinterest in many neighborhood youth and their lack of responsiveness. Community controlled neighborhood organizations have demonstrated extraordinary abilities to provide effective services for their residents in areas of housing, advocacy, and construction. In fact, a number of groups have started effective schools in inner city areas.

Independent schools with close ties to the community educate inner city children all over the country. The Washington, D.C., based National Center for Neighborhood

Enterprise has identified more than 400 minority-run, independent schools in various American cities, and has concluded that the actual number is "much greater" (Carlson, p. 1). The Center brought together a number of these schools for a conference on Neighborhood Based Independent Schools. In his opening comments, NCNE President Robert Woodson explained that "independent minority schools do not oppose public education. They merely seek to give low-income, minority families a choice" (Carlson, p. 1).

Chicago's Community Renewal Society investigated inner city private education in 1982. CRS is a multiracial, interdenominational organization which publishes a monthly newsletter, the *Chicago Reporter.* Their study found that "Chicago has at least 48 private, non-Catholic schools that are all-black or predominantly black. 35 are elementary, nine are high schools and four offer grades one through twelve" (Washington, p. 1). The investigation found that a substantial number of these students were low income: About 25 percent of the 7700 students attending these private schools are low income. One parent explained that sending her children to private schools means "you end up wearing the same coat for 10 years," but it's the choice she wants to make.

The Chicago survey identified a wide range of private schools. Several were started by former Catholic or public school teachers. The Learning Network, for example, has been open since 1972. While charging only $700 tuition, it has an impressive record: 95 percent of the 1980 graduating class tested at or above grade level in reading and math, members of the first graduating class of 1973 have all since graduated from college, every Network graduate has either enrolled in or graduated from high school. Other schools, such as the Faulkner School, are exclusive schools gradually taken over by Blacks as affluent Whites moved from the neighborhood. Virtually all of the schools emphasize both basic skills and awareness of Afro-American culture and contributions.

Kwame McDonald, a Black activist in St. Paul, Minnesota, and recently appointed director of the Governor's Council on Youth, agrees. "The most effective Black leaders in America have come from Black educational experience. . . .

The voucher system properly used could set up an educational institution that would educate Black people for our real challenge in this society" (McDonald, 1983).

There is strong evidence that many low income, minority families want more choice in education. The Gallup Poll of American Attitudes toward Education, published in September 1983 noted that while 51 percent of the general public favored a voucher plan, more than 60 percent of Blacks supported the idea.

A 1981 study of 64 inner city private schools documents the strength of that desire for choice (Blum, p. 17). The study examined schools in Los Angeles, New Orleans, Chicago, Milwaukee, Detroit, New York, Newark, and Washington, D.C. 90 percent of the schools were either Catholic or ex-parochial. Yet almost ⅓ of the families represented were Protestant. The study illustrates sacrifices many inner city families must make to send their children to these schools. 15 percent of the responding famiies had annual incomes of less than $5,000 per year, 35 percent had incomes of $5,000-10,000 per year, and 22 percent reported incomes of $10,000-15,000 per year. Thus, 72 percent of the families had annual incomes of less than $15,000!

Why do these families send their children to poorly equipped schools, often located in run-down buildings? The survey found that parents believe these independent schools provided a better education, one which

> includes religious and moral values, an education with rules and discipline, an education that treats their children with respect, an education provided by teachers and staff who care about their children and their image, and impress on them high levels of expectation, an education to which they themselves contribute labor and services, an education that makes their children so interested in learning that they discuss school at the dinner table. (Blum, p. 19)

Blum described several of the schools in the study, including St. Leo's in Milwaukee. This school closed as a Catholic school in 1970 and reopened in 1977. 90 percent of the 280 students are Protestant and 85 percent qualified for free meals under government financed breakfast and hot lunch programs. According to standardized test scores, these students generally came to St. Leo's two years below average in reading and math. After a year at the school they had progressed to within several months of the national average.

Another study was recently completed of parochial schools in Washington, D.C. (Schultz, 1983) 51 percent of the students in the District of Columbia's parochial schools are not Catholic. In some poor and working class areas, more than 80 percent of parochial school students were not Catholic.

It's ridiculous and inaccurate to suggest that all public schools are ineffective, or that all private/parochial schools are marvelous. There are independent schools in which teachers could tell their own horror stories of rigidity and intolerance. However, affluent parents can transfer their children. Low income families have very few choices.

An educational choice plan for families would allow many skilled people who love to work with youngsters and talented mature teachers to create new programs. One such project was established by a former suburban Chicago public school teacher and administrator, Jim Boyle. About six years ago Boyle approached five school districts and asked them to send him 10 to 15 of their most difficult high school students and pay him the per pupil allotment received from the state of Illinois.

Boyle called his program "Ombudsman." He rented store fronts throughout the northern suburban area, purchased a number of mini-computers and hired a talented staff. Boyle developed a list of competencies required for graduation. Students attend one of the Ombudsman centers at least three hours per day. They start at their personal skill level and move at their own pace. The center atmosphere is orderly, calm, informal, and optimistic that each student will succeed.

Visiting Boyle's centers is valuable for anyone who wonders whether it's possible to make a difference in the lives of young people. Ombudsman students test scores show enormous gains. Boyle is working with formerly disruptive students who hated their large well equipped suburban schools and showed their contempt through harrassment, vandalism, and truancy. He has transformed his students' attitude toward learning and themselves. The kids care deeply about what they were doing, believe it's worthwhile, and that they are learning for the first time in many years. Students feel well treated, encouraged, respected, and assisted. The Ombudsman program works for them. Boyle's operation is profitable. He has expanded to Arizona where several school districts have asked to work with him.

Another program operates in St. Paul, Minnesota, under the spirited direction of Bonnie McIntyre. McIntyre is a tough, committed Black and a former St. Paul public school teacher. She was angered by the district's bureaucracy and tendency to place too many low income and minority students in special education classes. She set out to demonstrate that many of these children have extraordinary talent.

McIntyre founded a school in the center of a low income area. Her program, called "McIntyre School for Gifted Children," has survived for seven years. She insists that every child is gifted in some way and should be so regarded. Some of her students were bored and starting to be disruptive in the public school they attended. Not at this school. McIntyre stresses individualization and discipline. She insists on parent involvement. Her school has achieved a great deal of credibility: More than half of the children's parents are public school teachers or administrators.

A similar program in Chicago has received national publicity. Another former public school teacher named Marva Collins founded a school which has attracted many youngsters described as "nonlearners" by their former teachers. Collins has been the subject of considerable controversy in Chicago because of her frank statements about education and her clearly stated educational philosophy. For example, Collins does not believe computers have a place in schools. Recently she told a national television audience that she didn't want computers in her school until her students knew how to build them. Obviously, Collins and I disagree. However, she's attracted a number of parents who agree with her and she's helped many youngsters.

These programs directly refute the contention that under a voucher program teachers would want to work only with the gifted, compliant students. Research by Washington's Center for Neighborhood Enterprise and the *Chicago Reporter* show that Boyle, Collins, and McIntyre are not unique. They are not the only people who care about inner city or alienated youth. Don't all youth deserve the chance to attend such programs?

Sometimes when people say that vouchers would destroy public schools, they mean that the ability of schools to bring together a vast array of American youth would be lost. They charge that *vouchers will destroy public school's central mission to provide millions of different youngsters with a common heritage and acceptance of each other.*

Some people cling to this goal as an ever higher percentage of families leave "public" schools to seek the best possible education for their children. Virtually all parents want the best for their children and do whatever they can (usually within legal limits) to obtain it.

The fact is that in the past many parents did not send their children to public schools. Since the earliest days of this republic, the most affluent people have created exclusive schools for their children. Before about 1850, there was no widespread public school system. Taxes in many places were used to support a variety of schools, including those established by religious groups. Even after the common school movement gained strength, many people objected to the "public schools" monopolizing all tax funds devoted to education.

Various religious groups shunned public schools, believing that parochial schools could provide more appropriate education. In fact, many of these inner city parochial schools are far more racially and socioeconomically integrated than public schools in the same city, much less the suburbs.

Public schools simply are not a place where all our country's children come together, learn to accept each other, and become productive, loyal citizens. This pleasant story deserves a place alongside the tooth fairy.

Many find these realities difficult to accept. Many of the people reading this book look back fondly on their public school days. They learned to read and compute. Public schools helped millions of immigrants learn our language, history, and culture.

Public school successes were not necessarily triumphs for democractic principles, as Colin Greer explains in *The Great School Legend*. He shows how public schools reinforced rather than restructured the patterns of wealth in this country. Public schools encouraged millions of citizens to accept boring jobs and insignificant roles in government decision making. Public schools helped convince millions that they had only themselves to blame for their lack of economic security. Greer shows that schools were established partly to serve as sorting mechanisms, preserving privilege and allowing a "talented tenth" to move ahead.

The schools succeeded in protecting wealth, power, and position. The single most common characteristic of wealthy people in this country is that their parents were also wealthy! (Jencks, *et al*) An expanding economy probably had far more to do with the growth in size of the middle class than with the schools.

Public schools never have been "value free." Science textbooks have extolled conservation while American history textbooks have praised industrialists who mistreated the land, fouled the water, and endangered entire species. Textbooks have encouraged cooperation while the school's structure has demanded intense competition among individuals. Teachers have stressed the value of individual initiative while many of them have demanded instant, unthinking obedience to their directions. Textbooks have described the importance of participation in voting while student governments generally have been relegated to picking bands for dances and choosing homecoming candidates. Until recently, most textbooks ignored discrimination encountered by immigrants to this country, be they Irish, Italian, German, or Hispanic. Contributions made by women and people of color often were ignored.

Millions of students dropped out before graduating. In the early years of this century, there were many jobs requiring little if any applied or technical skills.

In the 1980s and 1990s we face a world quite different from the one when most of us went to elementary and secondary schools. Low skill jobs will be far less available in the future. Our economy will require far more sophisticated knowledge and talent than it has in the past.

Expected to nurture a wide range of values and attitudes, public schools developed (and had forced upon them by courts and state legislators) a complex web of rules and regulations. Some of these inhibit effective education. For example, how much interracial harmony was gained by forcing people to send their children to schools in areas they feared? The most courageous educator I know, Jerry Winnegar, accepted an incredible challenge from a Boston court: to build a strong program which would attract Blacks into South Boston High School. I'll never forget the bitterness and hatred of the White Irish Catholics Jerry introduced me to: "Southies" who described their hatred of liberal Whites who sent their own children to 98 percent White public schools in Newton and other affluent suburbs while demanding that city schools be integrated. James Coleman and other scholars maintain that a major product of forced bussing was "White flight"—movement of middle and upper class Whites from urban public schools to private urban and public suburban schools. An increasing number of middle and upper class minority parents are now leaving urban public schools. Thus, in many urban public schools, we've had considerably less real integration than courts had hoped for.

What about those left in the public schools? It's not only racist Whites who hate forced bussing. Native Americans, Hispanics, and Blacks throughout the country have strongly resisted long bus rides for their children into neighborhoods where they are unwelcome. The nationally syndicated Black columnist William Raspberry summarized the major criticisms of a desegregation decision which involved forced bussing:

> The question that surely must have been in the minds of the plaintiffs—how best to educate the black children of the county—had no place in the eight week trial. The crucial point, however, is that racial statistics and bussing patterns offer no useful clue as to the quality of education Prince George's affords its black students . . . Wouldn't it have made more sense for the NAACP to apply its dwindling financial resources to finding ways to improve the education of black

children, rather than merely integrating them? My guess is that black parents in Prince George's want what parents everywhere want: the best possible education for their children.

It's hard to see how that desire is served by the NAACP's assumption that good education can happen only in classrooms with the "right" number of white children in them. (William Raspberry, St. Paul *Dispatch,* August 19, 1982)

Rather than improve racial relations or educational programs, many attempts at forced bussing produced more tension and hatred. There is little evidence that massive desegregation efforts have increased the low and moderate income Blacks' satisfaction with the quality of instruction their children are receiving.

We need effective, integrated schools to help youngsters understand the value and diversity of all our citizens. The best way to achieve this goal seems to develop the strongest possible educational programs. In city after city, this has attracted a racially and economically diverse student body, whether accomplished by private or public educators. This country need not rely on forced bussing or its existing public school structure to achieve successful integration.

Myths and realities must be identified. Millions of childrens' lives are being profoundly influenced by myths. Millions of parents have removed their children from schools which they regard as physically dangerous and academically ineffective. Billions of dollars spent on public school reform have not produced significantly safer or more effective public schools. Perhaps it's time to "remember the children" by providing all of them with a wider range of choices.

Another criticism of vouchers comes from those who feel that *although affluent parents may be able to choose what's best for their children, many poor and minority people can't.* This is not only arrogant and patronizing, but untrue. During the late 60s and early 70s, low income and minority people worked with various community organizations to develop responsive, respected, effective schools. These programs were operated by groups such as the Urban League, American Indian Movement, Raza Unida, plus hundreds of multicultural neighborhood centers. The schools had various names, including "street academy," "Red School House," "Casa de la Raza," "Guadalupe Area Project." Minority and low income people by the thouands sent their children to these programs. Many of them survived into the 80s by a combination of incredible commitment and practical politics.

Most criticism of vouchers which alleges limited parent ability to choose cites the Alum Rock project. Most low income and minority families chose the program in their immediate neighborhood. However, the Alum Rock project did not allow parents to send their chldren to programs operated by institutions in which they had greater faith than the public schools. Low income families often have more confidence in their churches and community agencies than they do in their public schools.

Research cited earlier shows that many low income urban families are selecting nonpublic schools for their children, even if it means putting off many other purchases. Recall Blum's research, for example, which found that "50 percent of those families sending their children to 64 inner city independent schools had family incomes under $10,000 per year" (Blum, p. 19).

An increasing number of Blacks, Hispanics, and Native Americans are questioning the attitudes and motivations of those making decisions for them. Most polls show little love lost between public schools and their constituents in low income and minority communities. In evaluating arguments for and against vouchers, it's wise to consider who is speaking for whom. Teachers' union officials are justified in speaking for their members. It's probably less appropriate for them to speak for low income and minority people.

Another major criticism of vouchers is that *they lead to greater polarization in this country.* Public schools do have at least some integration at present. Voucher opponents fear that this will be lost as each religion, race, and political group establishes its own program.

The experience of effective public and private schools around the country refutes this concern. Many Catholic inner city schools report that half of their students are not Catholic.

In St. Paul, Murray Junior High, Webster Elementary, St. Paul Open School, Benjamin E. Mays Fundamental School, and Central High School all draw young people of various backgrounds, races, and religions from throughout St. Paul. So do other "magnet" programs established in large cities across the country.

Nolan Estes and Don Waldrip edited a helpful book about such programs, entitled *Magnet Schools: Legal and Political Implications*. They point out that a well developed system of alternatives need not cost any more than is presently being spent, and that it can achieve the following goals: (1)Improved instruction through the school district; (2)Appropriate response to groups seeking controversial changes within the district; (3)Better response to needs of various students; (4)Increased racial integration within the school district through voluntary means; (5)Maintenance of a middle income constituency (Waldrip, in Estes and Waldrip, p. 131).

Strong schools can and will attract a diversity of young people. The student bodies of such programs as St. Paul's Webster Magnet Elementary and Skyline High School in Dallas reflect each city's racial and socioeconomic mix.

Most parents want schools which will help their children learn basic and applied skills in an orderly, safe environment. There are frank and honest disagreements about specifics such as school prayer, sex education, textbooks, instructional techniques, course offerings, school rules, and graduation requirements. Virtually all parents will support schools where children learn, their views are respected, and their assistance is encouraged.

People will choose different instructional approaches, ranging from traditional to progressive. Youngsters have different learning styles, and a school structure which is appropriate for one will be inhibiting or frustrating for another. Some youngsters who blossom in an "open" school are frustrated in a traditional school. Other children need the direct instruction and closer supervision offered in a traditional program. We do not attempt to tell people whether they should attend a huge university or small college. Some people prefer the broad range of courses available at a larger school while others prefer the greater "family feeling" available at a small school. Vouchers allow parents to choose schools which will match their children's learning styles.

Some narrow programs would be established under a voucher program, but no more than already exist. One consistent result of public opinion polls is that the vast majority of Americans reject extremes.

A legal objection to vouchers insists that *constitutional separation of church and state does not allow tax money to support schools affiliated with religious denominations.* The courts will have to resolve this issue. However, religious schools in many states already are receiving "public" funds for a variety of purposes. Title I of the huge Elementary and Secondary Education Act provided several hundred million dollars for math and reading instruction of low income children. Many of these funds already are going to "private" schools. In several states, tax funds are channeled through public school districts to provide a range of services for private school students, including transportation, counseling, and textbooks. Students attending religiously affiliated colleges often receive federal or state funds for scholarships.

The 1983 U.S. Supreme Court *Mueller v. Allen* decision showed that the court now believes providing benefits to parents whose children attend public and independent (private and parochial) schools is permissible under the Constitution.

Some people think the court was wrong. But they are hard-pressed to show how the law has harmed Minnesotans. Where is the evidence that it has produced excessive entanglement between the Minnesota government and religious institutions? Where is the evidence that Minnesotans have established one religion as more important or valid than others?

When the United States was established, most countries believed that national unity required one established church. Millions of people died because they would not convert to what was officially considered the one true church. The Spanish Inquisition tortured people who would not accept Catholicism. In other places Islam was regarded as the true faith, and one of the responsibilities of a believer was to convert or kill nonbelievers.

The founders of this country believed that unity did not require one established church. They thought that a nation could respect individual rights and tolerate a diversity of religious beliefs. They believed that the country would be bound together by certain philosophical beliefs: "We hold these truths to be self-evident, that all men are created equal, that they are endowed by their creator with certain inalienable rights, that among these are life, liberty and the pursuit of happiness."

As part of their respect for individuals, the writers of the Constitution wrote that "Congress shall make no law respecting an establishment of religion." Some people believe this phrase means that no tax funds should be used to support religious practices. Others view this phrase as prohibiting the government from setting one religion above others.

During the early 1800s, the Constitution was not viewed as barring public funds from supporting parochial education. Many early publicly supported common schools included Bible reading—using the Protestant King James Version of the Bible. Public school advocates in the 1800s didn't mind tax support for schools which taught religion, so long as it was *their* religion. These facts have been excluded from many history books, but they are readily available for anyone who investigates with an open mind.

Later, a number of states passed "Blaine amendments" to prevent tax support for religious schools. These actions were the product of people who were viciously anti-Catholic (Doyle, 1983). Liberals who insist the Constitution bars tax funds from supporting religiously oriented schools should read the debates about the Blaine amendments. They'll probably be shocked by the religious intolerance of ancestors who drafted laws barring such support. Educational historians such as Katz and Greer document that the "common school movement" included Protestants who hated and feared Catholics.

Opponents of tax support for independent and sectarian institutions aren't sure what to do with the G.I. Bill. Veterans were allowed to use tax funds to attend a variety of educational programs, including those colleges affiliated with various churches. The program was an enormous success and did not lead to excessive government entanglement in religions, as some people feared.

The American Civil Liberties Union has been a consistent and vigorous opponent of using tax funds to support parents' educational choices in parochial schools. Yet the ACLU insists that other groups have a right to freedom of speech and expression. The ACLU argued that public funds must go to support the right of Nazis to march through the streets of Chicago suburb which is the home of many Jews who survived Nazi concentration camps. Thousands of dollars were required to protect the rights of Nazis.

Aren't the rights of parents to freedom of religious expression as important as those of the Nazis? Some parents want their children to attend schools which stress certain religious values. And yet low income parents generally are unable to select parochial schools for their children because of the costs, modest as they are in many places.

Dr. James Skillen, Director of the Washington-based Association for Public Justice, believes the Supreme Court's decision in the Minnesota case was wise and consistent with the Constitution. Skillen believes that Americans have prospered, individually and collectively, by respecting religious rights of individuals. There have been some limitations on acceptable religious beliefs. Advocates of one creed are not allowed to kill people who disagree with them. Men are not allowed to have several wives. But religions have flourished in this country. And religious diversity has not hindered the country's development. Some would argue that respect for individual rights has unleashed human potential as in no other land in the world.

Skillen insists that the same liberal respect for religious diversity should govern educational policy. A strong country has evolved from respect for individual religious rights, and can come from respect for individual education rights. Skillen urges a shift in thinking about funds for education. "The policies of government should be founded on the recognition that the ongoing development of human culture can thrive only in responsible freedom" (Skillen).

For Skillen, the Association of Public Justice, and others, this means allowing public funds to support educational choices, including certain private and parochial schools. It is possible to have some restrictions without excessive entanglements. Tax funds have supported veterans' choices under the G.I. Bill. Tax funds have gone to religious groups that offer education programs for handicapped children. Tax funds have gone to religious groups that operate senior citizen homes. Earlier sections described specific restrictions that could be used to regulate programs. Public funds going to parochial schools will encourage rather than discourage liberty in this country.

Would a voucher program be beneficial if the courts ruled that church-related schools could not participate? Yes. There still would be opportunities for individuals and nonsectarian groups and community agencies to establish new programs. Some existing nonsectarian private schools would participate. Though parents would not have as many choices as in a system including parochial schools, there would still be some gain for parents and their children.

Some have argued that *vouchers may help urban students, but hold little benefit for rural students.* It's critical to understand that there is enormous variation in rural areas: Some people live within thirty minutes of two or three small towns, others live two to three hours from the nearest town.

The Vermont experience helps illustrate potential benefits of expanding choices for many people living in agricultural areas. People living within a reasonable distance of several small towns would have the opportunity to select among them or to select a school which might be located on someone's farm or ranch. Students and parents in Vermont readily can describe differences among nearby schools' educational philosophy and course offerings. It's reasonable to expect that such choices would develop in many rural areas.

Vouchers could encourage greater specialization. Most schools in an area would teach reading, writing, and math. Some, however, would teach German, and others French. Some would teach advanced math courses; others would offer an advanced science program.

Expanded choice gives families the option to band together, creating their own alternative if no one else responds to them. 17 families in the small southern Min-

nesota town of Northfield created Prairie Creek School when
their public school district wouldn't listen to them. Under the
plan proposed above, other families could establish a school
consistent with guidelines and receive tax support for their
program.

In extremely isolated areas, expanded choice would have
less impact. The legislature might decide to give an additional allocation to people located more than an hour from a
town (much as an additional allocation goes to a handicapped
student). This additional allocation could be used to attend
the nearest public school, a residential program, or perhaps to
participate in some form of advanced technology learning and
teaching. Frankly, expanding educational choices probably
would have less benefit for people in isolated areas. It could
produce some additional opportunities, but certainly not as
many as for someone living in a metropolitan area.

There is a final argument against voucher programs:
*Rather than decreasing the role of government bureaucracies
in education, a voucher program increases government's
role.* Noted economist Milton Friedman provides an excellent
refutation of this point. Friedman suggests that the appropriate role of government in education is similar to its role with
respect to restaurants. The government establishes and maintains minimum requirements geared to health, safety, and
advertising standards. Periodically restaurants are inspected
to determine whether these standards are being met.

As Friedman envisions a voucher program, there would be
periodic inspection of schools accepting vouchers. These
schools would have to demonstrate that they met appropriate
standards for student and employee safety, health, and non-
discrimination. However, the government would not tell
schools whom they must hire any more than it does restaurants. The government would not tell schools what to teach
any more than it tells restaurants what to serve.

Some scholars believe that tax funds going to private
schools would inevitably produce too much government interference with them. This would make the private schools less
distinctive and effective with the people they serve (Ravitch,
Wise, Darling-Hammond). Some private school staff and
parents share this concern.

State regulation of private schools varies enormously, from minimal to extensive. Recently the country witnessed a tragic confrontation in Nebraska, where the state insisted that a parochial school be closed because its teachers were not certified. The school pointed out that the children had been tested and were scoring above state and national averages. This did not deter state officials, who arrested and jailed parents and the school's minister when they refused to close the school. In such a situation, concerns about state interference are justified. (The Nebraska legislature has changed its law to permit private schools to hire noncertified teachers. However, the potential for excessive regulation remains very strong in some places.)

Just as the G.I. Bill provided remarkable opportunities for America's veterans and immensely aided post World War II development, a voucher program can be of enormous assistance to our country.

In recent years we've witnessed major changes in medical care. In many areas, employees are now able to choose among health maintenance organizations (HMOs) of various sizes and individual or small groups of doctors. Many teachers' groups have asked for such choices as part of their benefit package. Development of HMOs has not destroyed small family practice clinics. It has stimulated physicians to watch costs and provide a variety of services responding to patient needs. Similar benefits are possible under a carefully developed voucher program, which would provide incentives for teachers to create effective programs. Education would become a more appealing career, solving an urgent societal need. Schools could decide to pay able teachers higher salaries.

There are, of course, unresolved details. These include a transition period, financing court cases challenging vouchers, status of teachers already employed, and establishment of a monitoring agency. Each is an important question and must be answered. Throughout our country people are working on the answers.

Americans like to tell themselves that they believe in democracy and equal opportunity. We have never provided equal opportunity in education. If we stick to our present system of public and private schools, we will fall farther and farther short of our ideal.

Of course, equal opportunity is not the only democratic idea. This country has tried to provide enough liberty for each person to achieve his/her potential. For more than 200 years, there has been tension between providing equal opportunity and limiting individual freedom. The tensions are at the core of such issues as union organizing (i.e., the right of workers to join together versus the right of nonunion individuals to be employed) or free speech.

The voucher concept offers an opportunity to join these conflicting ideas. In a provocative essay reflecting 10 years of work on vouchers, Denis Doyle describes their potential: "Choice may emerge as a category of resolution, binding together the divergent virtues of liberty and equality" (Doyle, 1977, p. 251).

These proposals should help provide better learning opportunities for all the children in this country. Equality and excellence do not require uniformity. A voucher system builds on our finest individual and collective instincts. The American genius for creativity, energy, and invention will be encouraged by a well-designed voucher system. Vouchers are a necessary but far from sufficient solution to this country's educational problems. Earlier chapters described instructional strategies, discipline techniques, and graduation requirements to increase students' skills and improve their attitudes.

America represents a "light unto the nations" because we value individual potential. The present system of public schools does not allow teachers or students to achieve this potential. It's time to eliminate public school monopoly and make our schools more democratic.

REMINDERS
FOR
REFORMERS

We need to review past experiences with reform, particularly in the field of education, to get a sense of potential risks and dangers. Many efforts have involved coercion, standardization, or simplification. Some change efforts were formulated by small, isolated groups of people who tried to convince others to adopt their "package." Moreover, many reformers become frustrated with methods some journalists use to describe their actions. This chapter is presented with a certain sense of humility. In his book, *The Official Rules,* Paul Dickson quotes Finagle's Fourth Law: "No matter what occurs, there is always someone who believes it happened according to his pet theory" (Dickson, p. viii). These are my "pet observations" on reform strategies.

History frequently looks unfavorably on reformers, despite their passion, skill, and good intention. For example, idealistic and thoughtful people such as Helen Hunt Jackson worked hard for Native Americans in the late 19th century. They regarded the Dawes Act, which divided reservation lands among families, as one of their major victories. However, most historians regard the breakup of tribal held land as disastrous. As Edmund Spicer points out in his *Short History of Indians in the United States:*

> Even though it stemmed from strong humanitarian sentiments, the program [of the national white liberal organizations] was itself an expression of the new dominant conception that Indians had no political rights comparable to those of the White society. It played, moreover, into the hands of members of Congress who represented persons interested in acquiring still more of the Indian held land (pp. 67–68).

Other examples could be given, but the central point is that often change agents, despite their good intentions, have made situations worse. Any attempt to reform must carefully consider the variety of results which might occur.

The first chapter suggested that all schools should share a set of limited objectives. Schools should be held accountable for developing students' competence to live in and improve the world, and the belief and perspective to do so. These general objectives leave opportunities for schools to develop programs in response to teacher expertise, student interest, and parental values.

A number of school reform efforts involve coercion. Two examples illustrate this ill-advised strategy. Both have pushed millions of young children and their families out of public schools.

The first is the demand that all children take certain courses, such as sex education. Parents have raised a number of concerns about these classes. One is that the classes are taught in ways which suggest that any form of sexual expression is acceptable so long as both people are comfortable with it. This is a direct attack on some religious beliefs. Another concern is that young people learn about birth control and abortion, which may conflict with their families' moral and religious values. Bitter, emotional battles have broken out in some school districts with parents demanding that their children not be compelled to take these courses. In too many cases, educators have looked down their noses at parents and told them, "We know what's best for your child." A number of parents responded to such attitudes by saying, "Thanks, but no thanks," and removed their children from the public school.

A second example of ill-advised coercion is our unfortunate experience with forced bussing to achieve integration. This strategy was based on a fundamentally racist attitude: Minority children would be better off in schools with white children, and the presence of minority children would not have a negative impact on the white children's achievement. We know that, despite the best of intentions, forced bussing has not produced higher achievement levels. It has driven millions of youngsters from the public schools, as middle and upper income parents leave city schools to the poorest children whose parents can't move.

Millions of people in this country have worked hard, saved, and sacrificed to buy a home in a pleasant neighborhood. One of their dreams was that their children would have a better, easier life than theirs. Then along came Federal courts and officials which told them, "Sorry, your child will have to go halfway across town so that we can integrate the schools." When parents resisted these orders, they were branded "racists." Clearly, some of the people who resisted bussing hate blacks and other people of color. However, not all of the resisters were racists. They wanted their children to attend the best possible schools. They did not want their children used as tools. Is it any wonder that many people have come to believe our government produces, rather than solves problems?

It's worth noting that forced bussing has been unpopular in many minority communities also, who have been quick to pick up the fundamental assumption, "Your kids need to be in class with white children to get the best education." Many Hispanic, Asian, black and Native American parents don't accept that view; they want their children to attend schools with the strongest program—preferably in their own neighborhood.

Despite noble intentions, these two attempts at coercion failed. Millions of dollars were spent on litigation, people became more cynical, and through it all, kids suffered. Attempts to improve American education should not rely on telling parents what courses and which schools their children must attend. Coercion should be used only as a last resort. As noted earlier, creation of magnet programs has produced peaceful, voluntary integration in many cities. The costs of even the most expensive magnet programs are preferable to the social disruption and bitterness forced bussing produces.

Continuing attempts at standardization create some of the same problems. The Council on Basic Education's *Paideia Proposal* is only the latest attempt to describe a simple, set curriculum for all children to study. This program states: "Eliminate all electives from the course of study except the choice of the second language to be studied." (Adler, p. 82) It's the same old, "We know what's best for you" impulse which runs counter to democratic traditions.

Standardization advocates do not acknowledge families' differing values, students' interests, or teachers' creativity. They ignore possibilities that, for example, some students best learn researching skills in debating courses, while others learn by completing a research paper or holding an internship with a city government. As a result, standardization will increase the number of dropouts, because it does not pressure educational institutions to consider the interests and priorities of the communities they serve.

Standardization would usher in a new era of "blaming the victim": "We provided the finest possible education. Those children simply did not want to take advantage of the opportunities we provided." Standardization will continue to push people away from public schools—parents who can afford to, will turn to private schools.

Closely related to standardization is simplification. Simplification has haunted many who tried to develop solutions to complicated problems. More than a decade ago, people proposed that youngsters demonstrate competence prior to graduation. A few of us suggested that a variety of standards be used, so that youngsters would have to do more than pass a paper and pencil test. In an article published almost eight years ago, Wayne Jennings and I concluded that educational consumers were facing the classic consumer fraud known as "bait and switch" (Nathan and Jennings). An excellent idea—requiring that youngsters demonstrate skills before graduation—was the bait. The less satisfactory product which was then offered to consumers was the standardized test (the switch). Unfortunately, consumers in the form of state legislators bought this less acceptable package. They did so, despite recognition that a wider range of competence measures would not be more expensive to adopt.

Another example of unrealized potential reforms occurred

as school districts rushed to adopt "open education" in the early 1970s. Despite articles that explained how complicated the finest open schools were, and how much they demanded of teachers, the simplifiers and popularizers rushed in to capitalize, and transformed the reform into a fad. Publishing companies pumped out "learning center packets" which allegedly reduced the amount of preparation time for teachers. In many cases, publishers simply rewrote textbooks onto individual cards which could be placed in boxes around an "innovative" teacher's classroom.

Individualized instruction was one of open education's fundamental ideas. This did not mean that students would move at their own pace through predetermined text material, but that students would use a wide range of material available in libraries, textbooks, and the world beyond the school to develop strong research, reading, and writing skills. Providing redesigned textbooks as the major source of knowledge for students reduced the amount of research for teachers and students. It also reduced the amount of learning and benefit which occurred.

I remember talking with textbook manufacturers at teachers' conventions. When they learned I was at an open school, they would steer me away from most of their textbooks and toward the card files. Some of them laughed when I pointed out that the files were rewritten textbooks with questions at the end of each chapter. "What about the teacher and student writing some of their own questions to research? What about encouraging teachers and students to bring in other source material to learn from, or to go into the community to look for answers to their questions?"

"Boy, you sure are idealistic, kid," was a frequent response. "Most teachers don't want to do all that work. We produce what they want—simple, easy-to-use material. The innovative stuff you're talking about just won't sell."

There were other attempts to simplify open education. Many architects and educational authorities toured the country espousing "open plan architecture," a style which had few, if any, interior walls. Most teachers hated it. The drawbacks of this design were obvious to teachers from the beginning. What happened if a student and teacher got into an argument? Everyone in the school knew about it instantly. Wouldn't youngsters be distracted by the other activities around them? What happened if a teacher wanted to play some music while another teacher was giving a test?

I'll never forget the young architects who volunteered to help parents, students, and faculty plan the St. Paul Open School. After listening to the discussion for about 20 minutes, one of them pointed out "You'll have to remove all the walls, you know!" The response was unanimous and instantaneous: "Not in this school, we won't." The architects seemed genuinely hurt: "How can you have an 'open school' with walls?"

Everyone assured them that a quick way to kill the program would be to eliminate the walls. It would not be permitted. End of discussion. Some of the architects left in a huff. They weren't missed.

While not appropriate for everyone, open education can challenge and stimulate many young people. Herb Kohl's *Open Classroom* and *On Teaching* describe imaginative ways for teachers to use "curriculum webs." Kohl suggests using topics like "babies" or "houses" and weaving in a variety of investigations from which youngsters can choose. Regardless of their choice of subtopics, students would gain important experience in writing, researching, computation, and cooperation.

Tragically, many "open educators" allowed the public to believe that they were not committed to developing strong basic skills in their students. This dismayed and repelled parents who might have been attracted by the movement's creativity. Jonathan Kozol's book *Free Schools* caused a storm of protest when he argued that new programs must assure student acquisition of strong academic skills, not just a pleasant, comfortable school setting.

A reform's public image often hides its substance. Reformers must think about their relationship with the press. A chance encounter in Bangor, Maine, helps illustrate this point. The Maine Department of Education was hosting a conference at a local motel on high school graduation requirements. The sponsors invited me to discuss competence-based graduation requirements and called a local television station to suggest coverage. The TV reporter arrived just as we were breaking for lunch, and asked me to stand next to the motel's swimming pool where he would conduct an interview. Having some experience with television, I suggested that the interview be recorded in the cramped, smokey conference room where we met, rather than next to the pool.

The reporter became angry. "Aren't you willing to cooperate?" he demanded. "After all, we're giving you a chance to talk with half the state!"

"Of course I'll be glad to work with you," I responded. "However, the pool has nothing whatever to do with the conference, its message, or me. Filming by the pool might give some of your viewers ideas about this conference that wouldn't be too accurate."

The reporter muttered angrily but reluctantly agreed to film in the conference room. His questions were few and hostile. He left the room immediately after the interview. As the cameraman was putting away his equipment, he winked at me. "Good for you—ya saw right through him. This guy hates schools and teachers, and he's always looking for ways to put them down. You're absolutely right: Most of our viewers would have heard little of your message. They would have been thinking about those darn lazy teachers, taking off another day in the middle of winter to play around some fancy indoor swimming pool."

As in most professions, many journalists are honestly trying to do the best possible job. Unfortunately, their mistakes can have a major impact. One morning a reporter called from the Minneapolis *Star*. She interviewed me about problems schools face. She asked whether our school had been challenged by groups opposed to classroom discussions about values. We had been talking about the peer counseling program. I explained that the class was not required of anyone and that students needed parent permission to take the class. She agreed this made sense.

Then she asked about my response to critics who insist that schools stick to "reading, writing, and arithmetic" and forget counseling of any kind. She'd talked with some people who opposed all educational expenditures for school counselors, as well as programs like peer counseling. I explained that I felt many of those people were out of touch with a significant percentage of our students, who needed immediate help with their problems. Such students were not able to concentrate on their academic work because of more immediate problems: divorce, death, drugs, physical abuse, etc.

Several weeks later her article appeared. She had carefully written down my response, but unfortunately, I was answering a question she never asked!

> Videotape and cable television are expected to open new ways of presenting information. Computers will provide more immediate feedback to students. A more far reaching difference could come under a voucher system in which students receive a set amount of public money they can spend as they choose in public and private schools. Some educators are defensive about such thinking.
>
> "That's just terrific for them to sit out there and say those things, but then you come to this building and see what goes on," said Joe Nathan, assistant principal at St. Paul Murray Junior-Senior High School. "I'm dealing every day in this building with kids who are pregnant at age 12, with kids whose fathers are leaving them, with kids who are sobbing because they were raped last night. We've got to deal with all this reality" (Minneapolis *Star,* 3-18-82, Community Section, p. 4).

Stunned by the use of my quotation, I called the reporter. "Sharon, did you really feel I was defensive about vouchers? Weren't we talking about providing counseling services? In fact, I'm in favor of vouchers, but you never asked me about them. What happened?"

"Joe, I'm terribly sorry about the whole thing," she began. "You're absolutely right. The editor cut about four paragraphs I'd written between the sentence about 'some educators are defensive' and your quotation. It was very unfair to you."

She urged writing a letter to the editor. I figured the damage was done. Perhaps I should have followed her suggestion.

Of course, it's not accurate to suggest that all news stories are distorted. Most journalists try hard to present an accurate picture of any given event. Reporters and editors sometimes will view the same story in different ways. In 1975, for example, the Minnesota Governor's Crime commission issued a report about community-based residential corrections facilities in the state. The following headlines were used by three different newspapers:

"Corrections program hit." St. Paul *Dispatch,* 4-29-75, p. 1A.

"Corrections modes 'equal'." St. Paul *Pioneer Press,* 4-30-75, p. 24.

"Community penal programs supported." Minneapolis *Star,* 4-29-75, p. 8A.

Yet these headlines summarized exactly the same report. Moreover, the editors of one paper thought the story rated front page attention, while the others didn't.

There are other ways the press can help shape the public agenda for discussion and debate. Most people are familiar with "hard luck" stories publicized in newspapers or on television. Invariably, these people receive considerable attention and support from viewers and readers.

Parade, a national Sunday newspaper supplement magazine, once ran a story about our school's Consumer Action Service program. Their story produced extensive national press coverage and over 5,000 requests for our explanatory booklet.

A journalistic decision to identify some business's or agency's poor performance can have a dramatic impact. In the Twin Cities area, for example, WCCO TV's coverage of shoddy practices by a local Housing Inspection Bureau produced needed reforms and disciplinary action.

Unquestionably the press can shape, rather than simply report, the news. People committed to carrying out a reform must understand that power. We won't always be pleased with coverage, but we must do a better job of understanding press requirements for brief summaries, deadlines, clear statements, and interesting pictures. We also need to remember that journalists are not cheerleaders. Sometimes we'll wonder if the press is out to get us. Most reporters try to present information in a clear and balanced way. Other reporters say their job is to "Comfort the afflicted and afflict the comfortable!" Reformers may not like all this, but ignoring these realities inevitably will reduce their possibilities for success.

Schools should help young people understand ways in which the press influences their beliefs. I think every school should make available to its students a course on the ways radio, television, and newspaper reporters produce stories. Students should understand how reporters select some facts and opinions to include, and eliminate others. The pictures used and story placement also can have a dramatic impact on a reader or viewer.

Trying to improve learning opportunities is a complicated task. The experiences of scientists help illustrate this point. During the late 1950s and early 1960s a number of projects were funded by the U.S. government to improve course offerings in the sciences and humanities. Most of the funds went to universities, where the experts were presumed to be.

Some university professors at that time had an unfortunate tendency to look down on their colleagues in elementary and secondary schools. Much of the writing of this time focused on public school teachers' ignorance of new discoveries. This was a reasonable concern, but many professors took their criticisms a step further.

They boasted that the materials they were developing for elementary and secondary schools were so simple even the teachers who worked with them wouldn't be able to reduce their effectiveness. This attitude pervaded not only much of the writing, but many of the workshops universities held to promote their materials. Few people like to be told they are stupid and incompetent. This certainly applies to teachers. Many of the professors knew a lot about the latest discoveries in their field, but were ignorant about differences among young people.

One product of this period was "new math." Millions of dollars were spent trying to teach children basic mathematic principles by using a carefully developed set of ideas. The new math, as I understand it, tried to get young people to understand the concepts of mathematics before they started computation exercises. The intent was excellent. Unfortunately, the implementation failed. Many reasons have been given for its failure. (Recall Finagle's fourth rule, quoted at the beginning of this chapter.) It seems to me that there wasn't enough cooperation between the teachers of young children and the people who developed "new math." Many of the teachers who were expected to use the new techniques didn't understand them. Many thought they had more effective ways to teach math concepts. Of course, many resented the statements of some professors that the curriculum was "teacher proof."

Another example of this isolated approach to reform is the High School Geography Curriculum developed by university Geography professors. The project included some fascinating activities designed to help youngsters understand how an area's physical features influenced the way people developed it, and the patterns of their movement. So far, so good. However, one of the activities involved a board game. Many of the high school students I tried to use the game with found it too juvenile for them. Junior high youngsters (ages 12 to 14) really liked the game, and learned many of the lessons the professors had planned. Unfortunately, the reading material which accompanied the game was too advanced for them. Close collaboration between university professors and secondary school teachers would have produced a more effective program, which no one would have deemed "teacherproof"!

These examples suggest the following guidelines about educational reform:

1. Don't tell parents and their children which school they must attend and what courses they must study.
2. Don't develop programs that assume teachers or parents are incompetent or uncaring. Most aren't and will resent being included with those who are.
3. Help youngsters understand how they are affected by the press. Try to understand it yourself. Use your knowledge to communicate effectively with journalists and a broader audience.
4. Try to provide opportunities and encouragement for all involved in a school to use their best ideas and talents. Honor those people willing to suggest improvements, and those people willing to try something new.

The aim of these reforms is to simplify schools by returning authority and accountability to the people most directly involved in learning: parents, teachers, and students. I've also suggested instructional techniques and graduation processes which parents and other educators may wish to use. These suggestions appear to be consistent with those made more than a decade ago by Dan Levine, director of Kansas City's

Center for Study of Metropolitan Problems in Education, who called for efforts to reform urban schools by "rebuilding them as less complex institutions, . . . increasing student and parent participation in decision-making" (Levine, p. 258–259).

However, it is possible that our interest in simplification can have dangerous effects. For example, decisions may be made to eliminate requirements for equal access to schools participating in the voucher programs. All schools should have the opportunity to decide whether they will be involved. It's vital that one of the requirements for voucher schools be not only opportunities but guarantees for a cross section of applicants to be admitted into the school. This would help to assure increased opportunity for low income youngsters, most of whom presently are suffering in ineffective schools. Despite the value of this provision, it's possible that a legislature could eliminate it. If this happened, I personally would work hard against the proposal being enacted.

My emphasis here is on increasing educational opportunities, not limiting them. Attempts at coercion and standardization often are counterproductive. No school should be forced to accept the vouchers; a good way to doom this set of proposals would be to attempt to force everyone to participate. Conversations with some people affiliated with private religious schools make it clear that they want to have as little to do with the government as possible. They resent having to follow government directions in their schools. Some of these people would never accept the kinds of regulations which I believe must be a part of any successful voucher program.

Some affluent people probably will continue to demand exclusive programs for their children. The point of this proposal is not to restrict parental options, but to expand them. Private schools have correctly fought attempts to limit their independence. Their flexibility has been an important tool in responding to the priorities and interests of the families they serve. It would be tragic if those strengths were lost in the name of standardization.

Nevertheless, the proposals I am suggesting do include some standard requirements. I believe we must retain the demand for equal access to at least some of the openings in schools accepting vouchers. Minimal inspections to assure that programs are meeting health, safety, and "truth in advertising" requirements also are necessary to insure that young people and their parents are protected.

Providing more opportunities for parents, teachers, and students to help develop programs does not guarantee that all educational problems will be solved. Providing wider choices will not, by itself, produce effective, efficient, or pleasant schools for young people. Some programs developed for juvenile delinquents were dangerous and destructive. Some of the programs developed under "War on Poverty" guidelines had the same weakness as the worst ward politics. Political payoffs, corruption, inappropriate nepotism, and poor bookkeeping are all dangers of distributing power and authority more widely.

The strongest reform efforts have retained the genius of our system's approach to power, a system which incorporates checks and balances, while respecting individual liberty and encouraging initiative. Youth participation projects, competency-based graduation requirements, vouchers, school site management, shared facilities, and contracting offer extraordinary opportunities. We can honor and encourage some of the finest qualities in our country: initiative, creativity, cooperation, and innovation.

We must be honest and realistic. We owe that to everyone involved in education, but most especially to the young people who will spend their time learning—somehow, somewhere.

CONCLUSION

Schools reflect the dreams and demands of American culture. We have many expectations for them. Some hope they will help people overcome handicaps of race, religion, and family background. Others want schools to help children preserve family wealth and power.

We *can* have better schools, where children learn to think, compute, and communicate; where they gain sensitivity and self-confidence; where they come to see themselves in perspective with others throughout the world. Schools should stimulate thoughtful, creative approaches to complicated societal problems and provide opportunities for youngsters to serve others as they learn.

Effective schools require direct accountability between themselves and families. Teachers, parents, and other community members need opportunities to create the finest possible school programs. Cooperation can produce remarkable results, as the following story demonstrates.

One fall evening in 1971 several teenagers went for a bicycle ride in their St. Paul neighborhood. They had no idea that their evening exercise would produce a three-year struggle, several major technological breakthroughs and a change in the way 40 youngsters viewed themselves.

The young women noticed a very bad odor, which seemed to be coming from a paper plant. The girls mentioned the smell to their parents when they returned home. One parent explained that this had been a problem in the neighborhood for many years. The girls realized that they had not noticed the odor before. "Perhaps it's because we're taking an ecology class. We may be more aware now."

The next day the students mentioned their discovery in class. They talked about pollution and what to do about it. Part of the teacher's expectations were that the class participants would not just read and talk about ecology, but also try to do something to improve their local environment. Several of the students already had organized a block party-cleanup day and arranged for special garbage pickup from the Sanitation Department.

Students were divided over whether anything could or should be done about the odor. They had studied environmental "tradeoffs" and learned that sometimes factories were closed rather than retooled. Several speakers explained to the students that cleaner air and water is expensive. Students discovered that pollution control efforts can result in layoffs or money diverted from increased plant efficiency.

Nevertheless, several students decided to investigate the issue. They began by researching the State of Minnesota odor pollution laws. They discovered that the State used a "smell test" in which air alleged to be polluted was combined with "clean" air. The amount of unpolluted air added to the dirty air depended on the area's zoning. For example, in a residential area, one cubic foot of clean air was added to one cubic foot of polluted air. In an industrial area, the polluted air would be diluted by three or four cubic feet of clean air. An odor panel smelled the results. If an unusual smell was obvious to the panel, the source of the smell was required to eliminate it. Students were surprised at the unsophisticated nature of this law.

They determined to find out more about odor pollution, and went to a Law Library to continue their research. The youngsters summarized the odor pollution laws of Minnesota and the other 49 states.

Then they began to call the company they suspected was primarily responsible for the odor. Students phoned for several weeks, trying to arrange an appointment. The company officials kept putting them off. There may have been some miscommunication; company officials later explained they thought the students wanted a plant tour, which they were preparing but hadn't completed. The students insisted that they wanted to talk about odors coming from the plant. After being rebuffed by company officials, the students called the St. Paul Pollution Control Agency. An official there explained that the agency did not have enough staff to check all complaints. He also told the students they were the first to complain about the odor.

The youngsters were discouraged. They had not expected a rebuff from the Pollution Control Agency. They met with a local public interest group attorney who suggested that they start a petition, asking for an investigation of the odors. They collected several hundred names in the neighborhood. In the process, they learned a good deal about economic intimidation. Many owners of small businesses, such as barber shops, drug stores, and restaurants told the kids they agreed with the petition, but didn't want to sign it because they feared a loss of business from the large company.

One youngster was reading the local newspaper and saw a notice about a legislative hearing on pollution; the students went to the hearing and explained their experiences. The legislators' attitude seemed to be, "Aren't those kids cute!" However, a newspaper reporter at the hearing sensed a good story. He asked if they would be willing to have their names in the newspaper and get some publicity about the campaign. The students and their teacher agreed. They reported their conversation to the attorney, who was enthusiastic. "Something may start to happen now," he told them. The class was about to get an excellent lesson in "the power of the press."

Several days later a front page story appeared. The reporter noted that the area in question was sometimes called "the armpit of St. Paul." Some of the story's comments were revealing. The pollution control bureau chief said his agency was planning to investigate the students' complaint within a week. The company spokesperson denied knowing anything about the students' concerns. The company also denied producing any objectionable odor. The article quoted the company's representative promise that the students would be invited for a tour very soon. The class was ecstatic! They soon learned that action doesn't equal solution.

Things happened quickly for a while. The inspections were made and several companies (including the one students suspected) were found to be in violation of the pollution standard. Each of the three companies was ordered to develop a compliance plan. The companies asked for up to 18 months to make improvements. Those 18 months quickly stretched out to 24. Apparently there were no easy solutions to the kinds of odors the paper company was producing. Finally, however, the company did install the equipment, which worked reasonably well. Students were invited back to see what the company had done. The corporation's vice president then said something totally unexpected.

"Kids, we're really pleased you pushed us on this one. Oh, I know we weren't very happy several years ago." (Students had reminded the official of a conversation between the Superintendent of Schools and the corporation's president. According to the Superintendent, the businessman had demanded the students stop harassing his company. He threatened to encourage his workers to vote against a bond issue if the project wasn't stopped. To his credit, the Superintendent supported the project, told the company official that the students were learning about democracy, and that the company should be more cooperative!)

The official agreed that his boss was furious about the original newspaper article. However, he pointed out that the company now was getting excellent press coverage. Apparently the company's scientists had developed new technology to reduce the odor, and people from throughout the world were calling to inquire about it. The company was pleased and the official wanted the students to know it.

The project was an extraordinary learning opportunity for the youngsters, the community, and the corporation. The students wrote a 20-page booklet about their experiences. One of the kids summarized:

> I must admit that I was a bit skeptical at first—us against Big Business U.S.A. You bet! But I figured that I would only defeat myself and the project by being a pessimist. There is reason for optimism if people remember what we learned.

This class helped students improve basic writing, reading, and speaking skills. They became more confident about their ability to have a beneficial impact on the world. One of them became an attorney. Another is now a chemist.

We have a right to expect that schools will help all our youngsters achieve these things. Young people need to believe in themselves, in their personal worth and ability. Their skills ought to justify this belief: they *all* should be able to read thoughtfully, write clearly, compute accurately, and think logically. These are reasonable goals. They can be accomplished, as America has demonstrated that it can accomplish so many other complicated tasks. Problems are not solved by simply "throwing money" at them. Helping all children learn will require adopting new attitudes about learning and schools. We cannot use the same bureaucratic, production line approach to learning that we employ to produce cars.

Children are not like steel, plastic, and rubber. Each child is unique. Each child has dreams, interests, hopes, and talent. We do not seek to make each child the same, as we've sought to do on an assembly line which produces the same car model.

We have high expectations of our teachers. We want them to inspire and challenge each child. We are not content with teachers who use the same materials and instructional methods, year after year. Our best teachers don't treat all children the same; they recognize differences. They encourage young people to accomplish more than anyone thought possible.

The process of learning can and must become not only one of growing, but also of sharing. In helping others, youngsters come to understand the value of skills that older people are trying to help them gain. Reading, writing, thinking, and speaking are not goals in themselves—they are tools for progress.

Our present public schools help many young people develop these skills. This success is an enormous tribute to millions of individual teachers and administrators who cope daily with a web of rules, regulations, and restrictions. I believe we can do better by changing the system in which our finest teachers operate.

There are many ways to do this. Some retain the public school system as we know it. School boards could delegate more authority and accountability to individual schools, so that major decisions can be made at that level. Schools will improve if we involve young people in helping to care for the building, each other, and the broader community. More learning will take place if computers are used not just for "drill and practice" but to stretch and extend students' minds. More money will be available to pay teachers and provide materials if we create community service centers, in which schools are located along with other businesses and social agencies. Everyone involved with schools—parents, students, teachers, and community members—will be more satisfied if programmatic choices are available within schools or districts. These choices may include programs established by groups under contract to school districts, who are able to operate with greater flexibility than many of the more traditional programs.

Many people will be satisfied with such changes. Some believe that we should try them before adopting more radical reforms. Others, including me, believe that we need more fundamental change in the ways we fund and control learning. Philosophers and citizens representing the entire political spectrum join in urging new learning opportunities. Under these programs, the tax money will go to families to spend on education, rather than to local school boards. Teachers and parents would establish programs with direct and unmistakable accountability.

Many people probably will choose to keep their children in the public schools. Most of these schools have better facilities and equipment than private schools already in existence. Some families will use the opportunity to send their children to other schools with alternative programs created by concerned teachers, religious groups, and citizens. Respecting family choice would strengthen support for funding. For the first time, several million families would receive direct benefits from tax money allocated for education.

We've struggled for more than two centuries to achieve democratic ideals. We've had false starts and taken plenty of detours, but we've made substantial progress. We've been willing to rethink the kinds of institutions which best suit our needs. We've changed laws which inhibit progress or deny justice. We've discarded what no longer works well and tried new ideas which promise a better life.

This country should not accept an educational system which produces so many people with minimal skills. We've allowed many public schools to deteriorate to the point where their only students are from the poorest families with no other options. As many as one-third of our youngsters, most of them poor, leave school with such inadequate skills they are doomed to a life on the edge of our economic system. This situation is intolerable.

All our children deserve teachers who believe they can learn, and who will not be satisfied until they do. Democracy relies on informed citizens able to make thoughtful decisions. Justice demands that all parents have opportunities to select an appropriate, effective school for their children. Our future depends on creative people who are able to work together to solve complicated problems.

Yes, this country and its children do need and deserve the best. But it's unlikely that they'll find it in our public schools, with standard procedures, curriculum, tenure, and seniority systems. In far too many schools, people are unnecessarily restricted, discouraged, and confined.

Following the suggestions in this book will not solve all our educational problems. But we'll have recognized the value of our finest teachers and schools. We'll be able to honor and encourage them. The proposals in this book will unleash the creativity, energy, and human potential of this nation.

UPDATE
FOR THE PAPERBACK
EDITION

In the year following publication of *Free to Teach,* more than 35 reports by various national groups appeared. Beginning with the President's Commission which concluded that we are "A Nation at Risk," various groups made recommendations for improving our schools. In talking with people around the country about the ideas in this book, several themes emerged. First, there has been a positive response to the idea of businesses, community organizations, and schools sharing facilities. Next, an increasing number of parents and community members have asked about the impact and mechanics of expanding students' educational choices. Attention has been focused on ways to make the education profession more attractive to prospective and present teachers. Finally, many people are intrigued by the distinctions between increasing standards (which I favor) and increasing standardization (which I oppose). What follows clarifies and expands ideas which appeared in the original edition of *Free to Teach.*

ATTRACTING AND RETAINING THE BEST TEACHERS

Legislators and other policy makers will be making a tragic, costly mistake if they rely primarily on increasing salaries to

206

make teaching a more attractive profession. The evidence mounts daily that other steps must also be taken to attract and encourage effective senior instructors and talented prospective teachers. One of the most important is to provide new career opportunities for teachers. In the last year, several states have taken encouraging steps in this direction.

One important role for outstanding older teachers is to work with new instructors. In most places, this is done informally if at all. Several states have created new programs to provide incentives and opportunities for this to happen systematically. In California, the legislature authorized funds to fund "mentor teachers," who would be selected by committees of fellow teachers and administrators. These mentors spend at least 60 percent of their time with students, and no more than 40 percent of their time with beginning instructors. They receive an extra $2000 for their additional work and responsibility and are selected for a 3 year period. Local implementation of this plan has produced mixed results. In some places it works well. In other places, some decisions have discouraged teachers from participating. For example, the Los Angeles Board of Education decided that anyone selected to be a mentor teacher would have to work in an inner-city school to which it's difficult to attract staff. Many of the teachers who might otherwise apply did not want to leave the schools in which they were working. Thus, relatively few Los Angeles teachers applied. The mixed record in California shows why teachers must be involved in school improvement efforts.

The Toledo, Ohio, Federation of Teachers established a program in 1981 which has received national recognition (McPike, 1984). "Consulting teachers" have primary responsibility for the professional development and evaluation of new teachers. These experienced, expert teachers are released from other classroom duties, paid an extra $1250 per year, and trained to provide guidance and assistance. Recommendations concerning new teachers are made to a review panel composed of 5 teachers and 4 administrators. The President of the Toledo Federation of Teachers notes that the "consulting teacher"-review panel system has removed more new teachers from the system than did principals before the program started.

Additional responsibilities and a longer contract year can go together. The Tennessee legislature recently passed an educational reform package which includes opportunities for some effective teachers to work (and be paid) 11 or 12 months. The Charlotte-Mecklenberg School District in North Carolina recently adopted a similar program.

A Rochester, Minnesota, program illustrates another career option. The local school district and International Business Machines jointly hire several teachers each year. The district and corporation each pay half of the teachers' salaries during the school year. IBM hires the teachers during the summer. The teachers help train IBM engineers to give public presentations, work with entry level employees, and complete other projects. The corporation, school district, and teachers' organization agree that everyone participating sees the program as successful; everyone gains.

Many teachers around the country say they would like the opportunity to work part-time for a school district and part-time for a corporation or community agency. Writing teachers should be able to split their time between a school and a local newspaper or a business which needs manuals written. Art teachers could spent several hours with young people and the rest of the time illustrating corporate or agency brochures. The list could go on and on. Teachers need and want new options. Their lives and teaching would gain.

New career opportunities for teachers are one way to get around the "merit pay" debate which has developed in many communities. Teachers are legitimately worried that administrators will pick only their favorite teachers for additional (merit) pay. Wise programs will allow teachers, parents, and students some opportunity to select outstanding teachers. The best programs will allow teachers to take on additional responsibilities and work longer years.

If this country is to retain and attractive effective teachers, it must improve their career opportunities. The recent Carnegie Foundation study of American teachers found that they were "troubled not only about salaries but about loss of status, the bureaucratic pressure, a negative public image, and the lack of recognition and rewards." New career options can help to change that. Carnegie's President Ernest Boyer concluded, "The push for excellence must focus on those conditions that drove good teachers from the classroom in the first place, and this has to do with more than salaries" (Boyer, p. xiii).

What do the best teachers want? Some want the chance to use their expertise to help younger teachers. Others want opportunities to spend part of their time outside schools, learning in and contributing to social service agencies or corporations. Many teachers want the opportunity to spend all year in some form of teaching, rather than have to scramble to find a summer job. Some places have made a good start toward responding. Those who value effective education will listen, learn, and act.

ALTERNATIVE PATHS FOR TEACHER PREPARATION

What preparation should a teacher have? Raising this question insures a lively discussion among people concerned about the quality of our schools. During the past year this question was one of the most frequent I heard, given my strong criticism of "excessive reliance on teacher certification systems." A variety of groups have criticized university-based teacher education programs. Many people talk about how they considered entering teaching but were discouraged after taking dull, uninspired education courses in college. Some argue that people with undergraduate degrees in a certain curricular area (such as math, history, chemistry, English, etc.) have sufficient preparation to be effective teachers. I strongly disagree. The question becomes: What alternatives exist? This section describes several changes which would improve teacher training.

No form of certification is required for college and university professors. Colleges and universities frequently employ attorneys, accountants, politicians, doctors, real estate agents, etc., to teach some of their courses. And even those people who have academic backgrounds rarely participated in courses designed to help them develop classroom skills. Instead, their preparation has been heavily weighted toward knowledge in a particular field (i.e. history, biology, chemistry, English literature). No one insists that all college professors are excellent instructors, but there is no evidence that participation in teacher education programs would improve their skills.

Currently, each state requires teachers in its public schools to be certified. Some states require teachers in private schools to be certified. These rules have been challenged successfully in Maine and unsuccessfully in Nebraska. The National Commission on Educational Excellence described teacher preparation curriculum as "weighted heavily with courses in 'educational methods' at the expense of courses in subjects to be taught." Their survey of 1350 institutions training teachers indicated that 41 percent of the time of elementary school teacher candidates is spent in education courses (National Commission on Educational Excellence).

The Carnegie Foundation's 1983 study of the teaching profession found wide variations in certification requirements and process among the 50 states. Some states require passing a standardized paper/pencil test along with completion of a recognized collegiate teacher preparation program.

The standardized tests take several forms. Some are of particular academic content, such as reading, writing, mathematics, biology. Others are more generalized. For example, the National Teachers Examination includes a Test of Communications Skills, a Test of General Knowledge, and a Test of Professional Knowledge.

Another approach has been to require prospective teacher candidates to score at a certain level on a college admission test in order to be admitted to teacher preparation programs. As the Carnegie Report points out, "The development and use of tests is already having an impact upon the qualifications of those persons wishing to become teachers, particularly upon minority populations."

Many Black college students considering the teaching profession have difficulty with these tests. A November 1983 article in *Education Week* noted that only about ⅓ of Georgia Black teacher education candidates passed the state's teacher certification test. About 87 percent of White candidates passed the tests. In Florida, results in early 1983 from a similar certification test showed 35 percent of Black candidates passed on the first try, compared with 90 percent of Whites. In Alabama, about 50 percent of Blacks failed an elementary education test, while about 10 percent of Whites did not pass it. In California, a new standardized test was given to 6900 candidates. 71 percent of minority candidates (excluding Asians) failed the test. Aggregate figures for Whites were not available, but the overall failure rate was 38 percent.

Various explanations are given for these differences. Some believe that Blacks come into colleges with lower average skills than Whites. A former dean at the predominantly Black Valdosta State College says that many southern Blacks are "educationally deprived" and that colleges are not able to overcome these deprivations. Other people insist that colleges should be able to increase significantly skills of their students.

Several state legislatures seem to have accepted the latter assumption. In several southeastern states, approval by the state department of education of education school programs is now tied to students achieving an 80 percent pass rate on the certification test.

Some Blacks argue that these standardized tests are discriminatory and, in fact, part of a conspiracy against Blacks (*Ebony,* March 1984). They insist—with considerable justification, in my opinion—that resources traditionally allocated to predominantly Black elementary, secondary, and post-secondary programs in the South have been substantially less than those allocated to predominantly White programs. The question is, What should be done?

Fairness demands that resources be equalized. In many states this will require substantial change in state funding formulas. Real estate taxes still are the primary funding source for many school districts. Schools located in rural, poor areas often have much less to spend per pupil than those in affluent, suburban areas. This must change.

However, at the same time, I support making standardized tests *one* element measuring a person's readiness to be a teacher. Standardized tests help the state determine whether a person has at least some knowledge necessary to be a safe driver or effective attorney. As an earlier chapter in this book points out, there are valuable uses for standardized tests. This is not an endorsement for all standardized tests. However, particularly when effective teachers have worked with test makers, tests can help identify whether prospective instructors have vital reading, writing, computation, and instructional skills. The Carnegie Foundation concludes, "The testing movement now underway appears to have the potential for improving the quality of America's teaching force if only by raising the standard for the lowest acceptable candidates."

Not all states assume that a teacher preparation program is necesary for effective teaching. Several states have instituted policies allowing liberal arts graduates to begin teaching careers without completing a degree in teaching. A number of Massachusetts school districts are using interns who have a degree in math or science and are working part-time in their schools and part-time at an advanced technology company, Digital Equipment. The summer before the interns begin teaching, they go through an intensive series of workshops coordinated by the University of Massachusetts. The university hires "mentor teachers" from public schools who work with the young people in this summer program. Participating school districts must also identify a mentor teacher who works with the interns during the school year (and is paid several thousand dollars). Interns must commit themselves to half-time teaching for at least 3 years, and Digital Equipment has agreed to employ them part-time for the same period. The supervisor, a physics professor at the university, says that "districts are very pleased to get these young people," and notes that there were 100 applications for the 20 slots in the first year's program. Test scores and grade averages made the program's participants in the top 15 percent of college graduates!

A somewhat similar program operates in California. The legislature passed a massive education reform bill allowing districts to hire uncertified teachers in areas where they could document that no certified candidates exist. These uncertified teachers are required to complete two years of work under the supervision of a "mentor teacher" chosen by a committee more than 50 percent of whom are classroom teachers. New

Jersey's education commissioner and governor have pushed hard for a similar program.

New routes into teaching make a great deal of sense. At present there is no guarantee whatever that a prospective teacher will be placed in an effective teacher's classroom. Being paid an extremely modest fee, the teacher has little incentive to work with the college student. Many teachers simply turn over their class to the college student and go to the faculty lounge for coffee.

The California mentor teacher program provides an extra $4000 per year for those selected to monitor younger teachers' work. The experienced teacher must spend at least 60 percent of her/his time working with students so as not to lose touch with classroom reality.

Another approach is to provide opportunities for talented professionals in mid-career to opt into teaching with minimum restrictions. Harvard University has started a Mid-Career Math-Science program for mathematicians and scientists who will be eligible to teach in Massachusetts after a one-year concentrated program. These professionals are eager to spend some time teaching in elementary or secondary schools after spending years working on scientific research or development. Some will return eventually to former careers, others will stay in teaching.

Some people argue that schools should abolish certification requirements. UCLA professor Don Erickson wrote, "There is no evidence that certification is critical to student acquisition of skills essential to good citizenship. . . ." (Erickson, 1983). Erickson believes strongly that schools should not be limited to hiring certified teachers. Dr. Chester Finn of Vanderbilt University in Tennessee agrees, arguing that we should "abolish the presumption that the graduate of a teachers' college is automatically qualified to possess a teacher's license" (Finn, 1983).

A recent study pointed out that some of the most effective schools in our nation's capital do not favor certification requirements. Danielle Schultz notes that 51 percent of the students in Washington, D.C.'s Catholic schools are not Catholic. In some areas of Washington, more than 90 percent of the student body is non-Catholic. Monsignor Francis

Barrett, executive director of the National Catholic Education Association says, "Certificates are a farce. There is a distinct difference between qualified and certified. If anything, applicants with an education degree might be well advised to omit that fact when they're applying for a parochial school job" (Schultz, 1983).

While it is tempting, I do not accept the argument that no training program is necessary for people to be excellent teachers. In fact, we all are prisoners of our own experiences. Most people teach as they were taught. In secondary schools, this is primarily lecture, read the chapter, and answer the questions at the end. John Goodlad's recent study of more than 1000 classrooms around the country made this point clearly. Goodlad's team of researchers found that more than 80 percent of secondary teachers' time was spent talking at students and monitoring written work (Goodlad, 1983). If we want more creative, higher quality teaching, we will have to help potential instructors develop those skills.

National reports agree that the scores of college students going into teacher preparation programs are far below national averages. While teachers scoring highest on standardized tests are not necesarily the most effective instructors, it's clear that teachers who can barely read, write, or compute themselves will have difficulty helping young children master those skills. This is a critical, timely area for reform.

Overall, the approaches discussed in this section provide valuable and promising alternatives. Each provides opportunities for people with strong academic backgrounds to enter the teaching profession. Citizens are right to be concerned about the skills teachers have. One way to attract new, talented people into the profession is to provide a variety of paths into it. Models are available. It is up to those in decision-making positions to make use of these models and require careful evaluation of the results.

MISGUIDED REFORMS

This section was inspired by conversations with parents and teachers throughout the country. People usually asked what I thought of recommendations that academic standards be increased, school year extended, more homework assigned, and course electives eliminated or severely reduced. My answer was consistent: There is a national confusion between increasing standards and increasing standardization. We are in danger of accepting two myths: that there is "one best system" which is best for all, and that "more is better."

Parents and other community members ought to welcome higher standards while rejecting increased standardization. An earlier chapter in this book describes how and why students ought to demonstrate basic and applied skills before they graduate. Many sections in the book suggested that we need to increase our expectations of young people. They ought to be encouraged to participate in more challenging programs. They should be expected to provide service to others while developing basic and applied skills. They should be pushed, and pushed hard! Diplomas should represent real achievement, not just the passage of time.

People are legitimately frustrated now and looking for solutions. Some of the national reports in the last 18 months insist we need a return to a core curriculum with few choices for students or teachers. I sense an enormous national feeling supporting higher achievement for all students. But when I've explained how choices can help accomplish this sensible goal, there is immediate and strong support.

However, young people should have a variety of ways to gain the skills we all agree they need. They should be required, for example, to demonstrate certain writing skills before graduation. But they should be able to develop those skills in many different ways—by working on newspapers and magazines, by helping produce an oral history magazine such as *Foxfire*, by participating in traditional courses which focus on writing and research, by helping to identify, research, and propose solutions to various community problems. We know that young peoples' physical appearences differ considerably. Why is it such a surprise that they have different learning styles, and that no one pattern is best for everyone?

Teaching all teachers exactly what is to be taught and how to present it will not increase achievement. Bright young people will not enter a profession they view as offering little incentive or opportunity for creativity. Talented teachers who use unconventional methods will be increasingly frustrated by more instructions from above about how to do their job. Standardization is a reform which deserves immediate rejection.

What about extending the school year? Many reports compared our schools to the Japanese, German, and Russian programs, where students spend much more time in the classroom. At first a longer school year sounds like an attractive reform, but I'd ask several questions about it.

First, Will instruction be changed, or will traditional patterns be used? In some places, summer school has been used to offer creative, unconventional courses. Some summer biology courses take trips on rivers and lakes to gather samples and conduct experiments. Some districts have summer world language classes which take trips to areas where English is not the dominant language. Students are immersed in a different culture and with proper guidance quickly develop skills in a second language. Some summer health classes are presented in hospitals, team taught by school district teachers and hospital staff.

If extending the school year means using some of these creative, effective techniques, I'm all for it! If, on the other hand, it's just more of the same, then it probably won't have much impact. Earlier chapters documented that many students in this country do not feel challenged by their courses. "More of the same" won't solve that critical problem.

Anyone thinking about extending school days or school years ought to review fascinating new research just completed by two investigators at the Rand Corporation. They reviewed studies of teacher evaluation. They agreed that spending more time drilling students could improve standardized test scores. However, "teaching behaviors that increase student performance on standardized tests are different from—in some cases the opposite of—teaching behaviors that increase complex cognitive learning, problem solving skills and creativity" (Wise and Darling-Hammond). Citizens will have to decide what they want emphasized. Otherwise, test score improvements might actually be accompanied by decreases in other very important skills.

The second question is whether extending the school year is the best use of additional funds. If extending the school year provides new career opportunities for teachers, great! Some teachers should have opportunities to work 11 or 12 months and receive a substantially increased salary. While some teachers like taking 2 ½-3 months off during the summer, others must find part-time employment. It's not that easy or fulfilling. As Jerry Hughes, President of the Minnesota Senate points out, teaching is the only profession in which practitioners often don't use their skills for 25 percent of the year. Extending the school year will be valuable it it's used to create new career choices for staff.

People should also ask, How long is the school year presently? Researchers found significant variations among states and school districts during the past year. Some students are already getting about a month longer year than others. Some districts had only about 150 days in which students were actually in school, while others had 180. That month is significant.

Similar questions should be asked about demands to increase homework. In September 1983 many teachers had the clear message that people wanted more homework assigned. Unfortunately, that often translated into more worksheets and questions at the end of the chapter. Such exercises have some value. However, most students won't gain much from longer assignments. The expectation ought to be more *challenging,* not just *more* homework. The Effective Learning chapter tries to illustrate ways in which homework can call on students' creativity and idealism. Not all homework can or should do that. But increasing demands on students will be counterproductive unless their assignments are clear, monitored, and designed to stimulate, not simply occupy young people.

Americans want effective, appropriate schools for their children. Creative, thoughtful people in schools have made some progress in the last year. But the major push for reforms has come from outside. Dissatisfied, concerned businesspeople and parents should not be satisfied with "more homework, longer school year, and more standardized tests." Any list of major reforms should include the following:

1. New career patterns for teachers
2. Alternative routes into teaching
3. Shared facilities
4. Expanding educational choices for families, especially those families whose income presently limits their choices
5. Requiring demonstration of both "real world" and pencil/paper skills
6. Increased opportunities for young people to combine classroom work with community service.

BIBLIOGRAPHY

Adler, Mortimer. *The Paideia Proposal.* New York: Macmillan, 1982.
Aldrich, Hope. "Few Blacks Passing Georgia Teacher Test, Study Says." *Education Week,* November 9, 1983.
American Association of School Administrators. *Fiscal Impact of Natural Gas Deregulation on Urban School Systems.* Arlington, Va., A.A.S.A., 1983.
Barker, Roger, and Gump, Paul V.. *Big School, Small School.* Stanford, California: Stanford University Press, 1964.
Benjamin, Robert. *Making Schools Work.* New York: Continuum, 1981.
Bills, Robert. *Education for Intelligence or Failure.* Washington: Acropolis, 1982.
Blum, Rev. Virgil C. "Why Inner City Families Send Their Children to Private Schools: An Empirical Study." In Gaffney, Edward, ed., *Private Schools and the Public Good,* Notre Dame, Ind.: Notre Dame University Press, 1981.
Boyer, Ernest. "Forward" in Feistritzer, C. Emily, *The Condition of Teaching.* Princeton: Carnegie Foundation for Advancement of Teaching, 1983.
Branan, Karen, and Nathan, Joe. "Getting Ripped Off? Call a Kid," *Learning.* March, 1977.
Bridge, R. Gary, and Blackman, Julie. *Study of Alternatives in American Education, Vol. IV: Family Choice in Schooling.* Santa Monica: Rand Corporation, 1978 (Publication R-2170/4-NIE).
Calkins, Andrew. "Sparring Over Computers," *Electronic Learning.* March/April, 1982.
Callahan, Raymond E.. *Education and the Cult of Efficiency.* Chicago: University of Chicago Press, 1962.

219

Canter, Lee, and Canter, Marlene. *Assertive Discipline*. Los Angeles: Canter and Associates, 1976.

Carlson, Alan. "The Rotting Core of the American Experiment . . . and a Possible Cure." *Persuasion at Work*. Rockford Institute, December, 1983.

Carmichael, Lucianne Bond. *McDonough 15: Becoming a School*. New York: Avon, 1981.

Carnegie Council on Policy Studies in Higher Education. *Giving Youth A Better Chance*. San Francisco: Jossey Boss, 1979.

Center for Study of Public Policy. *Education Vouchers*. Cambridge: Center for Study of Public Policy, 1970.

Citizens League. *Rebuilding Education to Make It Work*. Minneapolis: Citizens League, 1982.

Coleman, James S.; Hoffer, Thomas; and Kilgore, Sally. *High School Achievement: Public Catholic and Private Schools Compared*. New York: Basic Books, 1982.

Committee on Vocational Education and Economic Development in Depressed Areas. *Education for Tomorrow's Jobs*. Washington: National Academy Press, 1983.

Coons, John, and Sugarman, Stephen. *Education by Choice*. Berkeley: University of California Press, 1978.

Currence, Cindy. "Scholars Call for Improvement in Teacher Training Programs." *Education Week*, November 9, 1983.

Davies, Don, ed.. *Schools Where Parents Make a Difference*. Boston: Institute for Responsive Education, 1976.

Dearman, Nancy B., and Plisko, Valena White, ed. *The Condition of Education, 1982 Edition*. Washington: National Center for Educational Statistics, 1982.

Dewar, Tom. *Rethinking the Professional's Legitimate Role*. Speech at Minnesota Association of Voluntary Social Service Agencies, October 13, 1976 (available from Humphrey Institute on Public Affairs, 909 Social Science Tower, University of Minnesota, Minneapolis, Minn. 55455).

Doman, Glenn. *How to Teach Your Baby to Read*. New York: Doubleday, 1975.

Doremus, Richard R. "Whatever Happened to . . . Contracting in Cherry Creek?" *Kappan*, May, 1982.

_____. "Whatever Happened to . . . John Adams High School?" *Kappan*, November, 1981.

_____. "Whatever Happened to . . . Melbourne High School?" *Kappan*, March, 1982.

_____. "Whatever Happened to . . . Northwest High School?" *Kappan*, April, 1982.

_____. "Whatever Happened to . . . Wayland (Mass.) High School?" *Kappan*, January, 1982.

Doyle, Denis. *Family Choice in Education: The Case of Denmark, Holland and Australia.* Washington: American Enterprise Institute (mimeographed), 1984.

_____. "Should School be Run More Like a Business." Speech at Governor's Conference on Education, St. Paul, Minnesota, July 28, 1982.

_____. "The Politics of Choice: A View from the Bridge." In *Parents, Teachers and Children: Prospects for Change in American Education.* San Francisco: Institute for Contemporary Studies, 1977.

Doyle, Denis, and Finn, Chester. *Educational Quality and Family Choice: Toward a Statewide Public School Voucher Plan.* Sacramento: Sequoia Institute, 1984 (mimeographed).

Dunn, Rita; Dunn, Kenneth; and Price, Gary. "Identifying Individual Learning Styles." In *Student Learning Styles.* Reston, Va.: National Association of Secondary School Principals, 1979.

Edmonds, Ron. "Some Schools Work and More Can." *Social Policy,* March-April, 1979.

Education USA. "Voucher System: A Maine Tradition," January 26, 1981, p. 173.

Educational Facilities Laboratory. *Community School Centers,* New York, 1982.

Erickson, Donald A. "State Regulation of Private Schools." *Education Week,* November 9, 1983.

Estes, Nolan, and Waldrip, Donald, ed. *Magnet Schools.* Piscataway, N.J.: New Century Educational Corporation, 1978.

Fantini, Mario. *Public Schools of Choice.* New York: Simon & Schuster, 1973.

Farrar, Eleanor; DeSanctis, John; and Cohen, David. "The Lawn Party: The Evolution of Federal Programs in Local Settings." *Kappan,* November, 1980.

Feistritzer, C. Emily. *The Condition of Teaching.* Princeton, N.J.: Carnegie Foundation for the Advancement of Teaching, 1983.

Ferlinghetti, Lawrence. "Truth is not the Secret of the Few." In *A Coney Island of the Mind.* New York: New Directions, 1955.

Finn, Chester. "The Goal of Education is Not Teacher Contentedness: A Reminder of the Real Purpose of Schools." *Education Times,* November 7, 1983.

Fogg, Susan. "One in 5 lacks reading skills to cope, study says." *Minneapolis Star,* October 29, 1975, p. 1A.

Ford Foundation. *A Foundation Goes to School.* New York: Ford

Foundation, 1972.

Fretheim, Tanya. "Unfair!" *Murray Junior High Flyer.* May 21, 1982, p. 3.

Friedman, Milton. "The Role of Government in Education." In Solo, Robert A., ed. *Economics and the Public Interest.* New Brunswick, N.J.: Rutgers University Press, 1955.

_____. *Capitalism and Freedom.* Chicago: University of Chicago Press, 1962.

Gagne, Robert. Quoted in *The School Administrator.* American Association of School Administrators, February, 1976, p. 2.

Gallup, George. "13th Annual Gallup Poll of the Public's Attitudes Toward the Public Schools." *Kappan,* September, 1981.

_____. "14th Annual Gallup Poll of the Public's Attitudes Toward The Public Schools." *Kappan,* September, 1982.

_____. "15th Annual Gallup Poll of the Public's Attitudes Toward the Public Schools." *Kappan,* September, 1983.

_____. "Majority supports school vouchers." *Minneapolis Tribune,* September 18, 1983, p. 28A.

Garibaldi, Antoine, ed. *In-School Alternatives to Suspension: Conference Report.* Washington: National Institute of Education, 1979.

Gartner, Alan; Kohler, Mary; and Riessman, Frank. *Children Teach Children.* New York: Harper & Row, 1971.

Gibbons, Maurice. "Walkabout: Searching for the Right Passage from Childhood and School." *Kappan,* May, 1974.

_____. *The New Secondary Education.* Bloomington, Ind.: Phi Delta Kappa, Inc., 1976.

Glazer, Nathan. "The Future Under Tax Credits." In James, Thomas and Levin, Henry. *Public Dollars for Private Schools.* Philadelphia: Temple University Press, 1983.

Goodlad, John. "What Some Schools and Classrooms Teach." *Educational Leadership,* April, 1983.

Greer, Colin. *The Great School Legend.* New York: Basic Books, 1972.

Grimes, Ann. "Public Teachers Pick Private Schools for Own Kids." *The Chicago Reporter,* May, 1984.

Hart, Leslie A. *How the Brain Works.* New York: Basic Books, 1975.

Haynes, Carrie Ayers. *Good News on Grape Street.* New York: Citation, 1975.

Healy, Judy. *Experiments in School Based Management.* St. Paul: Northwest Area Foundation, 1983.

Hedin, Diane, and Conrad, Dan. "Study Proves Hypotheses and More." *Synergist,* Spring, 1980.

Hedin, Diane, and Simon, Paula. *Minnesota Youth Poll on School Attitudes.* St. Paul: Center for Youth Development and Research,

1982.

Herndon, James. *How to Survive in Your Native Land.* New York: Bantam, 1972.

Hickey, Dr. M. E. "Letter to Representative Bob McEachern." November 18, 1983 (mimeographed).

Hoyt, D. P. *Relationship Between College Grades and Adult Achievement: A Review of the Literature.* ACT Research Report No. 7. Iowa City, Ia.: American College Testing Service, 1965.

James, Thomas, and Levin, Henry M., ed. *Public Dollars for Private Schools.* Philadelphia: Temple University Press, 1983.

Jencks, Christopher, et. al. *Inequality: A Reassessment of the Effect of Family and Schooling in America.* New York: Basic Books, 1972.

Jennings, Wayne, and Nathan, Joe. "Startling-Disturbing Research on School Program Effectiveness." *Kappan,* March, 1977.

Johnson, Grant; Bird, Tom; and Little, Judith Warren. *Delinquency Prevention: Theories and Strategies.* Washington: U.S. Department of Justice, Jus 436, April, 1979.

Katz, Michael B. *Class, Bureaucracy and Schools.* New York: Praeger, 1971.

_____. *Education in American History.* New York: Praeger, 1973.

Kohl, Herbert. *Basic Skills.* Boston: Little, Brown, 1982.

_____. *Half the House.* New York: Dutton, 1974.

_____. *On Teaching.* New York: Schocken, 1976.

Kozol, Jonathan. *Death at an Early Age.* Boston: Houghton Mifflin, 1967.

_____. *Free Schools.* Boston: Houghton Mifflin, 1972.

_____. *The Night is Dark and I am Far From Home.* Boston: Houghton Mifflin, 1978.

_____. *Tuition Vouchers/The Great Debate: A Scenario for the Future.* Unpublished manuscript.

Krajick, Kevin. "Punishment for Profit." *Across the Board,* March, 1984.

Lafferty, Elizabeth. "Soaring Dropout Rate--The Achilles' Heel of U.S. Public Education." San Francisco: Pacific News Service, n.d.

Levine, Daniel. "Concepts of Bureaucracy in Urban School Reform." *Kappan,* February, 1971.

Lincoln, Abraham. *Second Annual Message to Congress,* (December 1, 1862). In Bartlett, John. *Familiar Quotations.* Boston: Little Brown, 1980, p. 522.

Lortie, Dan C. *Schoolteacher.* Chicago: University of Chicago Press, 1975.

Macnow, Glen. "Michigan Teachers Oppose Merit Pay, Urge Reform." *Education Week,* October 5, 1983.

Mathematical Society of America. *Focus*, Jan.-Feb., 1982, pp. 1-6.

McClaughry, John. "Who Says Vouchers Wouldn't Work." *Reason*, January, 1984.

McDonald, Kwame. "Vouchers Can Be Good." *Twin Cities Courier*, November 24, 1983.

McGuire, Willard. "What Our Children Don't Know Can Destroy Us." *Newsweek*, October 4, 1982.

McPike, Liz. "Teacher Excellence: Teachers Take Charge." *American Educator*, Spring, 1984, pp. 22-29.

Meredith, Marsha. *Hodge Podge*. Rochester, N.Y.: Dynacomp, 1981. (Computer Program)

Merseth, Katherine. "Midcareer Math and Science Program." *Principal's Center Newsletter*, Cambridge, Mass.: Harvard Graduate School of Education (Winter, 1983).

Metzger, Devon. "Doctoral Study Evidence Supports Basic Walkabout Theory." *Walkabout Newsletter*, Bloomington, Ind.: November, 1977, p. 4.

Mirga, Tom. "High Heating Bills to Force Layoffs in City Districts." *Education Week*, January 11, 1984.

Munday, L. A., and Davis, J. C. *Varieties of Accomplishment after College; Perspectives on the Meaning of Academic Talent*. ACT Research Report #62. Iowa City, Ia.: American College Testing Service, 1974.

Murnane, Richard J. "Uncertain Consequences of Tuition Tax Credits, An Analysis of Student Achievement and Economic Incentives." In James, Thomas, and Levin, Henry. *Public Dollars for Private Schools*. Philadelphia: Temple University Press, 1983.

Nathan, Joe. *Attitudes Toward High School Education Held by Graduates of a Traditional and an Alternative Public School in St. Paul, Minnesota*. Unpublished Ph.D. thesis, University of Minnesota, St. Paul, 1981.

_____. "Can Kids Improve Their Community? You Bet!" *Learning*, January, 1975.

_____. "A Computer Specialist At Work." *Learning*, March, 1984.

_____. "Home School Connection." *Family Computing*, June, 1984.

Nathan, Joe, and Jennings, Wayne. "Educational Bait and Switch." *Kappan*, May, 1978.

National Center for Service Learning. "Service Learning in Secondary Schools." *Synergist*, Winter, 1980.

National Commission on Excellence in Education. *A Nation at Risk*. Washington: U.S. Government Printing Office, 1983.

National Commission on Reform of Secondary Education. *Reform of*

Secondary Education. New York: McGraw Hill, 1973.

National Commission on Resources for Youth. New Roles for Youth. New York: Citation Press, 1974.

National Commission on Resources for Youth (Schine, Joan; Shoup, Barbara; and Harrington, Diane). New Roles for Early Adolescents. New York: National Commission on Resources for Youth, 1981.

National Panel on High School and Adolescent Education. The Education of Adolescents. Washington: U.S. Department of Health, Education, and Welfare, 1976, HEW Publication #(OE) 76-00004.

National Task Force on Citizenship Education. Education for Responsible Citizenship. New York: McGraw-Hill, 1977.

New York City Educational Construction Fund. Information Bulletin. No date.

New York Community School District 4. 1983 Alternative Concept Schools. 1983 (mimeographed).

North Central Association Visitation Team. Report on Federation of Alternative Schools. Minneapolis Public Schools, mimeographed, February, 1984.

Olivas, Michael. "Information Inequities: A Fatal Flaw in Parochiaid Plans." In Gaffney, Edward McGlynn Jr., ed. Private Schools and the Public Good. Notre Dame, Ind.: University of Notre Dame Press, 1981.

Panel On Youth of the President's Science Advisory Committee. Youth Transition to Adulthood. Chicago: University of Chicago Press, 1974.

Papert, Seymour. Mindstorms. New York: Basic Books, 1980.

Paulson, John. Early Games for Young Children. Minneapolis, 1982 (computer program).

Paulu, Nancy. "Minnesota's Private-School Parents Await Decision in Tax Case." Education Week, June 15, 1983, p. 5.

Pearl, Arthur; Grant, Douglas; and Wenk, Ernst, ed. The Value of Youth. Davis, Calif.: Responsible Action, 1978.

Peirce, Neal, and Hagstrom, Jerry. The Book of America. New York: Norton, 1983.

Pepin, Constance, and Hunt, David. Education Vouchers: Theory and Practice. Minneapolis: Citizens League, 1983 (mimeographed).

Phi Delta Kappa. Why Do Some Urban Schools Succeed? Bloomington, Ind.: Phi Delta Kappa, 1980.

Pinney, Gregor. "Alternative School Movement Fades From View." Minneapolis Tribune, February 23, 1976.

Proctor, Pam. "What Your Kids Really Think About School." Parade Magazine, April 1, 1979, pp. 4-5.

Raspberry, William. "The Question of Excellence Never Came Up." St.

Paul *Dispatch,* August 19, 1982.

Raywid, Mary Anne. *Current Status of Schools of Choice in Public Education.* Hempstead, N.Y.: Project on Alternatives in Education, 1982.

_____. "The First Decade of Public School Alternatives." *Kappan,* April, 1981.

Rebell, Michael A. "Educational Voucher Reform: Empirical Insights from the Experience of New York's Schools for the Handicapped." *Urban Lawyer,* Summer, 1982.

Rogers, David. *110 Livingston St.* New York: Vintage Books, 1969.

Sale, Kirkpatrick. *Human Scale.* New York: Perigee, 1980.

Sarason, Seymour. *The Culture of School and the Problem of Change.* Boston: Allyn and Bacon, 1971.

Schultz, Danielle. "Lessons from America's Best Run Schools." *Washington Monthly,* November, 1983.

Seeley, David S. *Education through Partnership: Mediating Structures Education.* Cambridge, Mass.: Ballinger, 1981.

Shanker, Albert. "The worst decision, at worst time." *USA Today,* July 5, 1983, p. 8A.

Shaten, Jessica, and Kolderie, Ted. "Contracting with Teacher Partnerships." Sacramento: Sequoia Institute, 1984.

Sher, Jonathan. "McDonaldization of Rural Schools." *Rural America,* Spring, 1982.

_____. "School-based Community Development Corporations: A New Strategy for Education and Development in Rural America." In Sher, Jonathan, ed. *Education in Rural America: A Reassessment of Conventional Wisdom.* Boulder, Colo.: Westview, 1977.

Skillen, James. Speech in St. Paul, Minn. May 22, 1984.

Spicer, Edward. *A Short History of the Indians of the United States.* New York: Van Nostrand Reinhold, 1969.

Thomma, Steven. "Students say Boredom is Worst Problem." St. Paul *Dispatch,* August 11, 1982, p. 1C.

Tompkins, Ellsworth, and Gaumnitz, Walter. *The Carnegie Unit, Its Origin, Status and Trends.* Washington: U.S. Department of Health, Education, and Welfare, Bulletin 1954, /7.

Turnbull, William. "A Partial View of Educational Testing Service." *Kappan,* October, 1977.

Tyack, David B. *The One Best System.* Cambridge, Mass.: Harvard University Press, 1974.

United States Department of Education. "State Education Statistics." January, 1984. (Chart)

Vance, Victor, and Schlechty, Phillip. "Distribution of Academic Ability in the Teaching Force: Policy Implications." *Kappan,* September, 1982.

Washington, Laura. "Chicago's Black Private Schools: Separate But More than Equal." *Chicago Reporter,* January, 1982.

Wasserman, Miriam. *Demystifying School.* New York: Praeger, 1974.

Weintraub, Frederick. "Non-public Schools and the Education of the Handicapped." In Gaffney, Edward McGlynn Jr., ed. *Private Schools and the Public Good.* Notre Dame, Ind.: University of Notre Dame Press, 1981.

Willet, Edward J.; Swanson, Austin; and Nelson, Eugene. *Modernizing The Little Red Schoolhouse.* Englewood Cliffs: Educational Technology Publications, 1979.

Willower, Donald J. "Educational Change and Functional Equivalents." *Education and Urban Society,* August 1970.

Wise, Arthur E. *Legislated Learning.* Berkeley: University of California Press, 1979.

Wise, Arthur, and Darling-Hammond, Linda. "Educational Vouchers: Regulating Their Efficiency and Effectiveness." *Educational Researcher,* November, 1983.

_____. "Current Teacher Evaluation Won't Support Merit Pay." In *ASCD Update,* March, 1984, p. 1.

Wolf-Wasserman, Miriam, and Hutchinson, Linda, ed. *Teaching Human Dignity.* Minneapolis: Education Exploration Center, 1978.

World Health Organization. Untitled. In Sale, Kirkpatrick. *Human Scale.* New York: Perigee Books, 1980.

Zaltman, Gerald; Florio, David; and Sikorski, Linda. *Dynamic Educational Change.* New York: Free Press, 1977.

Conversations with the following people, in Vermont unless noted otherwise:

Yvonne Bailey, education writer, *Rutland Herald,* Rutland

Wendy Capobianco, Washington County Community High School, Montpelier

Pat Carini, Director, Prospect School, Bennington

Jack Cummings, Admissions Director, St. Johnsbury Academy, St. Johnsbury

Susan Curnan, National Youth Practitioner's Network, former director, Smokey Hill, Danby

Linda Dean, New School, Plainfield

Lee Dietz, Executive Director, United Cerebral Palsy Association, Montpelier

Charles Glenn, Director, Bureau of Equal Education Opportunity, Massachusetts Department of Education.

Dan Gregg, Social Studies Consultant, Vermont Department of Education

Celia Houghton, Professor, Goddard College, Plainfield
Donald Jamieson, Superintendent, Barre City Public Schools
Steve Kaagan, Commissioner of Education, Vermont Department of Education, Montpelier
Richard Koehne, Director, Riverside School, Lyndonville
Jim Lengel, Director of Basic Education, Vermont Department of Education, Montpelier
Bob Luce, Counsel, Vermont Department of Education, Montpelier
Viola Luginbuhl, Chair, Vermont Board of Education, South Burlington
John McClaughry, former state legislator and White House Senior Policy Advisor, Concord
Bob Meldrum, Superintendent of Schools, Granville, New York
Jerry Mintz, Director, Shaker Mountain School, Burlington
Cynthia Parsons, Chester, free lance writer, former education editor, *Christian Science Monitor*
Anthony Polina, Director, Washington County Community High School, Montpelier
Diane Ravitch, professor, Columbia University, New York City
Martha Richardson, Assistant to the Director, Putney School, Putney
Sandra Robinson, Director of Adult Education, Vermont Department of Education, Montpelier
Liz Rocklin, Consultant, Special Programs, Vermont Department of Education, Montpelier
Ed Ryan, Chief, Education Field Services, Vermont Department of Education, Montpelier
Peter Smith, Lt. Governor, Vermont, Montpelier
Maida Townsend, President, Vermont-NEA, Montpelier
Tom Ward, Director, Smokey House Project, Danby
Alan Weiss, Director, Department of Continuing Education, Vermont College, Montpelier, former Superintendent of Schools, Montpelier
Marjorie Witherspoon, Director, Vermont State Economic Opportunity Office, Waterbury
Warren Witherell, Director, Burke Mountain School, Burke
Lynn Wood, former member, Vermont Board of Education, St. Albans
Judy Woods, Assistant to Headmaster, Burke Mountain School
Al Wroblewsky, Development Director, College of St. Joseph, Rutland

Plus conversations with community members in a number of general stores around the state and students in several schools